SCIENTISTS MAY NOT BELIEVE IN GOD,
BUT THEY SHOULD BE TAUGHT
WHY THEY OUGHT TO BEHAVE AS IF THEY DID.
MAX F. PERUTZ, Nobelist in chemistry, 1962

This quote comes from a letter to The Independent
*newspaper of London (March 22, 1993), following establishment of
the Starbridge Lectureship in Theology and Natural Science
at Cambridge University, endowed by author Susan Howatch.
Biologist Richard Dawkins, an atheist, had railed in a letter
to* The Independent *(March 20) that "the achievements
of theologians don't do anything, don't affect anything, don't
achieve anything, don't even mean anything.
What makes you think that 'theology' is a subject at all?"
Perutz made the above comment to dissociate
himself from that attack by a fellow scientist on the new
lectureship. Perutz said he would have preferred a chair in
"science and ethics," but considered a chair in science
and theology the "next best thing" to counter "the increasingly
prevailing law of the jungle in the scientific world."*

Reformation-based churches profess
that all truth is God's truth,
yet few give as much encouragement
to young people going into scientific fields
as to those going into the mission field.
This book helps redress the balance.
An introduction to serving God
in the study of nature.

NANCY R. PEARCEY,
author of *The Soul of Science:
Christian Faith and Natural Philosophy*

BEING A CHRISTIAN IN SCIENCE

Walter R. Hearn

InterVarsity Press

Downers Grove, Illinois

The writing and distribution of this book has been supported by the generous gifts of the M. J. Murdock Charitable Trust of Vancouver, WA, and the Stewardship Foundation of Tacoma, WA.

InterVarsity Press® is the book-publishing division of InterVarsity Christian Fellowship®, a student movement active on campus at hundreds of universities, colleges and schools of nursing in the United States of America, and a member movement of the International Fellowship of Evangelical Students. For information about local and regional activities, write Public Relations Dept., InterVarsity Christian Fellowship, 6400 Schroeder Rd., P.O. Box 7895, Madison, WI 53707-7895.

Scripture quotations, unless otherwise indicated, are from the New Revised Standard Version of the Bible, copyright 1989 by the Division of Christian Education of the National Council of the Churches of Christ in the USA. Used by permission. All rights reserved.

Cover photograph: Terry Vine

ISBN 0-8308-1898-7

Printed in the United States of America ♾

Library of Congress Cataloging-in-Publication Data

Hearn, Walter R., 1926-
   Being a Christian in science / Walter R. Hearn.
     p. cm.
   Includes bibliographical references.
   ISBN 0-8308-1898-7 (alk. paper)
   1. Scientists—Religious life. 2. Science—Vocational guidance.
 I. Title
 BV4596.S35H43 1997
 500'.88'204—dc21   97-19047
                                                           CIP

20	19	18	17	16	15	14	13	12	11	10	9	8	7	6	5	4	3	2	1
14	13	12	11	10	09	08	07	06	05	04	03	02	01	00	99	98	97		

Preface

So many individuals contributed to this book that it would be impossible to name them all. Dozens of members of the American Scientific Affiliation (ASA) offered specific suggestions. Many others, simply by example, provided insights on what it means to be a Christian in scientific work. Not all would agree with everything I have written, but in my experience ASA members are a charitable lot.

John Wiester and David Price, coauthors with me of ASA's *Teaching Science in a Climate of Controversy,* have given encouragement and wise counsel over the years. John took the lead in obtaining foundation support for *Being a Christian in Science* when it was first envisioned as a booklet.

I am indebted to the Stewardship Foundation of Tacoma, Washington, to the M. J. Murdock Charitable Trust of Portland, Oregon, and to the individuals behind them, for backing this project and for waiting patiently while it came to fruition.

I am grateful to ASA's past and present executive directors, Bob Herrmann and Don Munro, for years of gentle nudging when they were no doubt being asked "Where's the book?" by the foundations underwriting it. Dennis Feucht did me a great service by taking over as ASA newsletter editor in 1993, freeing me after twenty-four years of bimonthly deadlines to devote more time to this project.

ASA executive council members were willing to establish an ASA Press to publish the book. Then managing editor Jim Hoover of InterVarsity Press took it on despite a potentially limited market. Jim Sire, Terry Morrison, Randy Bare, John Bower and other InterVarsity staff nevertheless saw its ministry potential. Thanks to them and to students in IVCF graduate groups at the University of California at Berkeley and Stanford University for field-testing an early draft.

The training of a scientist, or of a Christian, includes learning what to consider important. Of immeasurable importance to me were my parents, Bradford and Jessie Hearn, now deceased. From them I received my genes and language and first understanding of the gospel. From my wife Virginia I have received so many other good things over the past thirty years.

Besides raising daughter Christine and son Russell Houston, Ginny and I have been through many adventures, including droughts, an earthquake and a disastrous fire in the Berkeley-Oakland hills from which our beloved Troll House was spared. Six months before I began work on this book, I had a silent heart attack, later detected by cardiologist David Anderson. I owe my life to David's alert care and to the skill of surgeon Leigh Iverson for the quadruple bypass operation he performed four and a half years later.

Though mostly written in Berkeley, this book was born, or at least conceived, one clear August night in a rustic cabin owned by the late Helen Lindgren south of Lake Tahoe. I am indebted to her and to our neighbors Bill and Dorothy Frey, in whose Tahoe chalet I later isolated myself to begin playing out the endgame of this book.

I know Who it is to whom all thanks are ultimately due. Besides being grateful to God, I thank the many friends who have offered prayers on my behalf. Some prayed during my heart surgery and recovery. Others have been praying specifically for this book.

Now I must turn everything over to my in-house editor, standing by with her editorial scalpel. Ginny, one of the best book doctors in the business, with nearly two hundred books to her credit, has lately been referring to this one as my life's work. That could be because I've put so much of myself into it or because it has taken so long to finish it. Either way, here it is.

Walter R. Hearn

Prayer for Scientific Ministry
Eternal Father,
in the heart of your Son
and through the Holy Spirit,
I pray to you most humbly:
make me,
make all of us
instruments of your wisdom,
so that contemporary intellectuals,
particularly scientists,
may meet you in all of us,
through us
and with us,
and all of us together
may love you wholeheartedly.
Amen.

Used by permission of the author, physicist Enrico Cantore, Jesuit priest and founder of the World Institute for Scientific Humanism in New York. Originally titled "Prayer for Scientific Apostolate."

1

Jesus in the Laboratory?

IT COULD BE ARGUED THAT WHILE he was on earth, Jesus Christ had nothing good to say about science. That is true—because he said nothing about science at all.

For that matter, Jesus said nothing about capitalism either. Or about representative democracy, or computers, or bicycles. None of those things had been invented when Jesus walked the shores of Galilee and the streets of Jerusalem, or a few years later when historical accounts of his life were written down, forming the Gospels of the New Testament.

Yet twentieth-century Christians who function in a capitalistic economic system and participate in the democratic process have written about "following Jesus" in those pursuits. Today such authors use word processing software on computers to write their books, probably without asking whether that is what Jesus would have done—had he written any books. Christian parents teach their kids to ride bikes (though Jesus never rode a bicycle). Many Christian young people go to college (though Jesus never did), preparing to serve Christ as ministers or missionaries, or in such professions as medicine, law, education or business.

What about science as a profession? As one Christian physics professor,

John McIntyre of Texas A&M University, has observed,

> There is a steady unconscious pressure on our young people to devote their lives to the approved activities and, of course, to admire others who do so. One hears Christians speak proudly of their sons or daughters who have married seminary students or missionaries.
>
> But where is the encouragement for our young people to enroll into the graduate schools of our great research universities to enter a life of scholarship? I have yet to hear a Christian father speak proudly of his son or daughter marrying a graduate student. No wonder our young people are discouraged from entering the rigorous life of learning and research.

Does it have to be that way? Invited to a banquet honoring "the forty-eight American Jews who have won the Nobel prize," Professor McIntyre said he had difficulty recalling even one Nobelist who was an evangelical Christian. In America many more Jews than evangelicals must have gone into science over the years. Why?

McIntyre attributed the discrepancy to the fact that "for two millennia the learned Jewish rabbi has occupied a place of honor in the Jewish community. Consequently Jewish young people strive to enter the most challenging universities to prepare themselves for a life of scholarship." Of course, Jesus himself was a Jew. Today young people of Asian descent constitute another subculture in America heavily represented in scholarly pursuits.

What has happened, McIntyre concluded, is that evangelical Christians have allowed themselves to be cut off from their roots in the Protestant Reformation. That sixteenth-century movement countered the then-prevalent idea that the clergy (priests and monks) were the only "full-time" Christians. Everybody else (the laity) had to earn a living in practical ways and also support the clergy. Before the Reformation, lay people who carried out the business of the secular world, from farming to trading, seldom saw their occupation as a form of Christian service. Then along came Martin Luther (1483-1546) and those who followed him, emphasizing that all honorable work done by Christians is acceptable to God if done for God's glory.

The new Christian freedom to probe wholeheartedly into the material world drew many Reformed Christians into science. By 1660, over half of the founders of the Royal Society of London were Puritans. Reformer John Calvin (1509-1564) had encouraged Christians to take up one of the few well-established sciences of that time, as either a profession or a serious pastime:

> For astronomy is not only pleasant, but also useful to be known; it cannot be denied that this art unfolds the admirable wisdom of God. Wherefore, as ingenious men are to be honored who have expended useful labor on

this subject, so they who have leisure and capacity ought not to neglect this kind of exercise.

Over four centuries later McIntyre concluded, "It's time to rejoin the scientific establishment," and offered a number of suggestions for helping the evangelical community "return to its roots." This book can be regarded as one response to McIntyre's plea.

Being a Christian in Science is written for young people attracted to the fascinating field of science. It is addressed to all students interested in such matters, but particularly to those on the verge of entering the profession: graduate students in one of the scientific disciplines and undergraduate science majors. It should also help high school students who are pondering various career options, by giving both them and their parents "a feeling for science."

Science is no doubt the most self-consciously secular of all occupations. Although *secular* and *sacred* are often understood to be antithetical terms, the two are not opposites. In the Middle Ages, *secular* came to mean "living in the world," so that priests and monks living outside of cloistered communities were known as secular clergy. (By that definition, almost all Protestant ministers today would be considered secular.) *Secular,* which basically means "temporal" (akin to "temporary"), is more logically contrasted with *eternal.*

Determined opposition to Christian thought comes not from secular activity itself but from *secularism,* a worldview denying the importance or even the existence of anything beyond the temporal. Secular*ism* is an unwarranted idolatry, but one must not jump to conclusions about words ending in *-ist.* A secularist could be an opponent of Christianity or merely be employed in a secular position. A naturalist could be a student of nature or someone who argues that there is nothing beyond nature. A humanist may be an atheist who thinks humans invented God, but might also be a Christian scholar of the humanities.

What then can be said of *scientists?* Are they to be understood as promoters of idolatrous *scientisms?* Scientisms are philosophical positions or worldviews falsely claiming to be established by scientific discoveries. No, in this book, as in general usage, a scientist is anyone trained in the practice of science. That practice is focused exclusively on what is natural and temporal, so science can in no way establish the claim that nothing supernatural or eternal can be real. Whenever such a claim is made, it is not scientific but *scientistic.* A career in science is a valid option for a Christian; embracing a scientistic belief-system is not.

Creator and Redeemer
Being a Christian in Science is meant to be a practical guidebook for living

"life in the lab." It is not intended to be a theological treatise, nor to offer a philosophical justification of Christianity. It is not even addressed exclusively to those who consider themselves Christian. It simply begins where a Christian must begin, with a biblically informed understanding of the world, including ourselves as part of that world. As in mathematics, on which science so heavily depends, we must begin with certain propositions accepted as self-evident—the kinds of statements mathematicians know as "axioms."

In the major theistic religions (Judaism, Christianity and Islam), the unifying proposition is that everything in the universe, including ourselves, did not happen by accident, but was intentionally created by God. Further, theists believe that the one God who created and sustains the universe has attributes of a divine *person.*

God can be described as a "heavenly Father," a caring parent who brings human persons into existence and continues to watch over them. Part of that caring is shown in God's desire to communicate with us. With other theists, Christians are "people of the Book," accepting the Old Testament as Holy Scripture, God's self-revelation. To Christians, the books of the New Testament are an extension of God's self-revelation. (See Close-Up 1: The Core of Christian Faith.)

The distinctive mark of a Christian is trust in Jesus Christ as "God with us." Christians believe that the Creator has communicated most directly and persuasively by entering the human race on a specific occasion at a specific time and place. According to the New Testament, God has addressed us in person, as it were—in the person of Jesus Christ—and invited us into a living relationship with the Creator of the universe.

To non-Christians, the claim that a person can be spiritually united through Christ to "the Maker of heaven and earth" may sound preposterous or arrogant. Writing in New Testament times, the apostle Paul saw clearly that what Christians call the good news of salvation must look like foolishness to many others, although he added that "God's foolishness is wiser than human wisdom." There is no getting around the offensiveness of the gospel to some, except by convincing them of its truth by the way we live, in the lab and elsewhere.

There is also no getting around the New Testament proclamations of Christ as creator and redeemer. To a Christian, a study of any part of the natural world is a study of something that God has done through Christ. Science is not only an honorable profession but, in this light, also a worshipful one.

Does that mean that the Bible should serve as a textbook for those who take up the scientific study of God's creation? In one specific sense, yes. The whole Bible is an indispensable guide to the worshipful aspects of a scientific career, though the Old Testament predates modern science by millennia and the New Testament predates it by many centuries.

The Bible does not set forth a detailed description of the created world, as scientists seek to do, but repeatedly refers to that world as evidence of God's purposeful activity. The biblical answer to the question, "Why does anything exist at all?" has not been superseded by scientific discoveries or surpassed by philosophical reasoning. (See Close-Up 2: The Bible and Science.)

The word *laboratory* comes from Latin, meaning "a place for work." Anyone who has worked in a lab, struggling to wrest secrets from nature, can appreciate that the Latin word stems from a wrestling term for "struggle" or "pain." That sense of the word *labor* is retained in obstetrical usage. Though without etymological significance, another point easily remembered is that *laboratory* also contains the word *oratory*. An oratory is "a place for prayer," such as a small chapel. To Christians in science, a lab-oratory is a place to pray about one's work as well as to do that work.

Reality Is Seldom Simple

Christians cannot function in what is commonly called the real world without running into challenges to their basic religious beliefs. Challenges made supposedly on scientific grounds generally come not from science but from various forms of scientism. Scientisms like naturalism, materialism or even evolutionism essentially function as substitute religions.

It is important to recognize scientisms and to distinguish them from authentic science. All Christians should learn to take scientific data and conclusions seriously without accepting the presuppositions of scientific materialists, philosophical naturalists, or secular humanists—who may or may not be scientists themselves. Rampant scientisms pervade western culture, tending to put Christians on the defensive. A young person going into scientific work will, of course, get an insider's view of real scientific theory and practice. Ideally, the more familiar we are with authentic science, the less vulnerable we should be to scientistic alternatives to true religion.

On the other hand, most Christians in science will be expected to help others come to terms with so-called scientific challenges to biblical faith. With relatively few Christians going into scientific work, meeting that challenge can become a heavy responsibility, perhaps even a distraction from doing the quality of research for which Nobel Prizes are awarded. Yet no matter how much time we devote to apologetics or evangelism, most of us in science have a very specific responsibility. We are called to represent Christ faithfully in our laboratories and to represent science faithfully to the world outside the lab, especially to the church. We become witnesses in both directions.

The vocabularies of the scientific community and the Christian community differ widely but are not without points of contact. Many Christians know that the word *worship* is closely related to *worth;* to worship means "to honor what is worthy." Many scientists probably use the word *axiom* without realizing that it comes from a Greek word for "worthy." Consider also the plural word *data* (singular *datum*), from the past participle of the Latin word *dare,* "to give." Science is built on (1) what is worthy of acceptance as being true (axioms) and on (2) "given" information about the natural world (data).

Scientists tend to shy away from the word *truth,* but the search for truth is a goal shared by scientists and Christians alike. Human beings experience the real world in chunks, particular bits of experience that may or may not fit what we have come to expect. Our understanding of reality is formed from what we make of such data-points of actual experience. In the practice of religion, as in science, one tries to "connect the dots" to see their relationship to each other and to the rest of human experience.

Scientists quite literally do that, plotting points on a graph and drawing a smooth curve through them, comparing the pattern of their empirical observations to other curves from theoretical calculations. Religious believers try to make sense of the totality of their data by theological formulations. Either approach requires choices, about which axioms to accept as true and which data-points to consider, but the aim is to get at the meaning of isolated experiences. In order to yield dependable results, both approaches require honesty in making and recording observations, plus willingness to reevaluate tentative conclusions.

It is dangerous, though common, to assume that either scientific or religious conclusions could represent the whole story. Scientists are generally quite tentative about their conclusions, though when scientism takes over, reservations are conveniently dropped. For many "true believers," in science as well as in religion, the way one wants things to come out can override a more modest assessment of what we can know about reality.

Any book about how to be both a serious Christian and a practicing scientist should exemplify honesty, openness and humility. The rest of this chapter is an effort to be up front about important matters, to face some of this book's limitations and possible biases. Think of these sections as a series of reality checks.

Being a Christian

Oversimplification is a risk whenever we try to clarify complex issues. This introductory chapter had to begin with a simple definition of a Christian without pointing out the varieties of Christian experience or the theological distinctions between different branches of Christianity. Christians probably come in more varieties than scientists, partly because of the church's much longer history.

In the eleventh century the institutional church experienced a schism into Eastern Orthodox and Roman Catholic branches, with the Protestant Reformation splitting the latter branch some five centuries later—about the time European science was getting off the ground. Today the number of groups that consider themselves part of the Protestant tradition is vast.

An outstanding job of defining and describing what it means to be a Christian was done by British literary scholar C. S. Lewis (1898-1963). In *Mere Christianity* he gave a thoughtful definition meant to be acceptable to most readers. He acknowledged differences in doctrine, practice and emphasis among believers, but pointed to an essential unity that he found "remarkably robust" across many cultures. What Christians believe, he wrote, is "not only positive but pungent." Lewis saw Christian faith as "divided from all non-Christian beliefs by a chasm to which the worst divisions inside Christendom are not really comparable at all."

My working definition of what it means to be a Christian (as discussed above and in Close-Up 1) may not fully jibe with your experience, or with what is emphasized in your branch of the faith. That need not hinder you from gaining help from this book in making science your Christian calling. Definitions are important, but scientists have learned to get on with their task without waiting for definitions that satisfy everybody.

Being a Scientist

Perhaps surprisingly, saying precisely what *science* means is as problematic as defining what it means to be a Christian. The boundary between authentic science and "fringe science" or pseudoscience is so hard to specify that some writers have facetiously evaded the issue by saying that science is simply "what scientists do." But real scientists do many different things.

A precise definition of science has always been of greater concern to philosophers of science than to working scientists. This "demarcation problem" came to public attention following the trial in 1982 over teaching "creation science" in Arkansas public schools. In his decision, Federal Judge William R. Overton declared that creation science was not science at all but "religion masquerading as science" (i.e., a form of scientism). Most Christians in scientific work probably agree that Judge Overton made the right decision, but some philosophers of science were dissatisfied with the criteria he laid down for what is, and is not, real science.

Again, for present purposes, a working definition will do, or even a tacit agreement on the general characteristics of the scientific enterprise. Like Christianity, science has three major divisions, commonly designated as the physical, biological and social sciences.

Most people recognize science as the study of natural phenomena by observation and experimentation. Scientific explanations are best characterized as simple chains of cause-and-effect restricted to physical (i.e., secondary or proximal) causes, and thus excluding primary, ultimate or supernatural causes. To a theist who trusts in God as both beyond nature and active within it, scientific statements can be only partial descriptions of the way the world works, not comprehensive explanations of the real world.

In *The Limits of Science,* philosopher of science Nicholas Rescher concluded his argument concerning scientific realism this way:

> Realism prevails with respect to the *language* of science (that is, the asserted content of its declarations); but it should be abandoned with respect to the *status* of science (that is, the ultimate tenability or correctness of these assertions). What science says is descriptively committal in making claims regarding "the real world," but the tone of voice in which it proffers these claims is (or should be) provisional and tentative.

Most scientists, like most Christians, are realists of one kind or another. Philosopher of science Larry Laudan cautioned that "scientific realism fails to offer a viable account of scientific values and aims." Though most people believe that science describes a real world, *any* human description of reality remains to some extent a distortion because of its incompleteness. Scientists seldom claim to understand the world as a whole. Each studies only part of the totality of reality.

For example, a psychologist's study of visual perception in humans or in rats will hardly resemble a physicist's study of that phenomenon. The physicist's concern with the properties of the electromagnetic radiation impinging on the organism's visual receptors will differ even from a biochemist's focus on the photochemical reactions within those receptors. A physiologist studying the processing of information from the receptors in the central nervous system will be less concerned with the organism's external behavior than the psychologist would be. To an astronomer, these phenomena are all out of range of the telescope, and thus of little interest, though astronomers themselves depend on visual perceptions of electromagnetic radiation.

Each of the above investigators would honor, as valid scientific work, the efforts of the others. On the other hand, if a biochemist uses rat brains to study the chemical reactions from which physicists' theories arise, or worse, if a social psychologist or cultural anthropologist starts exploring the motives of physicists, watch out. The physicist is likely to accuse them of going beyond the bounds of hard science. Many philosophers of science (to say nothing of physicists) regard physics as "the right stuff," the model of the way all science should be done.

All branches of science are characterized by an interplay of theory and observation. Yet formulating theories and choosing among them (hot topics in the philosophy of science) are more central to some disciplines and subdisciplines than to others. Some physicists describe themselves as experimentalists, others as theoreticians.

To an outsider, psychology seems rife with theoretical schools. Some psychologists do straightforward experimental work, though for obvious reasons clinical psychologists generally obtain their data by observing rather than experimenting on human beings. In the twentieth century, physics was revolutionized by the success of the new quantum theory; in the twenty-first century, biology may be ripe for new theoretical inputs.

In general, the methods of the social sciences are distinguishable from the "exact sciences" of physics and chemistry, with most geological and biological studies located between those extremes. Geophysics and biochemistry are examples of well-established hybrid fields. It was once generally assumed that all of biology would eventually come under the rubric of the physical sciences. Today, what we have learned of the complexity of biological systems keeps that from being a foregone conclusion.

A classic fable illustrates the different levels of exactness of different branches of science, or perhaps merely the disdain of "hard" scientists for anything "softer" than their own branch. One version of the tale has three English scientists hiking through Scotland on holiday. The social scientist spots a sheep on a hillside and says, "Look, the sheep in Scotland are black."

The biologist replies, "Don't jump to conclusions. What you mean is, 'In Scotland there is at least one black sheep.' "

The physicist scoffs, "No, no. Why can't you be more precise? All we can conclude from this observation is that, 'In Scotland there is at least one sheep, one side of which is black.' "

"Natural sciences" is a common term, though few who use it could describe either an unnatural science or a supernatural science. Perhaps it is meant to exclude the human sciences or behavioral sciences. Yet physics deals with the behavior of particles and waves, chemistry with the behavior of atoms and molecules. And as this book emphasizes, science is always done by human persons; hence all science is both natural and human.

To the extent that human beings can be studied by scientific methods, they are as natural as any other object of investigation. What *more* we may be is a question of major concern to Christians. Is the human mind merely an epiphenomenon of a human brain? What humans can do that computers may not be able to do is a current scientific problem bearing on the older philosophical question of what it means to be human.

Another distinction can be made between strictly experimental science and the historical sciences, which try to establish what has happened in the past but cannot be repeated. Cosmology (dealing with the formation of the universe as a whole), historical geology and macroevolutionary biology are examples. Biology was once known as natural history, in contrast to natural philosophy (physics). Some Christian writers distinguish between "operation science," which is experimental, and "origin science," which is more or less equivalent to historical science.

Pure science and applied science were once poles apart. The modern trend is to refer to fundamental research versus strategic research. The distance between the poles was greatly shortened when discoveries in electronics and genetics were rapidly transformed into commercially exploitable technology. Although fundamental researchers sometimes set themselves apart from applied scientists, engineers and technologists, it is obvious that many agriculturalists, engineers and medical practitioners do scientific work.

What tends to unite all who consider themselves scientists is the value placed on empirical data from careful, repeatable observations and experiments. A scientist's focus is on the raw data, despite philosophical argument that all data are theory-laden. Philosophers of science stress that even the initial choices of what data to consider depend on ideas about nature already held by the observer. Scientists stress the reverse proposition. That is, any theories to be taken seriously must be data-driven. That attitude is at the heart of an empirical approach to understanding the world.

In an excellent section on "The Essence of Science" in *Science as a Process,* philosopher David Hull put in simple terms the role of the scientific enterprise in increasing human knowledge:

> Scientists are not infallible. Science is not a process by which we go from no knowledge to some knowledge, or from some knowledge to total knowledge. Rather it is a process by which scientists go from some knowledge to more knowledge. The important feature of science is not that it *always* produces increased knowledge but that *sometimes* it does.

In general, scientists regard their empirical approach as a way of moving toward a closer approximation of reality. To claim more than that is to move beyond the limits of science into philosophy. There is nothing wrong with doing philosophy, but it is not the focus of this book. Science by itself is almost too broad a category for our purposes. Communication across the many scientific disciplines is already difficult enough.

Being a Christian and a Scientist

With so many variations in theory and practice among Christians and among scientists, it is obviously unworkable to lay out a single pattern to follow for those who seek to be both. The function of this book is not to tell you exactly how to be a Christian in the scientific world; it is to show you some challenges faced by others who have already taken that dual path. What difficulties did they encounter and how did they resolve them? What have they been able to accomplish?

Being a Christian in Science has another purpose: to inspire you to go beyond what others have done. Graduate mentors worth their salt want to turn out young scientists more competent than the mentors had been at that same stage in their careers. To be fair to their students, mentors have to do that, because rapidly developing branches of science tend to leave behind those who do not develop with them. Christian mentors or spiritual advisors feel the same way. Aware that we have not accomplished in God's service all that we could have, we try to help a new generation to be more faithful to Jesus Christ than we have been.

One problem of the mentoring relationship is finding the proper fit between student and advisor. Many a graduate student has switched to a different mentor, or wished that departmental rules allowed such a switch, because of a clash in views about the way science should be done or life should be lived. Likewise, young Christians sometimes find themselves outgrowing the limits of a particular church group in which they had earlier experienced spiritual growth.

Christians starting out in scientific work have sometimes felt bereft of role models to pattern their lives after or of heroes to inspire them. In their experience, exemplars in both the scientific career field and the spiritual path they have chosen have been difficult to find. That feeling can be particularly strong if respected voices in either or both communities have told them that they are making a mistake in trying to follow both courses at once.

Many voices speaking through this book will assure you that it is possible to take up science as a Christian calling, to make positive contributions to both communities, and to do so with joy. Further, these men and women want to stir up that joy within you at the very beginning of your journey. That way, if you later run into difficulties, you will have positive experiences to fall back on to keep you going. Words of encouragement that speak through this book will be here to return to after the voices that spoke them are gone. Some are gone already.

Certain ways of putting Christian training to scientific use, and scientific training to Christian use, may not yet have occurred to you. *Being a Christian in Science* draws on the experience of many travelers along different routes. Ideas have come from Christians retired from their scientific careers and from graduate students still in the pipeline. Many of the mature scientists said they wished they had had such a book when they were students. Readers of early drafts offered a variety of suggestions to make the book ring as true as possible to life in the lab.

Science relies on what is called intersubjective verification. It is a process like that counseled repeatedly in the Bible: Check what seems to be true against the experience of others with access to the same Spirit of Truth.

The Publisher(s)

Being a Christian in Science was produced under the auspices of the American Scientific Affiliation (ASA), headquartered in Ipswich, Massachusetts. ASA is a nationwide (and to some extent international) fellowship of several thousand Christians in scientific work. Founded in 1941 to serve an evangelical Christian community then (and still) wrestling with intellectual problems, ASA has always limited its membership to persons with degrees in science. Probably more than half of its members hold doctorates.

ASA is identified as a Christian organization by its Statement of Faith, a succinct *credo* appropriate for scientists accustomed to freedom in expressing theoretical formulations. Besides accepting the authority of the Bible "in matters of faith and conduct" and confessing orthodox Christian doctrine as summarized in the Apostles' and Nicene Creeds, all members pledge "as stewards of God's creation, to use science and technology for the good of humanity and the whole world." (See Close-Up 3: The American Scientific Affiliation.)

To hard-nosed materialists or secular humanists who accept the positivistic notion that science is the only approach to truth, no "real scientist" could express such personal devotion to Truth beyond the reach of science. In fact, though, the American Scientific Affiliation is composed of real scientists and is organized more like a scientific society than a religious body. Its scholarly journal, *Perspectives on Science and Christian Faith,* has always been edited by scientists, using the same referee system used by strictly scientific journals.

The ASA was little known in either the Christian community or the scientific community before the wide distribution in 1986-87 of the first two editions of its guidebook for high school biology teachers, *Teaching Science in a Climate of Controversy.* The same ASA committee responsible for that guidebook then undertook to meet another need: a guidebook for young people headed for careers in science. For *Being a Christian in Science,* ASA worked out a publishing arrangement with InterVarsity Press of Downers Grove, Illinois.

InterVarsity Press (IVP) is the publishing arm of InterVarsity Christian Fellowship (IVCF), a ministry to students on college and university campuses. IVCF came to the United States via Canada in 1941 (the same year ASA was founded) as an offshoot of a parent organization in Great Britain. IVP was established to produce popular books expounding the Christian faith to intelligent readers, plus scholarly works relating that faith to academic pursuits, including science. With IVCF-related groups of graduate students and faculty now existing at major research universities, the combined contacts of ASA and IVP in academia made feasible the publication of this book.

The Book Itself

Teaching Science in a Climate of Controversy took shape as a direct response to a 1984 booklet called *Science and Creationism,* published by the National Academy of Sciences (NAS). ASA's Committee for Integrity in Science Education published its alternative booklet to counter several overstated claims made in the NAS publication.

In the 1980s Congress was expressing concern over widely publicized reports of unethical or questionable conduct in research supported by government grants. Certain "watchdogs of science" threatened that Congress might hold hearings on scientific conduct and pass laws to regulate research more closely. Scientific societies rallied by holding symposia on ethical behavior. Guidelines were published both to educate young scientists and to convince Congress that the situation was under control. In 1989 NAS published *On Being a Scientist,* a booklet dealing with how scientists should behave.

This time the flaw in the NAS publication was not what it said, but what it left out. In its earlier booklet on creationism, NAS had warned science teachers not to get mixed up with something other than science, namely religion. Now it was saying that unless scientists demonstrated ethical principles and moral values, science would suffer. Yet NAS found it hard to say more than something like, "Being dishonest in reporting one's work can hurt one's career and in the long run will hurt science." The rationalistic, objective picture of itself painted by the scientific community offered rather barren soil for cultivating personal values.

Since Christians are accustomed to forceful instruction about honesty and other moral issues, the ASA committee began putting together a supplementary response. Along the way what was envisioned as a small booklet became this book. (Because bookstores are reluctant to stock magazine-like publications, ASA turned the 1993 version of *Teaching Science in a Climate of Controversy* into a paperback with a spine bearing the title.)

Despite a reported distribution of over 200,000 copies of *On Being a Scientist,* few scientists and fewer students seemed to have read it, providing another reason for this book to stand on its own. NAS has since published a revised and enlarged edition of *On Being a Scientist* (1995). Its summary of the way science works makes an excellent introduction to this book. In addition, a valuable bibliography on ethics in science has been added.

So much for the story behind *Being a Christian in Science.* What kind of story does the book itself tell? This chapter is the first of six in Part I, which provides a big picture of science and its challenges for a Christian. Chapter two examines science as both an (exciting) intellectual process and a (sometimes troubling) cultural institution. Chapter three looks at personality traits and investigative styles of scientists, to help you determine if science is indeed your calling. To face that question is important even if you are already in the process of becoming a scientist. Struggling in advanced courses or perhaps flubbing your first research efforts can make you wonder if you have made the right choice.

The next two chapters get down to the nuts and bolts of daily life in the lab. Chapter four emphasizes that a life in science may differ from other lives, but that all of us who follow Christ must learn to live crossculturally in *some* culture. Chapter five shows how specific problems encountered in the scientific subculture can become opportunities to experience and demonstrate the power of the gospel.

The challenge of living in two different cultures simultaneously could leave a false impression that Christians in science must live split lives. The last chapter in Part I stresses the need to live with integrity (from Latin for "untouched," i.e., whole, as an *integer*). The resources suggested can help you develop spiritually and professionally without compartmentalizing your life, and keep at it throughout your career.

Part II includes five Close-Ups, focused examinations of certain aspects of life as a Christian in science. They provide details on our identity as Christians, on using the Bible properly in science, on the American Scientific Affiliation, on how the Internet is changing the way we go about our business, and on exemplars who have paved the way for us.

In a book dealing with two subcultures, certain stylistic choices had to be made. Books aimed at evangelical Christian readers are commonly loaded with biblical references, citing chapter and verse right in the text. Strictly scientific works bristle with numbered references to earlier works.

To avoid interrupting the flow of thought, this book uses neither style. Instead, extensive notes on each chapter and Close-Up appear at the end of the book, documenting quotations, suggesting related readings, and amplifying what is said in the text. These research notes form a running commentary supplying additional information.

Throughout this book, gender-inclusive language is used even when that requires compound forms like "he or she" and "his or her." Generally, awkwardness has been avoided simply by speaking of scientists, Christians, or other groups, in the plural. Readers (whom I hope are in the plural) can then picture human persons of either sex. It was not until 1971 that the standard biographical reference work, *American Men of Science,* which had always listed women as well as men, was retitled *American Men and Women of Science.* It is no wonder that women were annoyed, or that men found it easy to overlook women's contributions.

Nevertheless, traditional male pronouns have been used in this book when speaking of God, partly because such usage is traditional and partly because each possible alternative has serious flaws. Clearly the Creator of the universe is not a sexual being in any anthropomorphic sense, so using pronouns like *he* and *his* for God does not accede to male glorification.

Using the word *God* repeatedly whenever a divine pronoun is called for becomes awkward and, despite the doctrine of the Trinity, the biblical God is not plural. This book follows Jesus' example in speaking of God as our heavenly Father. The parental appellation is also inherently more personal than a functional, epicene term like "Creator." Language, like science (and also religious faith), has limitations.

The Author
Readers of the technical literature of science get accustomed to the passive voice and an indirect third-person style. Sentences like "The sample was analyzed" are meant to convey objectivity. For other readers, such expressions, or repeated references to "the author(s)," even if humanized occasion-

ally by an editorial *we*, get tiresome. For at least the final paragraphs of this first chapter, and at the end of each subsequent chapter, *this* author will drop into a personal style of communication. I do not want to focus attention on myself, however, even when drawing on my own experience. *Being a Christian in Science* is really your story rather than mine.

Would the truest picture of science come from someone working in the field or from a less partial observer looking in from the outside? I am not sure, but the fact is that I have been both. After some twenty years as a practicing scientist, university professor and mentor of graduate students, I hung up my lab coat to become an editor and journalist.

In my second career I was not totally removed from science, though, because one of my editorial tasks was to edit the newsletter of the American Scientific Affiliation. I was one of the founders of ASA's Committee for Integrity in Science Education in 1984 and subsequently a coauthor of *Teaching Science in a Climate of Controversy.* By that time I had published six or eight chapters in books, at least half of them on the relation of science to Christian faith, plus many articles, reviews and even poems.

To sum up, the author of this book is a real person who has had one satisfying career as a scientist and another as an editor and journalist. During that span of four decades, I have had time to do a lot of reflecting on the integration of biblical faith with my particular professions. The problem is in that word *particular,* which limits all of us to our own experience and requires us to broaden ourselves by contact with others, through books and in person.

I have been a particular kind of scientist (a biochemist), but with good friends in many other disciplines, from astronomy to zoology. I am an evangelical Christian, brought up as a Baptist but with close ties to spiritual siblings across a broad range of Christian experience.

As a university professor I worked with colleagues ranging from conservative Christians to militant secularists. Some of the latter probably pegged me as a fundamentalist, partly because I kept a Bible on my desk beside the *Merck Index* and *Handbook of Chemistry and Physics.* Any real fundamentalists would have known better, recognizing that I was more open to contrary opinions than they were. But I tried to listen to all my colleagues and to learn from them.

That is who I am. Now the question is, Who are you? And is science where you belong?

2

Science
Inside Out

THE BEGINNING OF THE twenty-first century is a wonderful time to be entering a research career. Science in all its branches challenges young people with the opportunity to solve significant problems.

The scientific community, like the rest of western society, is kept in a state of flux by developing technologies. Technical fields that hardly existed before, such as genetic engineering, have become household words. Agriculture and medicine are ancient biological technologies, but today the term *biotechnology* refers primarily to direct manipulation of the genetic material, something unimaginable in the past. DNA's molecular structure was unknown until X-ray crystallographers worked it out a scant five decades ago.

In less than one individual's lifespan, laboratory work has been transformed by the wide availability of sophisticated instruments. Scientists today obtain measurements with amazing speed and precision. They routinely analyze data in ways that make the work of past generations seem primitive in comparison. In laboratories, as in everyday life in industrialized countries, computers have changed the way almost everything is done.

The computer entered the laboratory as a general purpose number cruncher to deal with numerical data obtained in the old-fashioned way (by hand). Before long, instruments were feeding data directly into "dedicated" computers, which could also program instrumental protocols. The graphics capability of powerful computers soon enabled chemists to visualize extremely complex molecular structures. Societies like the American Chemical Society began publishing and distributing peer-reviewed specialized software.

Meanwhile, word processing and desktop publishing were changing the way information flowed from the lab. The ability to store vast amounts of information on compact disks introduced new techniques for searching the literature. Electronic exchange of information via international networks is developing so rapidly that even scientists who use the Internet daily can hardly keep up. (See Close-Up 4: On to the Internet.)

A Troubled Institution

Despite such heady developments, for many scientists the late 1990s are not a happy time to be in the lab—or to be looking for a job. Despite ready access to desktop and benchtop computers, much research requires ever more expensive instruments and technical assistance. Rising costs have put a squeeze on laboratory budgets. Senior scientists who remember "the way things used to be" consider the situation discouraging, if not for themselves then certainly for the younger people in their laboratories.

Even before the current budget-cutting wave swept into Congress, established researchers with a proven track record could no longer count on their grant applications being funded. Many scientists hope that this situation is a phase that will pass; others see it as a long-term trend. Some accept it as inevitable; a few fight it with whatever political clout they can muster.

In January 1991, Nobel laureate Leon Lederman, professor of physics at the University of Chicago, produced a pessimistic report titled *Science: The End of the Frontier?* This report appeared as a special supplement to *Science,* the weekly journal of the American Association for the Advancement of Science (AAAS). Lederman, then president-elect of AAAS, based his report on some 250 responses from leading scientists in American universities to a survey of their situation and that of their colleagues.

One section of Lederman's report posed the question, "Why Is the Morale of American Scientists So Low?" The next section, "Impacts of the Funding Situation," seemed to provide a big part of the answer.

From 1968 to 1990, federal expenditures for basic and applied research at U.S. colleges and universities rose from about $1.5 billion to almost $8 billion. With research costs rising faster than the general rate of inflation, Lederman calculated that this amounted to only a twenty percent increase in research support. But in the same period, the number of doctoral-level scientists and engineers at those institutions doubled, from about 100,000 to 200,000. Contending that "the United States is underinvesting in research," Lederman warned of an increasing shortfall in producing the number of scientists and engineers needed to solve the country's problems. He urged all scientists to lobby Congress for a twofold increase in federal support for academic science.

In a 1991 cover story on "Crisis in the Labs," *Time* magazine brought the Lederman report to public attention. The story's subhead read: "Beset by a budget squeeze, cases of fraud, relentless activists and a skeptical public, American researchers are under siege." Even if the *Time* story was over-blown, Lederman's recommendation touched off a sharp debate among scientists, including some of the very people who had responded to his inquiry. According to senior correspondent Wil Lepkowski of the American Chemical Society's weekly *Chemical & Engineering News,*

Lederman's report engages the issue of whether academic science wants to be seen as a messianic claimant to world progress deserving an immediate doubling of support, or whether it should be seen as a group of favored intellectual citizens grateful for whatever they get from the public at a time of human suffering in every urban alleyway and rural enclave.

One critic of the Lederman report, then National Academy of Engineering president Robert G. White, saw the trials of academic science as equivalent to those of other segments of society going through a shakeout in hard economic times. According to White, "We have a crisis of rising expectations that will not be met." Materials scientist Rustum Roy of Pennsylvania State University doubted that subsidized academic scientists (whom he once sarcastically called "welfare queens in white coats") deserved to be treated any differently from "other workers" in a shrinking economy.

AAAS is considered the leading scientific society in the world, with over 143,000 individual members and nearly 300 affiliated science organizations. Its members may have been divided about Leon Lederman's passionate plea, but the AAAS leadership clearly recognized that young scientists faced a serious problem in the job market of the 1990s. In 1991 *Science* published a pull-out section on *Science Careers,* containing helpful advice along with an assessment of the way things were going. In that section, news writer Constance Holden began an article on "Career Trends for the '90s" with these words:

There ought to be a fin de siècle air of excitement for the newly fledged science postdoc these days: after all, he or she will hit the most productive years of scientific life not merely in a new century but in a new millennium. The horizons should seem limitless: Except . . . everywhere our young hopefuls look, their scientific elder statesmen are grousing.

In academia, administrators and investigators alike are hounded by money shortages. In industry, vice presidents of R&D [research and development] are bemoaning the sluggish economy, which they blame for holding down research budgets. Policy gurus in government are anguishing over where the next generation of scientists will come from. Lab heads are worrying about what new hoops the government science police will make them jump through. And nearly everyone connected to science fears for the morale and motivation of young investigators.

Confusing as all this is, there's yet more to confound the budding scientist. As Heraclitus might say, all is in flux. Traditional boundaries are dissolving. High-tech firms are bridging the gap between academic and industrial science; universities—and many academic labs—are looking more like businesses. Lines between basic and applied research are blurring. Disciplinary divisions are becoming irrelevant—even counterproductive—as many of the most striking research advances are occurring on the interface of multiple fields. Even geographic boundaries count for less as science becomes increasingly globalized. And all of these potentially exhilarating but disorienting trends are being accelerated by the emergence of incredible new tools—the computer being the most obvious—that are altering and speeding up the process of science at a dizzying rate. (Reprinted with permission from *Science* 252 (1991): 1110; copyright 1991, American Association for the Advancement of Science.)

Some young scientists have spent years in a series of temporary postdoctoral posts, their futures on hold as they send résumés to every department in the country. A projection that two-thirds of the full professors in American universities will need to be replaced by the year 2000 is little comfort to junior scientists unable to find a job this year to put them on that tenure track.

In the long run, prospects for technical employment should be bright, partly because the world faces many economic challenges. For example, environmental problems brought on by population increase and unwise use of technology will not be solved without employing technically trained individuals. Yet the future of science depends on many human choices and many factors beyond the control of scientists and technologists.

A few decades ago, continued growth of the scientific enterprise seemed inevitable, at least in the absence of an all-out nuclear war. The nuclear threat has diminished considerably, but political turmoil and social unrest make the future uncertain. Populations cannot expand indefinitely without using up biological carrying capacity. It seems equally reasonable that the number of scientists and the amount of scientific research that can be supported must someday level off.

Constance Holden pointed to a number of "career trends" of which young scientists should be aware. For example, demographic changes make it hard to predict whether there will be a shortage or surplus of trained scientists in the future. In the 1980s, while the total U.S. population of scientists and engineers was doubling (to over four million), college enrollments began to decline. That decline should bottom out in the late 1990s, just as many professors reach retirement age, creating a demand for new academic scientists.

The size of the demand for new teachers and researchers in the U.S. will vary from discipline to discipline; the supply factor is complicated by the influx of foreign-born scientists, which may increase. Many industrial scientists lost their jobs in the late 1980s and early 1990s as labs were downsized. Physicist Daniel Kleppner of the Massachusetts Institute of Technology said he felt "more and more uneasy about advising students to enter science."

Those who do find employment also find profound changes in the lab environment, some of which reflect "the intensely competitive milieu in which scientists must now work." In some fields, multi-billion-dollar "big science" projects like the Superconducting Super-Collider (the SSC, now canceled by Congress) or the Human Genome Project (still underway) have eaten into government funds for new grants to individual investigators. Debates continue over other funding questions: Do "fundamental" projects or "strategic" projects give better long-range payoffs? Should research money go primarily to a few "centers of excellence" or be spread around geographically to build up lesser institutions (and attract broader congressional support)?

Holden concluded by advising scientists to become "more flexible than ever as the funding environment becomes less so." That could mean shifting to nontraditional career patterns, or simply lowering one's expectations and altering one's preconceptions. Whatever else it might mean, Holden stressed that young scientists will have to be creative in developing their careers.

The most distinguished scientists are not in agreement on the future of science. In 1979 Nobelist Peter Medawar urged young people to enter science as an unending frontier. Fellow Nobelist Max Perutz responded that although that might be true of Medawar's field (immunology), in many fields there may not be "a whole world of physical phenomena that has escaped detection." Scientists are aware that turn-of-the-century predictions of the end of physics were demolished by the unexpected discovery of quantum phenomena. Nevertheless, some are again beginning to ask if the end is near, at least for the "big questions" in certain branches of science.

Science May Need You

Christian young people contemplating a scientific career should not be put off just because science as an institution seems to be in trouble. On the contrary, its present difficulties make the laboratory a more challenging place to live out the Christian faith, provided we have our own priorities straight.

The current generation of younger scientists was not born when John F. Kennedy gave his 1961 inaugural address, inspiring young Americans with the appeal, "Ask not what your country can do for you, but what you can do for your country." Kennedy was paraphrasing a statement by a former Supreme Court justice, an exhortation to selfless service that most Christians would see as echoing a much earlier source: the Gospels.

When two of his disciples began asking for special favors, Jesus said that no matter what other people do, his followers should not put their own interests first. Pointing to his own role, he said that "the Son of Man came not to be served but to serve, and to give his life a ransom for many." None of Jesus' modern followers should go into science, or any other profession, determined to squeeze out of it as much as they can for themselves.

The Christian ideal is to serve others, to live creatively and responsibly, and, in the process, to support ourselves and contribute to those in need. Christians believe that to trust in the Lord "with all your heart," acknowledging God "in all your ways," will lead to "length of days and years of life and abundant welfare." No matter how tight the job market, each individual needs only one job—and our heavenly Father knows our needs.

Does such idealism sound hopelessly unrealistic? Ironically, idealism may offer the most realistic hope for science. What the institution needs even more than a solution to its funding problems is to attract young men and women with high ideals. Even if the deleterious effects of declining research budgets can be overcome, other problems have revealed deep cracks in the foundation of the scientific edifice.

Questions of Value

Establishing priorities forces individuals, institutions and entire societies to consider which of two options is better than the other. Should I go into science or into some other line of work? Should our lab devote its energies to open-ended research or try to solve some practical problem? Should the nation spend billions of dollars on a space station or use that money for other purposes?

Scientists try hard to be "objective" in making choices, or at least to project an image of objectivity to people outside science. They may tell the public that "Science can say nothing about beauty, meaning, morals, ethics, values, and a host of important matters that lie outside its purview." Of those concepts, the one that seems most compatible with objective reasoning is *value*, a term used in various ways in quantitative scientific discourse.

Mathematicians solve equations to find the value of x; chemists and physicists look up the numerical values of certain constants or physical properties in tables; biologists consider the "survival value" of various genetic traits. Yet many of the value questions on the minds of scientists today lie outside the bounds of science.

The Value *of* Science

The general public obviously considers science valuable, and continues to support it with tax money. Efforts to sell the public (and the Congress) on the value of science frequently emphasize its role in technological innovation. The golden age of research in the United States came about after people saw the all-important role played by industrial technology in winning World War II and protecting America during the cold war that followed.

In that period the number of scientists grew so rapidly that it could be said that over ninety percent of the scientists who have ever lived were then living. What was also true (but seldom said) was that a very large percentage of the world's scientists and engineers were working on military objectives.

Not all scientists favored the military justification of research support, some opposed it, and many are still ambivalent about doing defense work. The Strategic Defense Initiative (SDI, the "Star Wars" of the Reagan years) was considered an unworkable concept by a number of scientists who never-theless supported their fundamental research by SDI grants, because that was where the money was. Major cutbacks in U.S. spending for defense R&D since the dissolution of the Soviet Union have cost many scientists and engineers their high-paying jobs.

We are now in a relatively peaceful era, or at least one with no immediate military threats to the United States. Science-based technology for peaceful purposes is valued by most Americans. Advocates for scientific research, however, have learned to be nimble in identifying technological successes with science. After all, highly publicized technological failures also occur, as when the Challenger spacecraft exploded in 1986 or when the Hubble space telescope initially showed flaws requiring an expensive and problematic shuttle mission to correct.

A cynic might observe that every time an expensive project succeeds, the public has science to thank; if it fails, technology was at fault, not science. When construction of a base in space was first proposed, scientists working for NASA probably saw in it great potential for advancing science. Other scientists, fearing that their research would suffer from the drain of funds, were more inclined to see it as a gigantic boondoggle.

In recent decades a large segment of the American public has developed a heightened environmental consciousness. People no longer see all peaceful technological advances as desirable or as environmentally benign. Even in medical fields, citizens now sometimes question the value of a breakthrough, generally credited as a *scientific* achievement.

Most medical advances are achieved at great cost, and troublesome side effects may eventually come to light. Although few people would prefer to live without antibiotics, we now know that their widespread, often careless use has produced potentially uncontrollable strains of antibiotic-resistant pathogens. Even when research diminishes the toll of a major killer like heart disease, many realize that living longer makes them more likely to die of Alzheimer's or cancer or some other debilitating disease.

In a sense, bottom-line value questions have arisen because the scientific enterprise has been so successful. With many technical problems now solved, doomsayers tend to devalue science-based technology, pointing to some serious problems it has caused. At the other extreme, even technological optimists must weigh the benefits of more research against its rising costs. How much is society willing to invest in science? Have other public needs been neglected? If scientists can land astronauts on the moon, why can't they provide housing for the homeless? Such complaints give the impression that science may have been oversold.

Values *from* Science

The acknowledged success of science has raised a second set of value questions, which have to do with the scientific process itself rather than with its products. The 1995 NAS publication *On Being a Scientist* summarizes the core values on which the research enterprise is based as "honesty, skepticism, fairness, collegiality, and openness." Scientists who value science for its own sake sometimes seem shocked that other people do not share their enthusiasm.

In the past the American public has placed high value on the scientific approach, so nonscientists have often tried to get that prestige to rub off on their own activities. All kinds of enterprises are labeled as scientific by their proponents: Christian Science, Divine Science, Scientology, noetic science, even domestic science. Advertisers repeatedly tell the public that scientific research shows a certain brand of toothpaste or gasoline or headache remedy to be superior. Such claims seldom enhance public perceptions of science, however, especially if the product is shoddy.

Chapter three will look more closely at qualities valued highly by scientists as characteristic of genuine science. The point made in this section is simply that competition sometimes exists between those values and other human values not considered intrinsic to scientific work.

In academic circles, scholars in the humanities or the arts sometimes feel envious of what seems to be a preferential treatment of the sciences. Labs full of scientific equipment are more expensive than the requirements of English departments. Chemistry professors employable in industry or government command higher university salaries than history professors. Of course, when the price of crude oil dropped precipitously, geologists laid off by petroleum companies suddenly found academic salaries more appealing. More recently, the demise of the Super-Collider sent hundreds of suddenly unemployed physicists chasing after relatively few academic openings.

Academic conflict over cultural hegemony goes deeper than competition for limited budgets. It also surfaces in debates about curriculum. Should college students be required to take more or less science than they do now? Must all students learn to think like scientists in order to become good citizens? Or might the vaunted scientific approach tend to depersonalize or dehumanize individuals by its insistence on dispassionate objectivity? Could stress on quantitative reasoning contribute to a devaluation of other aspects of our humanity?

After a lifetime of scientific work, Charles Darwin commented on his "curious and lamentable loss" of interest in poetry, music, and art—all of which had appealed to him in his youth—as his mind became "a kind of machine for grinding general laws out of large collections of facts." He felt that the loss of those tastes, caused by "atrophy of that part of the brain" on which they depended, amounted to "a loss of happiness, and may possibly be injurious to the intellect, and more probably to the moral character, by enfeebling the emotional part of our nature."

Such single-mindedness has frequently been caricatured in "mad scientist" cartoons, or in a vignette that goes something like this: A physicist, invited to an artistic friend's apartment in a high-rise building, sits for a few minutes as though in another world: listening to Mozart, gazing at a beautiful painting on the wall, contemplating a volume of Shakespeare on his lap. Suddenly he jumps up, takes out a stopwatch, and in turn drops the stereo, painting, and book from a window, timing their fall to the ground below. Then he turns to his appalled friend and says with a satisfied smile, "See? Galileo and Newton were right!"

The view that scientific values and spiritual or religious values war against each other depends, of course, on how those values are defined. Economist Kenneth Boulding examined the values of science and those of the rest of society in his 1980 AAAS presidential address on "Science: Our Common Heritage." He referred to the initial explosion of scientific thinking in western Europe as a "cultural mutation" following an "ethical mutation"—a change in the human value system. Certain features of the scientific ethos began to distinguish science as a subculture from the rest of humanity.

In the first place, Boulding said, scientists place a high value on curiosity, coupled with the testing of ideas. Thus a "curiously uneasy" combination of imagination and logic in forming and testing theories came into existence. That distinctive emphasis was accompanied by a high value on telling the truth, because scientists must be able to trust the records of others. Boulding commented that veracity is "a sporadic value in folk cultures and a rare value in political cultures."

Another major characteristic is "abandonment of threat as a means of changing people's opinions and behavior." In the scientific ethos, minds should be influenced by evidence, not by coercion. Religious cultures have been known to use coercion and almost all political cultures have relied on it or been prepared to do so. Even in the scientific culture, Boulding acknowledged, exceptions occur—as when students are forced to conform, or when extreme practices lead to expulsion from the organized scientific community. Threat returns to science when science becomes politicized: witness the T. D. Lysenko tragedy in Stalinist times, when an illiterate charlatan gained absolute control over Soviet biology and agriculture. Even the AAAS itself, Boulding admitted, had used threats during the war in Vietnam, officially changing the location of its annual meeting from one city to another in order to use its economic clout as a form of political pressure.

Although Boulding pointed to the positive values of science, he added: "There is constant potential tension between the scientific community, with its peculiar ethic, and the social environment in which it finds itself and which supports it." Conflict has surfaced in the past, he warned, and might do so again.

Values *in* Science

We have seen that science is not only valued by outsiders but has its own positive values to offer the world. Lately a third set of value questions has been on the minds of scientific leaders, questions that more or less directly triggered the writing of this book. These questions concern values that scientists have to learn outside of science but incorporate into their practice to keep the scientific enterprise afloat.

In the past decade, a few scientists have been caught fabricating data, reporting results of experiments that never took place, using research funds for unauthorized purposes, and suppressing or distorting research findings for the benefit of an employer. Further, the general public has found out about it.

Today scientists seem no more immune than politicians to corruption by the "root of all kinds of evil." With big money at stake, distinguished scientists have brought suit over the priority of discovery. Some have hastily called press conferences to announce preliminary results rather than waiting to publish in a refereed scientific journal. Some have lobbied Congress for pet pork-barrel projects from which they stand to gain.

Researchers are often under tremendous pressure to produce publishable results. In the past, even a strong suspicion that a novice scientist had altered data or engaged in some other shady research practice was sufficient grounds to remove that individual from a laboratory position. Recently, though, when a congressional oversight committee investigated publication of allegedly false data, a senior investigator (and Nobel laureate) was accused of stonewalling the investigation and covering up misconduct that had occurred in his laboratory. He subsequently resigned his post as president of a major university, although he claimed he would continue to do research.

Another highly publicized case sent ripples through the academic pond. A prominent scientist resigned the presidency of another university over alleged misuse of funds for overhead expenses allowed on government grants. An audit showed that money for support of research had been used for redecorating the president's home. It may be that the scientist-turned-administrator merely went along with accepted practices, or failed to exercise proper oversight. Even a scientifically illiterate public can discern that it is wrong to mismanage funds given for research. On-the-job training may be the only way young scientists learn how to manage research funds, but they are expected not to cheat and not to condone cheating.

News stories probably stretch some charges of misconduct out of proportion, since reporters love to expose the foibles of "high and mighty" establishment figures. Yet reports in almost every issue of *Science* or *The Scientist,* periodicals addressed to working scientists, raise ethical questions concerning some new incident within the citadel of science. Scientific leaders see a need to instruct graduate students about ethics, but they also want to defend scientific freedom against encroaching regulation. From within the citadel, regulation is generally seen as congressional meddling.

Many scientists who began their careers around the time of World War II are dismayed at what is happening to science as an institution. In letters published in scientific periodicals, mature scientists sometimes confess that if they were starting out today they might choose some other occupation. The whole enterprise has not gone sour, but such a large barrel may well contain some bad apples.

A pair of science reporters blew the whistle in a 1982 book, *Betrayers of the Truth: Fraud and Deceit in the Halls of Science.* Authors William Broad and Nicholas Wade examined dozens of cases of misconduct that "failed to conform to the model of science implied by the conventional wisdom." The scientists they cited who published false data had successfully defied all the safeguards of logic, replication, peer review and objectivity, sometimes over a long period. Broad and Wade concluded that although fraud and deceit have always been a hidden part of science, the situation is getting worse.

Those who wish to denigrate science and those determined to protect it from outside interference continue to debate the impact of such "sin" on the institution as a whole. Most scientists seem to doubt its importance (though many have heard of at least one example in their field). The prevalence of scientific sin is downplayed by some who study science as a social phenomenon. In *Science as a Process,* David Hull included a long section on the institution's built-in social mechanisms for preventing or weeding out anomalous behavior.

After arguing that errors tend to remain undetected only in the "backwaters" of science, Hull discounted the conclusions of Broad and Wade. Seven of the thirty-four cases they documented took place more than two centuries in the past. Five of the perpetrators could only marginally be considered scientists (e.g., a parapsychologist), four had committed plagiarism rather than falsifying research findings and five or six cases were not of outright fabrication but the kind of "fudging" or "judicious finagling" of data found even in the work of the exemplary Isaac Newton. Finally, of the eighteen examples of outright fraud, many were committed by graduate students, especially by those "trained in countries without much in the way of a scientific tradition."

Thus, while some writers (e.g., Broad and Wade) see documented cases of fraud and deceit as much more than a passing blemish on the face of science, others (e.g., Hull) emphasize that scientists in general adhere to the operative norms of research. Nevertheless, there is agreement on the kinds of pressures that cause some scientists to yield to "the ordinary human passions of ambition, pride, and greed."

Broad and Wade described science as an arena in which participants have always striven for two distinct goals: "to understand the world and to achieve recognition for their personal efforts in doing so." The same duality of purpose was expressed by Hull in his description of science as "a matter of competitive cooperation." Since scientists must use the results of each other's research, to be recognized they must not only publish accurate data but also cite accurately the work of others. Erroneous claims, intentional or not, are likely to be discovered and punished in one way or another. Such errors "are liable to hurt one's opponents, but they are even more likely to damage one's allies."

Science is clearly a human activity in which people have opponents and allies, vices and virtues. Unless the incidents that have surfaced are but the tip of a giant iceberg of self-serving motivation, the ethical situation is not desperate. Yet it is taken seriously by the National Academy of Sciences, Sigma Xi (the Scientific Research Society) and the American Association for the Advancement of Science, all of which have called for greater emphasis on ethical behavior in science.

Where Do Values Come From?

To consider one kind of behavior preferable to another requires us to think about what is good and about what is bad or evil. Questions of good and evil are ethical questions, the subject matter not of science but of religion and philosophy. The behavioral or human sciences can tell us *how* human beings behave, but the question under consideration is how human beings *should* behave, and specifically how *scientists* should behave.

To avoid entanglement with politics and religion, scientists have generally described what they do as merely trying to uncover cause-and-effect relationships at work in the physical world. Many hold that studies of those *proximate* linkages can be carried out without reference to *ultimate* causes or concerns. In other words, scientists can explore the links of a very long natural chain without considering what that chain might be anchored to at either end. Where we ultimately came from and where we are ultimately headed are religious questions. Of course, a scientist, like anyone else, may ponder those questions but, like anyone else, must seek the answers outside of science.

Religious believers do not automatically behave more ethically than religious skeptics, but philosophers recognize that codes of conduct are rooted in "ultimate concerns." Any scientist reluctant to acknowledge the religious basis of ethics needs to be reminded that even the logical foundation of the scientific ethos stemmed from a religiously based conviction. That belief, in Kenneth Boulding's words, was that "the real world not only existed but would itself respond to inquiry." Boulding was willing to speculate that "it was not wholly an accident that science arose in a Christian society." Restricting scientific work to proximate questions, of course, enables non-theists to participate in it fully, despite its origins in the theistic belief that we live in a created world.

When the ethical responsibility of individual scientists is under consideration, it is almost impossible to dissociate science from religious conviction. Although religion and morality can be studied by social scientists, by definition one cannot be objective about one's own beliefs, or about one's behavior based on those beliefs. Science as an institution rests on millions of personal moral decisions made by hundreds of thousands of scientists every day.

Modern science took hold in a culture in which ethical norms were consciously grounded on biblical foundations. The Ten Commandments of the Old Testament spelled out absolute principles of right and wrong. Most members of that older culture knew that telling a lie was a sin, not merely that it was bad for society, or would get them in trouble. Because the Bible recorded "Do not bear false witness" as a direct order from God, even born liars knew that it was wrong to lie. It was also wrong to murder, to commit adultery, to dishonor one's parents, and so on.

Christians need not get into arguments with atheists or humanists over the biblical foundations of modern science; historians will eventually sort that out. Nor should we expect anyone who denies the Creator's existence and power to acknowledge that God has revealed moral guideposts. We are not accountable for the behavior of others.

Further, we can acknowledge that any code of ethics, revealed or otherwise, must be applied to real-life situations. Jesus himself did so when he pointed to anger as the inner problem leading to murder, and lust to sexual misconduct. In fact Jesus summed up "all the law and the prophets" by exhorting his followers to love God with all their hearts and to treat others as they would want to be treated.

If some scientists have other foundations for their behavior, so be it. Christian behavior is rooted in biblical precepts and in loyalty to Jesus Christ. We need not apologize for bringing those precepts with us into scientific work. Moreover, in addition to a rigorous standard of conduct, Christians have something equally important for living an ethically oriented life: assurance of forgiveness. The gospel tells us that we will not be forsaken if we find ourselves unable to do perfectly what we know to be right.

What science needs, in order to pull itself out of the dumps and then to thrive, cannot come from application of any "scientific method." What is needed most to keep the scientific enterprise on the right track is a continual influx of bright young people with high ideals.

Where do such young people come from? It may seem strange to say that the future of science depends on babies being born into loving families and brought up, before they ever think about science, to choose what is right over what is wrong. Yet that has always been true. Scientists who celebrate Christmas with their families should understand it, because in the Christian understanding of history, a newborn baby changed everything.

Lessons from History

Perhaps a decline of personal moral values among scientific workers was to be expected. Most of the earliest pioneers of modern science were devout believers in the God of the Bible, to whom they felt personally responsible for their actions. Soon, though, an upstart scientific establishment was challenging an aging religious one over the question of which establishment would exercise cultural control. The contest was not the "warfare between science and theology" that some writers have made it out to be, but the outcome could be described as a kind of uneasy truce. Scientific institutions were content to leave ultimate philosophical questions to the church in order to focus on proximate cause-and-effect questions.

Over the next few centuries, Christians in scientific work accommodated themselves to the task of describing the workings of creation on the basis of physical forces alone, without reference to God's supernatural presence or influence. That methodology was acceptable as a "rule of the game" because no one then considered science the only game in town. There were warnings, however, that if science were to become a dominant cultural force, its characteristically nontheistic way of thinking would pave the way for an atheistic erosion of belief.

Though many now see evidence in society of an erosion of belief, it would be difficult to pin the blame entirely on science. What is clear is that by dropping the God of the Bible from its conversation, institutional science has lost its absolute, transcendent basis for ethical judgments.

Trouble in institutional science could also have been anticipated by looking at the historical experience of the Christian church. For roughly its first three hundred years, Christianity was essentially a fellowship of joyfully creative yet serious people who surprised the culture around them by their wonderment and absorption in "unworldly" pursuits. The early Christians were often misunderstood and even persecuted as a dangerous counterculture—until Christianity rather suddenly became an established religion. With the conversion of the emperor Constantine in A.D. 323, the church received government recognition, but at the price of entanglement with political establishments.

By about a dozen centuries later the church had become a dominant cultural force in Europe, but an institution thoroughly beholden to secular powers. That was when European science got *its* start—as essentially a fellowship of joyfully creative yet serious people surprising the culture around them by *their* wonderment and absorption in another kind of "unworldly" pursuit.

The transformation of science into an established institution was inevitable once scientists sought patronage from wealthy rulers. Scientists dependent on government support were expected to support governments in return, serving as consultants and using their skills to develop new industries and new weapons systems. Even Galileo helped sell the civil authorities on his new telescope by pointing out its military and commercial usefulness. In 1863 the U.S. government chartered the National Academy of Sciences to aid its military effort.

So, in about the same number of centuries it had taken for the church, science also turned into an influential cultural establishment, deeply entangled with political powers. In industrialized nations today, public policies as well as consumer products are sold on the basis of how "scientific" they are. In a vast social experiment in our century, certain national governments officially embraced science while officially denying religious faith. The results of communist efforts to replace faith in God by faith in science are still coming in, some of them tragic.

Like the Christian church after Constantine, science has enjoyed great freedom. Like the institutional church over the centuries, science has influenced government policies and people's deepest beliefs. And like the medieval church, perhaps, modern science may have promised more than it could deliver. To ordinary citizens it has begun to look like an expensive, self-serving institution run by a powerful elite. Its priests speak a specialized mathematical language as arcane to ordinary people as medieval Latin. This surrogate church claims to have the keys to (economic) salvation, if the citizenry would only turn over their children to be educated from their earliest years along scientific lines.

The idea of scientists as priests of a religion whose cult is bound up with power has not gone unnoticed by scholars. They have observed that when the secularized profession of research gets entangled with "science policy," it becomes a collective faith, even a state religion:

> To an important extent, indeed, scientific research has become the secular religion of materialistic society; and it is somewhat paradoxical that a country whose constitution enforces the strict separation of church and state should have contributed so much public money to the establishment and propagation of scientific materialism.

As one senior professor of humanities put it, despite all that science has accomplished, public confidence has waned partly because "what in fact has been achieved is so much below what had been promised and guaranteed from the end of World War II on." Not only that, but

> the immense prominence and the hugely enhanced visibility of the scientists have made prominent and visible the incessant controversies, differences of diagnosis and evaluation, increasingly shrill, even bitter . . . and . . . outright, advertised political orientation of scientists, [which] have inevitably diminished public respect for men of knowledge. The same erosion of status that began with the clergy in the last century is to be seen today in the ranks of scholars and scientists.

Christians today bear the weight of church history, with its costly mistakes as well as its spiritual breakthroughs. We are also accustomed to jeers from outsiders about institutional hypocrisy. The current troubles of institutional science thus sound very much like something Christians have heard before. The press and the general public delight in seeing another arrogant establishment get its comeuppance.

What science needs, of course, is not better public relations but a renewed vision of its real self. Christians need that, too, but we have many visionaries to remind us that the institution is not what really counts.

At its heart, science is not an institution. Rather, it is committed individuals working with others of like mind toward the goal of understanding how the world works. The scientific enterprise depends on shared values, but an impersonal, heartless scientific establishment cannot generate those values. They must come from beyond science, in the personal lives of those who enter the profession.

Theists bring values with us into the practice of science, as do atheists, agnostics and others. Our religious faith offers an ultimate basis for the ethical decision making that leading scientists recognize as so badly needed.

A Personal Testimony

As someone who eventually left the practice of science, I need to be straightforward about my experience. The facts are that my twenty-year career in academic science was thoroughly satisfying and that I left the field before many of the problems mentioned in this chapter had surfaced. To keep from embellishing (after more than another twenty years), I will confine my reflections to what I wrote in two essays about the time I left scientific work.

In 1972 at the University of Michigan, the Institute for Advanced Christian Studies (IFACS) sponsored a conference on ethical issues in science. Several papers responded to B. F. Skinner's positivistic *Beyond Freedom and Dignity,* which had just been published. Others dealt with drug research, genetic control, and—with an unpopular war in Vietnam dragging on—the question of whether Christians in science should do "war work."

In my paper I took a personal approach, pointing to three small-scale ethical problems arising in my day-to-day practice of biochemistry. All three actually boiled down to the effects of competition on my desire to treat others the way I would want to be treated—that is, to follow the Golden Rule, important to me as a Christian.

One dilemma I described was over what to say in grant requests: I wanted to be honest and realistic but was aware that my career was on the line each time I competed for limited funds against requests from the best and brightest in my field. Second, in writing up research results I knew I had to be truthful, but I also needed to attach importance to my work, lest my papers fall into that fraction of "less valuable" papers rejected by referees or editors (up to fifty percent in the best journals).

Third, I had begun to experience the pressure of what I called the "mechanization" of scientific work. I told the story of how, after wangling the purchase of an expensive piece of analytical equipment to solve a problem I was working on, I felt obligated to keep it in service. I had to hire a technician, solicit samples from other investigators, and otherwise organize my life around the presence of that instrument in my laboratory. I wrote:

> In science, as in other fields, the machines we have increasingly come to rely on are highly complex, "almost human." But as machines take on more human attributes, we see human beings not freed to become more human, as we had hoped, but constrained to become more and more like machines. This mechanization of people seems to come not so much from understanding ourselves mechanistically as from competing among ourselves for the available resources. Machines perform subhuman tasks more efficiently than humans can. One makes a machine of oneself simply by limiting oneself to a single objective at a time. That is the way to "get things done." Competition forces us to that kind of efficiency. In the course of a scientific career we may have to drop other aspects of life to become first a grade-grinding machine, then a data-collecting machine, a computing machine, a grant-getting machine, a teaching machine, and finally a machine-tending machine. Scientific work is intense and competitive. And although it is a human enterprise, it is not necessarily a humane one.

In that paper, which I called "Whole People and Half Truths," I said that young scientists generally start out as whole people seeking the whole truth, but learn to settle for less than the whole truth. The problem is that to gain even those half-truths, we may have to sacrifice something of our wholeness and then ignore or suppress that sacrifice to continue to do good scientific work. At the time, I still had about a month left of a year's leave (without pay) taken to think about my career. The intensity of my quandary showed in a final paragraph:

> If we remain as whole people, we see that we are dealing with half-truths. But the whole truth may contain the knowledge that we are making half-people of ourselves. What shall we do? Is everyone in the same situation? Is there anything better than science we could do? Or is there a better way to do science?

Five years after switching to a new career, which of course had its own ethical dilemmas and competitive pressures, I looked back on my years in science in an article published in *Radix* magazine. I explained that as a university scientist I had been doing "the most satisfying work I could imagine getting paid to do" and had been paid so well that "I was sometimes embarrassed to be enjoying my work so much." By age forty-five,

> I had put twenty years as a Ph.D. into my profession, into several academic communities and into the lives of countless individual students. I worked among congenial and intelligent people in a parklike campus setting with

an atmosphere of freedom and integrity.

Nevertheless, God seemed to lead me out of that career just as he had led me into it. Like Thoreau, who said in *Walden* that he left the woods "for as good a reason as I went there," I had something else to do, and was still young enough and adventurous enough to take a crack at it. Having done what I could to humanize my profession, my department and the university, I could make a different kind of contribution simply by resigning, so my department could replace me with a woman, a member of an ethnic minority, or at least some younger Ph.D. anxious to get started on the tenure track.

Although I alluded to the ethical questions I had mentioned in "Whole People and Half Truths," the reasons I cited for leaving were even more personal. I wanted to be more of a generalist than my department could afford. My wife and I wanted to share a profession, pay more attention to family, and move toward a simpler life.

I had allowed myself to be drawn away from working at the lab bench alongside my graduate students, into administering research done by them and the technicians working in my lab. I did not enjoy a management career and was not very good at it. Mentoring graduate students had been my most important work, I thought, but

eventually, even that benign policy began to get to me. "How long can that go on?" I asked. "Where will *their* research money come from? And what if I have trained them to enjoy repeating the process, training more graduate students, who in turn will train more, and so on? Resources are limited on our planet, and who has the right to do more than reproduce himself? Is it really society's needs that demand the training of more scientists in our image—or is it the demands of our own egos?"

Questions that *I* asked after twenty years of doing science and having a great time doing it may differ from the ones that will occur to you twenty years down the road. As a young person just setting out, you have other questions to face. The most important question to consider now is whether science is the right career path for *you*.

3

Science as
a Christian
Calling

IT HAS BEEN SAID THAT SCIENCE deals with problems, religion with mysteries, and philosophy with questions. Implicit in that aphorism is the idea that problems can be solved but mysteries have to be accepted.

In the above sense, a mystery is a deep truth that remains beyond our full intellectual grasp no matter how much we explore it. In popular usage, a mysterious circumstance is either something "spooky" or something that will eventually turn out to be merely an unsolved problem. In murder mysteries, for example, a baffling crime is a "mystery," but only until a clever detective reconstructs the crime and identifies the actual perpetrator. The detective has treated an apparent mystery as a problem and solved it by scientific methods.

What Scientists Do

Most scientists would probably accept the analogy that the work they do is something like playing detective. Scientists search for clues, test various hypotheses, and eliminate possibilities until a particular problem is solved. Science is best described not merely as a body of knowledge but as a group of methods for solving a particular kind of problem. It is often referred to as "a way of knowing." In the words of Stanford materials scientist Richard Bube:

Science is a way of knowing based on human interpretation of publicly obtained sense data through interaction with the physical world. Science is *a* way of knowing, but not *the only way* of knowing. The fundamental purpose of science is to describe the events and phenomena in the natural world, to provide models (metaphors) for the description of these phenomena, and to provide insight into the answers to the questions of *how* these phenomena occur. Science has both a theoretical component (the human interpretation) and an experimental component (interaction with the physical world).

Bube added that although science provides partial insights into some part of the universe, it "does not answer many questions of fundamental importance, and does not give us an absolute understanding of anything."

The general public probably has a clearer picture of what detectives do than of what scientists do, even if their understanding is based largely on fictional detective stories. Few accounts of real scientists at work have become bestsellers. Even fictional accounts of scientific work, except for fantastic or futuristic tales in the sci-fi category, tend to lack compelling excitement or action.

Even though criminal investigations grip the imagination of readers or television viewers much better than scientific investigations, the same painstaking attention to detail is characteristic of both professions. Both lines of work generally follow a similar pattern: long periods of tedious, frustrating, even boring routine, punctuated by shorter periods of fierce intensity when accumulated evidence begins to lead to an inescapable conclusion.

Almost anyone who enjoys solving puzzles is familiar with the pattern. Dumping the pieces of a jigsaw puzzle out of the box is followed by a lot of random searching for any two pieces that will fit together. Then, as things begin to take shape, one is surprised to have missed certain connections that now seem obvious. Satisfaction comes as the last few pieces complete the picture. Solving a well-constructed crossword puzzle gives the same feeling when everything finally fits into place. Scientists frequently use such phrases about their work. Then one moves on to the next step—a new phase of research, the next criminal case, or another puzzle—and the pattern repeats itself.

The work itself may not be continually exciting, but the excitement of occasional discovery along the way and anticipation of the final result keep one going. Fictional detectives, and no doubt real ones as well, have individual personalities and styles of working. That is also true of scientists:

Scientists are people of very dissimilar temperaments doing different things in very different ways. Among scientists are collectors, classifiers and compulsive tidiers-up; many are detectives by temperament and many are explorers; some are artists and others artisans. There are poet-scientists and philosopher-scientists and even a few mystics.

That observation of Peter Medawar is quoted in the 1995 edition of *On Being a Scientist,* one of the best and most accessible accounts of how scientific work is done. Recognizing that scientists do more than collect and analyze data to test hypotheses, the NAS booklet focuses on the life of the scientific community, in which results are communicated, other scientists' work is reviewed, and a new generation of scientists is continually being trained.

On Being a Scientist describes a "rich interplay of competition, elation, frustration, and cooperation at the frontiers of scientific research." From all that profoundly subjective human activity comes "objective" knowledge, its reliability safeguarded by social conventions such as the refereeing of journal publication. The NAS booklet shows how easily conflicts over accuracy of data, interpretation of results and priority of discovery can arise in the scientific community. It presents hypothetical case studies to prepare young scientists to make good judgments in real-life situations.

A more detailed account of social mechanisms in science was given by David Hull in *Science as a Process.* Hull's examples of functioning and dysfunctioning science came from his own investigations into systematic biology and from documented cases in other fields. One of his conclusions was that for science to function well, scientists do not have to possess noble motives, because the institution is so structured that "they are rewarded for doing what they are supposed to do and punished when they do not." Hull continued:

Scientists need very little encouragement to adhere to the institutional norms of science. Scientists do not band together in weekly support groups to urge each other to mend their sinful ways. They need not because by and large their individual goals coincide with the institutional goals of science. Scientists adhere to the norms of science because it is in their own self-interest to do so. Outright fabrication of data is very rare in science because it is in the self-interest of other scientists to uncover fraud.

Hull undertook his scientific study of the scientific enterprise from an explicitly Darwinian perspective. He focused on selection processes at work in the scientific community but offered no explanation for a number of factors that make the system work: the existence of human curiosity, the desire to get credit for one's work, or the regularity of the real world that allows experiments to be checked by others. He took those things for granted, he said, in order to explain "other things in terms of them." Although he did not call them such, Hull accepted those phenomena as "givens"—that is, we might say, as mysteries—at least for the time being.

This chapter began with a distinction between problems, mysteries and questions. If problems are to be solved and mysteries accepted, what about *questions?* In real life, we frequently face this kind of philosophical question: "Should I treat this situation as a problem, and try to solve it—or is it a mystery, which I must learn to accept?" We have no reason to assume that any real situation is exclusively one or the other, but if we are open to more than one way of knowing, we must grapple with the question.

Serious questions lead serious people to seek satisfying answers, in the form of lasting truth that one can live *by* or of some provisional truth that one can live *with*. Living, whether "by" or "with," is an individual responsibility. No consensus of professional philosophers (or of scientists or theologians, for that matter) about what is universally true, even if it could be arrived at, would automatically provide a final answer to any personal dilemma. After solving a problem or accepting a mystery we can turn to something else, but it is the nature of philosophy that even when we arrive at an answer, the question remains with us.

Philosopher Michael Polanyi, whose first career was in physical chemistry, wrote a book in the 1950s called *Personal Knowledge*. He made the point that *all* knowledge is personal because it must be held by a knower who contributes to it by the very act of commitment to it. That does not mean that truth is whatever we want it to be or "whatever works for us"; it means that we cannot fully know the truth without being devoted to it. "Truth," wrote Polanyi, "is something that can be thought of only by believing it."

The most important "truth questions" are those of life and death, change and permanence, and so on—all summed up in that all-encompassing biblical phrase: good and evil. Is life good in all circumstances? Is knowledge better than ignorance? If things change, will they get better or worse? Is impending death something to fight against or something to be accepted as a given? What is worth living for—or dying for? What should I do with my life?

Should I Be a Scientist?
When Jesus said, "God is spirit, and those who worship him must worship in spirit and in truth," he likely used an Aramaic word related to the idea of "air" or "breath." The English word *spirit* retains those connotations in words like "respiration" and "inspire." Spiritual matters do not enter into scientific theories forged exclusively from physical or material concepts. Yet leading

scientists, when trying to describe how they arrived at a particular idea, have written of a "moment of inspiration" or even a "revelation." A "given" insight may have led them to trust in the rightness or fitness of a hypothesis long before it was adequately supported by empirical evidence. Arrivals of such insights are treated as welcome mysteries.

If hard-nosed scientists, trained to ignore the spiritual realm in their work, are nevertheless willing to consider the possibility of a mystical element in personal experience, no Christian should be reluctant to cultivate deeper spiritual understanding. For the most important questions in life, people need the most profound kind of wisdom, which begins with personal devotion to truth.

Even for those who take up science as their only route to truth, the language of science is not a native tongue. Science is something like a second language that must be learned in order to do scientific work. Phrases like "seeking God's will" or even "trying to do what is right" are from a more universal language, the language of devotion.

The possibility of divine guidance is familiar to Christians, as it is also to Jews and Muslims. In chapter one that concept was said to be the distinguishing mark of a theistic belief system. In the eighteenth century many people influenced by science became deists, accepting that the natural world was created by a supernatural deity but denying any ongoing supervision from beyond nature. After initially being wound up like a clock, a deist would say, the universe has been running (down) on its own. Theists, in contrast, accept the biblical picture of God as a parent who cares for his children.

In Christian theology, God is both transcendent (above and beyond the creation) and immanent (present in creation or influencing it from within). Various formulations attempt to explain how both can be true at the same time. Such complex theological proposals are generally of no more help in everyday life than a physicist's Grand Unified Theory of everything in the universe.

Just as multiple interpretations of quantum reality have not daunted explorers of quantum phenomena, multiple interpretations of how God interacts with his creatures should not hinder devotional exploration. The point is that we must act on any knowledge of God we already possess, while remaining open to a deeper understanding of the One in whose image we are made.

Over the centuries it has been the testimony of Christians that the Creator takes a personal interest in human lives. The most immediate Christian understanding is not a philosophical abstraction but a shared spiritual experience that God wants to be approached by us in a respectful, childlike way. No amount of potential ridicule from atheists, deists, humanists or skeptics should keep us from trying to discern what God wants us to do, especially when facing major decisions.

Of course, the ways in which Christians find God's desired path for our lives are as varied as methods used in studying natural phenomena. Even the terminology is not universal: Protestants generally use terms like *calling* and *ministry* for what Catholics call *vocation* and *apostolate.*

How should you decide whether or not to go into science? Common sense dictates that before making any important decision, you should first consider the most realistic possibilities. Then seek counsel from reliable friends who know you well. For Christians, the basic research methodologies also include delving into Scripture with an openness to its message and seeking God's wisdom directly through prayer.

Picking a verse from a randomly opened page of the Bible is a caricature, though some may have found legitimate guidance in that unusual way. Christians inclined toward science are likely to have strong analytical tendencies that will play a role in their Bible study and prayers. For some Christians, prayer is a serious conversation with God; for others it is primarily a quieting of their own thoughts to experience God's presence. Whatever one's style, the goal is to bring our thought life and prayer life into harmony.

Each person puts the elements together in a different way, and not all will find clear-cut direction. Some who seek God's guidance will reach a sense of exactly what they are to do. Others must take a cautious first step without seeing very far ahead. Some have little knowledge about what they are getting into but a strong conviction about which direction to take. Others continue to weigh various possibilities as they "wait on the Lord."

The Christians in scientific work who contributed to this book have all "been there," each with a unique story of how they got there. Your story will also be unique because you are unique among God's many children. Others can offer information and inspiration, but the decisions are yours to make.

What It Takes To Be a Scientist

Some people should not go into science. Success in scientific work requires certain aptitudes that are unevenly distributed in the human population. It is unreasonable to assume that God would want you to go into science without providing you with the right equipment: curiosity about nature, intelligence, perseverance, common sense, and better-than-average conceptual ability.

We are all gifted, the apostle Paul said, but not with the same gifts. He was writing about spiritual abilities most essential to the community of faith, abilities like preaching and teaching, but it hardly stretches his meaning out of shape to think of any ability as a gift. In another letter, Paul encouraged a young follower of Jesus to "rekindle" or "stir up" his particular gift by developing and exercising it.

It is not improper to speak of having a gift for science. To test that gift, take all the mathematics and science courses you can, and work hard at mastering them. Think of your studies as mind-building, the way athletes and bodybuilders benefit from physical exercise at a gym. For most of us, the challenge of mastering science courses in school will either develop our interest or reveal that God has another direction for us. Good grades in math and science courses serve as reasonably good indicators of our attitude toward science as well as our aptitude for it.

As a rule of thumb we can expect God to call us into a life's work that we will enjoy. Scientists generally work extremely hard, partly because it is expected but also because they tend to enjoy what they do. Any scientist needs emotional resilience, determination and self-discipline to keep going through long periods when joy is hard to come by. Sometimes theoretical calculations just will not come out right. The most carefully planned experiments can keep going haywire. The atmosphere in a lab can be discouraging because we may be surrounded by colleagues with similar frustrations.

Few Christians in science would expect to solve problems in the lab without putting in the same amount of effort as anyone else. Yet many testify that at least on occasion they have experienced God's special presence in the laboratory. Sometimes that means seeing the breakup of a mental logjam that has held back progress. More often it means being sustained by hope when things are not going well.

The apostle Paul referred to faith, hope and love as the "greater gifts," with love being the greatest of all. Any individual able to exercise those gifts can make an outstanding contribution to a scientific laboratory. A Christian who demonstrates resilient hope based on an abiding faith, and who can lovingly pass a spirit of hope on to coworkers, can have a salutary effect on the morale of a whole research group.

Flexibility is another important characteristic. Studies of psychological profiles indicate that successful scientists have a strong desire to find solutions, but can tolerate a lot of ambiguity and delayed gratification along the way. The most creative scientists can carry around in their heads a dozen competing hypotheses, seriously considering ideas that may turn out to be false or even ridiculous. Scientists must be able to play with ideas even when they know that not every one of them can be correct.

Thoughtful Christians often display that same kind of intellectual flexibility. Anyone who has grappled seriously with apparent theological paradoxes comes to realize that each extreme position may hold some partial truth but neither tells the whole story.

Scientists are trained to withhold judgment, to remain objective until all experimental results are in. Of course all possible results of all possible experiments are *never* in. Flexibility can harden into overarching skepticism, reluctance or inability to commit ourselves to any position. In practice, scientists will vigorously support an appealing hypothesis, the one they consider least likely to be falsified, because they believe in it.

In theory, at least, a scientist's commitment to any hypothesis remains tentative. Yet no one gets to be a scientist without making a serious commitment of his or her life to the scientific community. Those who disparage religion caricature it as taking blind leaps of faith. Those who actually *live* by faith generally keep our eyes wide open—to see where we are going to land.

Lifestyles and Role Models

We speak of belonging to the scientific community or the Christian community, but what we actually belong to in either is one of many subgroups. The group loyalty of those who work in a particular scientific discipline roughly parallels the loyalty of most Christians to a specific church or denomination. Anthropologists and biochemists tend to read their own journals first, as evangelicals and charismatics do, and Baptists and Episcopalians.

Yet it is not entirely misleading to refer to either science or Christianity as one large community made up of smaller distinct communities. No matter how many differences exist within the outer walls, insiders generally recognize a common bond and show some degree of solidarity if the larger community is demeaned by outsiders.

Although still considered members of the community, many individuals trained as scientists do not continue in research. Nevertheless, all enter the profession by that route. Some stay in the lab (or the observatory or the field) throughout their working lives. Others become administrators in universities or government agencies, editors of scientific publications, science writers, teachers, managers or even sales personnel in high-tech industries.

The role of research as the core of the scientific community is somewhat analogous to the centrality of the gospel in the Christian community. We have all become Christians through the passing on of the *evangel* of Jesus Christ, but not all Christians—nor even all "evangelical" Christians—are engaged in doing what the public understands as evangelistic work. Some, in fact, are doing scientific work.

Christians in the scientific community are represented in all the disciplines and types of work done by other scientists. Some are to be found among the explorers of the unknown, driven by curiosity to find out how the world works without immediate concern for practical goals. They thrive on the unraveling of a supposed mystery, the sheer fun of doing something new, the joy of learning more about God's creation. Christians in basic research have a noble tradition, reaching back to the earliest pioneers, of wanting to "think God's thoughts" about the universe.

The solvers of practical problems do a kind of research often better understood by the public. Although their work sometimes leads to open-ended exploration, it is judged primarily by its usefulness. Christians have contributed to increased food production and to improved medical treatment, honoring Christ's commandments to feed the hungry and heal the sick with their technical skills. Scientific investigations offer a variety of opportunities to help needy people in the Lord's name.

Some Christians in science see themselves primarily as teachers of the next generation. As scientific knowledge accumulates, great wisdom is needed to decide how much of it should be transmitted and in what manner. Mentoring graduate students is a great responsibility, but teaching younger students can be even more challenging, and requires different personal qualities. The highly publicized "crisis" in science education calls for wise teachers with the self-giving spirit that lies at the heart of Christian faith. The most effective teachers love not only the subject they teach but also their students.

Most Christians in science also see themselves as representatives of Jesus Christ and of a biblical understanding of right and wrong. Ethical standards are rooted in personal conviction. Christians who try to be open about what is most important to them bear witness in the lab, in the church and elsewhere, seeking to be light in a dark world and salt where the flavor of goodness has been lost.

Most Christians continue to carry out several of these functions, perhaps majoring in one or the other at different stages of their career. A sense of calling and the daily experience of walking with God are great advantages in a rough-and-tumble world, even in the relatively civilized world of science.

At times it may be difficult to honor a profound commitment to Jesus

Christ while participating wholeheartedly in "the game of science," but many have done it. If God is guiding you, so can you.

Welcome to the Family

After describing at the end of chapter two the way things were when I stepped out of my research career, let me tell you how that career began.

Young scientists today face a number of problems that I did not encounter. Any obstacles in my way were more like hurdles than the land mines some face today. For me, becoming a scientist was a series of relatively safe steps, each preparing me for the next. The process opened up a new world, or, if that sounds too grandiose, it expanded my sense of belonging.

I came from a family with no academic tradition. There were no doctors or lawyers in our extended family and, apart from a teacher or pastor, I seldom met anyone who had studied beyond college. In my family I became a first-generation college graduate. My father had quit elementary school to help support his widowed mother and three younger siblings. My mother had left college her first year to assist her mother.

By the time I entered high school, my father had worked his way up to a responsible position through disciplined self-education. I inherited some of my parents' common sense and readily absorbed my father's love of books. Because I did well in high school it was assumed that I would go to college, though my parents knew little about the cost of higher education. Halfway through college I learned about that cost myself from Navy buddies who had attended other schools. The small private university I attended had high academic standards but, until recent years, no tuition. Moreover, Rice Institute, as it was called then, was within walking distance of my home, so I also had no dormitory bills.

A love of the outdoors picked up from scouting was the source of my interest in biology. My father knew that the oil company he worked for employed geologists and chemists but, except for the example of my high school biology teacher, neither of us knew how anyone could make a living in biology. So I majored in chemistry. What seemed at the time to be a sensible compromise I later saw as the touch of God's hand, shaping the beginning of my career in just the right way at just the right time.

Having skipped an elementary grade, I graduated from high school at age sixteen, a few months after the United States entered World War II. Rice went on a year-round wartime schedule, so I was already in my junior year when I received my draft notice. With two years of physics under my belt, I easily qualified for electronics training, which later proved valuable in working with scientific instruments. My two years in the Navy not only helped me mature but made me eligible for benefits under the GI bill. I saved them for graduate school, including the typing of my Ph.D. dissertation.

By then, as in the words of "Amazing Grace," I had come through "many dangers, toils, and snares" and had learned to trust God in small details as well as in the big questions. All along I prayed for wisdom, yet had to face many forks in the road with too little knowledge to make a wise decision on my own. I still find the grace of some of those turns amazing: discovering biochemistry as a field of study, being accepted at the University of Illinois, joining Professor Herbert Carter's antibiotics research group, landing a teaching assistantship and soon a research assistantship, completing a Ph.D. in three years.

Almost everybody in our group spent their evenings at the lab, partly because nobody wanted to miss out on anything if Dr. Carter came around at night, as he often did. The whole gang might go to Farwell's across the street for part of the evening, where we would seek advice from "the boss" on how to interpret our results and on what experiments to try next. We absorbed a lot of lore: chit-chat on new developments, historical anecdotes and tales of our mentor's encounters with well-known scientists.

In that congenial group, the apprentices learned lab techniques from those who had come the year before, and so on. From the example Dr. Carter set, we got the idea that "if research isn't fun, then it shouldn't be done." That spirit of camaraderie stayed with me, enabling me to see professional colleagues and eventually my own students as peers, and even as family.

A big wall chart in Noyes Laboratory showed the scientific lineage of each professor in the chemistry department. I could trace my line through Herb Carter back to famous European chemists whose names I already knew. I discovered that I was an intellectual descendant of Friedrich Wöhler, who synthesized the first organic compound (urea) from inorganic chemicals. Wöhler earned a medical degree in 1823 at Heidelberg under Gmelin (of the encyclopedic *Handbuch der Chemie*), but also studied in Sweden under Berzelius, to whom we owe our present system of symbols for the chemical elements.

If I had come from a family with academic roots I might not have been so moved by my acceptance into a community of scholars. In the evangelical Christian community, where I had already found my place, my belonging was independent of scholarly accomplishments. Now I was a member of a different community, one in which spiritual awareness played no role but in which strong bonds could be forged out of common intellectual interests.

The two communities may seem exclusive because each makes certain demands on anyone who wishes to enter. My inclusion in both as a young person convinced me that science and evangelical Christianity are not mutually exclusive worlds. That is a primary message of this book.

As a Christian apprentice in scholarly endeavors, I met a few others like myself, at first primarily through church and parachurch student groups. After receiving my doctorate I began to find peers with whom to pray in my own research group or department, or down the hall in some other group or department. As a graduate student, though, I discovered the American Scientific Affiliation, and during a postdoctoral year at Yale I was able to attend a national ASA meeting in New York. That "fellowship of kindred minds" enriched both my Christian life and my professional life from then on.

If scientific work is your calling as a Christian, you will be welcomed into a wonderful family. Through ASA I know of thousands of men and women serving Christ with their scientific training, and I have been able to meet hundreds of them. Toward the end of this book you will meet some of them too.

That Good Company you will meet in Close-Up 5 needs to be replenished with younger Christians serious about science, though (as I learned around that table at Farwell's) to be serious about something does not mean that you have to be grim about it.

4

What to Expect

THE ARGUMENT HAS AT TIMES been made that although Copernicus, Galileo, Newton and Faraday actually believed in God as divine Creator, such a belief was possible only because those early scientists lived before Darwin's time. That argument is refuted by thousands of contemporary Christians with successful scientific careers. For many practicing scientists, as for many other intelligent people, scientific rationalism has not outmoded religious faith.

Nevertheless, one still encounters "secular fundamentalists" who persist in the belief that no scientist could possibly be a supernaturalist. From the viewpoint of a hard-nosed philosophical naturalist, to be a professional scientist and a committed Christian at the same time just does not compute. Something must be wrong: either people who make that claim do not *really* believe that God acts in the world (though they say they pray and take the Bible seriously), or they cannot be *real* scientists (even with a Ph.D., a tenured faculty position and refereed research publications).

When secular fundamentalists cite Darwin's theory as warrant for their naturalistic beliefs, they drive religious fundamentalists to oppose everything to which the term "evolution" is attached. In academic life, a Christian who tries to stay out of that quarrel may be considered as partisan as those who take sides. Among scientists, misunderstandings of Christian faith probably turn up as regularly as in the general public.

Young believers who go into science should not feel professionally insecure; in the United States at least, academic scientists who publicly express antipathy toward religion constitute a minority of the scientific community. Occasionally a believer not yet established in research may run into opposition orchestrated by secularist hard-liners, but outright academic martyrdom is probably rare. The New Testament suggests that for followers of Jesus it is better to accept persecution for one's faith than to fight it. Besides, religious bias is hard to prove.

The best way to overcome bias or opposition is to do acceptable or even outstanding work while bearing a faithful witness from the very beginning. Where there are misunderstandings about Christianity, do your best to clear them up. When trying to remove a splinter from another's eye, though, remember Jesus' caution to watch out for logs in your own. A chip on the shoulder toward the scientific community is another hindrance to avoid.

Living Crossculturally

In *The Two Cultures and the Scientific Revolution,* Sir Charles Snow depicted a gulf separating members of the scientific culture from all others engaged in intellectual pursuits. Snow, trained as a physicist, had been in charge of Britain's scientific recruitment during World War II. He was also a successful novelist, so he wrote as an insider to the literary culture as well. Although he deplored what he saw as a widening of the gulf (he wanted scholars in other fields to be better educated in science), his own life demonstrated that a person dedicated to excellence in both literature and science could bridge a wide gulf.

Christians in science are people with two strong allegiances, holding citizenship in two distinct communities. Bridging that gulf means sharing some values held by scientific colleagues and some values of importance to fellow believers. We may not be fully accepted or "vote with the majority" in either group, but we can live crossculturally without becoming intellectual schizophrenics. After all, people do marry into another extended family without totally abandoning their own family ties.

To assume that we could not function as scientists while maintaining our identity and integrity as Christians would be like denying that a football player could also be good at chess. Even if one cannot play both games simultaneously, there is no reason why a successful quarterback or defensive tackle could not win a chess match. Rather than casting scientists and Christian believers as opponents in a winner-take-all contest, it is helpful to picture science and Christian faith as two different "games."

We are not negating the rules of one game when we concentrate on the other, though having to shift our focus from one to the other will not be understood by anyone who plays by a single rule book. The moves of knights and bishops do not pertain to the gridiron and offensive guards do not block for the queen's moves on the chessboard.

Science and Christian commitment are both complex human activities. They cannot be summed up as a simple contrast between facts and faith, reason and emotion, or objectivity and subjectivity. Scientists do try to establish facts, and they reason to conclusions as objectively as possible; but they also believe in their own abilities, trust the work of others, get passionate about their discoveries, and recognize that their lives are invested in their work. Christians, as forgiven sinners, do trust in God, but they also try to think critically and dispassionately about theology, everyday life and scientific findings. Christians in science may sometimes think or behave more like other scientists and sometimes more like other Christians, but how else could one live crossculturally?

Consider the task of Christian missionaries, who hear the gospel in their own culture but try to transmit it to people in a different culture. Missionaries must learn new cultural patterns in order to identify with those whom they serve. Yet if the gospel is really foreign to that culture, no matter how genuinely the missionaries adopt new patterns of thinking and acting, their lives will always display an element of difference. After all, if they had nothing new to contribute, they need not have gone in the first place. Missionaries must try to decouple the gospel itself from the trappings of the culture in which they learned it, lest they unintentionally communicate ideas irrelevant to the new culture.

It would be wise for all Christians to think of ourselves as living crossculturally, even if we do not go overseas, learn a new language, engage in a secular career, or even move from our old neighborhood. Neighborhoods change. Living languages change continuously. The culture in which we were brought up has by now been influenced by new technologies, new art forms, new political situations. For that matter, as we grow older, *we* change. Gradual changes may go unnoticed, but differences in thinking and behavior strike us forcefully when we are thrust into a new environment.

Some crosscultural adjustments are extremely difficult to make. Even after years of speaking a second language, for example, expatriates may retain a lingering accent from their native tongue.

One factor that makes living as both a Christian and a scientist easier is the restricted nature of the scientific enterprise. One might say that the language of science is appropriately spoken only in special circumstances. The goal of describing physical phenomena quantitatively does make science rather elitist. It is not surprising that many scientists find it hard to explain their work to nonscientists. A biochemist excited about prodigiosin biosynthesis in *Serratia marcescens* generally has to find something else to talk about to stay in a general conversation.

To become a professional scientist requires, among other things, a relatively high intelligence quotient. To become a professing Christian there is no such requirement, though to be an intelligent Christian takes all the intelligence one can muster:

Anyone who is honestly trying to be a Christian will soon find his intelligence being sharpened; one of the reasons why it needs no special education to be a Christian is that Christianity is an education in itself.

Neither a college degree nor a course in calculus is a prerequisite to finding forgiveness in Jesus Christ. Christianity is basically a family open to any scientist, whereas science is a profession open to Christians only if they possess ability and dedication. Any believer with those qualifications is capable of actively pursuing scientific knowledge without abandoning the saving knowledge of Jesus Christ.

Scientific knowledge and religious knowledge are compatible partly because of a significant difference in the way they are acquired. That difference is illuminated by a memorable distinction made by Jewish scholar Martin Buber between an "I-it" and an "I-Thou" basis for knowledge. Science is based on logical analysis, on a rational or analytical understanding: what I can learn by studying something (it) as an object. Religious knowledge is not illogical or irrational, but is characteristically fiducial: what I can learn by interacting with another knower (thou).

In practice, as scientists doing our best to be unbiased, we try to keep ourselves "out of the equation" as much as possible, though aware that as observers we are never completely objective. As Christians seeking wisdom in order to make personal decisions, we must put ourselves *into* the equation as much as possible. Scientific conclusions generally take the form of statistical generalities making no demands on the knower. In contrast, the moral aspect of religious knowledge puts doing the truth on a par with knowing it. Without a prior commitment to do what Truth tells us, we shut ourselves off from its discovery.

Religious knowledge, though less amenable to validation by others, affords a more compelling sense of truth. Because scientific knowledge lacks that quality, to apply moral judgments to scientific behavior requires going beyond the rules of the scientific game.

Nobody Said It Would Be Easy

Living in two cultures simultaneously may take more than twice the effort of living in only one. Since being a Christian and being a scientist each has its ups and downs, one might expect that, statistically, the ups of one endeavor should balance the downs of the other about half the time. The same goes for rewards. It is exhilarating when your Christian life and scientific work are both going well, but you may also experience some "double down" times of doubt and discouragement.

The life of most scientists, as depicted in chapter three, is a mix of joys and disappointments, responsibilities and rewards, and times of comradeship as well as of loneliness, with occasional periods of intense excitement separated by long periods of hard work. Each scientist's experience depends on many personal choices made along his or her career path, plus many circumstances beyond his or her control. Whether the career is "his" or "hers" can also make a big difference. Women have made definite strides in recent years, but women in science still face greater obstacles than men.

Making Hard Choices

Not many scientists deal with science as a whole or even with their own discipline as a whole. What most of us encounter at each stage of our career are colleagues in a particular university department or in a research group in a specific company or government agency.

Our intellectual foundation for professional life comes from textbooks and teachers at the beginning, and from the scientific literature later on. All along, though, we absorb the ethos or lore of professional life by interacting with other people—those with whom we work or compete or rub shoulders at seminars, scientific meetings and other gatherings.

The way we process all that informational input depends on who we were before we entered the profession and on how new experiences, professional and otherwise, continue to shape us. The lives of Christians in science will thus differ in some respects from those of colleagues who face the same problems and opportunities. We will continually be making choices, some of them difficult, that will not only affect our professional life but will also indicate to our colleagues what sort of people Christians are.

In the long run, certain of our religious beliefs may stand up to scrutiny no better than some of our scientific hypotheses. Yet faith can be intelligent even if not scientific; after all, few scientists would claim that their decision to study science was made on strictly scientific grounds. Christians should never be intimidated by those who look down on religious faith, but in turn we should not parade our faith in an intimidating way. To speak of our Christian faith in any culture, at home or abroad, requires sensitivity in the ways we express ourselves.

Whatever else may be in question, a Christian's view of the world begins with allegiance to the God who created us in his image and gave his son Jesus to draw us to himself by dying for our sins. If others have a different "bottom line," so be it. Nobody said the Christian life would be easy or popular.

Many distinguished writers have championed "the Christian worldview" as the most satisfying picture of reality. In coherence, consistency and completeness, a system of thought based on Christian belief can certainly compete on equal terms with other belief-systems. Everyone starts somewhere, yet Christians as well as others face a problem when trying to forge an airtight, all-encompassing philosophical system.

Any worldview that can adequately account for everything in its own terms leaves no way to break into that worldview from outside to criticize it. In other words, if a closed system of thought gets off the track, the "worldviewer" inside will never know it. It might be better to drive one's stake in a somewhat smaller piece of real estate, and from that point of view, see the world in as many ways as one can manage.

So far this book has posed a series of questions for Christian students to settle before taking up science as a profession: Is science a worthy pursuit? Could it use something I have to offer? Am I called to such a career? Should I expect a welcome from the scientific community?

Answers to such questions stem from one's basic outlook or worldview and affect one's subsequent actions. Hence they are truly philosophical questions, though a professional philosopher might not consider them the most basic questions facing Christians in science.

Excursus into Philosophy—with Some History Thrown In
This excursus deals with the sort of public philosophical questions with which one must continue to grapple because public discourse provides no consensus. The two cultures we have been considering (broadly, science and religion) have their own developed philosophies, and their interaction raises many profound questions.

As has been said, science came into existence in the sixteenth and seventeenth centuries under the cultural hegemony of a European religious establishment. Although the attitude of the Christian church toward science was not always negative, it has been painted that way by polemicists with an axe to grind. Two famous works of the Victorian era were J. W. Draper's *History of the Conflict between Religion and Science* (1875) and A. D. White's *A History of the Warfare of Science with Theology in Christendom* (1895). They promoted a "warfare" myth engineered by philosophical naturalists:

> In late nineteenth-century England, several small groups of scientists and scholars organized under the leadership of Thomas H. Huxley to overthrow the cultural dominance of Christianity—particularly the intellectual dominance of the Anglican church. Their goal was to secularize society, replacing the Christian worldview with scientific naturalism, a worldview that recognizes the existence of nature alone. Though secularists, they understood very well that they were replacing one religion by another, for they described their goal as the establishment of the "church scientific." Huxley even referred to his scientific lectures as "lay sermons."

Thus, though the historic relation between science and the church was much too complex to be summed up that way, we have inherited an enduring warfare mythology. That was the beginning of a genuine culture war, initiated by persons using science for their own pseudoreligious or antireligious purposes. Even when the protagonists had no scientific standing, science tended to get the blame for many philosophical attacks on religion:

> It was one thing to have a disagreement between scientific opinion and religious doctrine, quite another for an individual scientist to attack Christianity, because scientists might oppose religion for a variety of reasons having nothing to do with science. In the nineteenth century there was more conflict between "historical study and accepted views of the Bible" than between science and theology, but the public, failing to make such distinctions, labeled any challenge to the Bible as "science."

Polemic writers like Draper and White gleefully pointed to the censoring and house arrest of Galileo by the Roman Catholic Church in 1633 as a typical example of out-and-out religious persecution. In fact, though, Galileo's real enemies were rival academics who found themselves on the losing side of a festering intellectual argument. Astute politicians, they knew how to silence the arrogantly overconfident astronomer by manipulating ecclesiastical leaders to use their power against him. Even though what happened was not a noble episode in church history, Galileo himself remained a faithful Christian throughout the ordeal.

Galileo, along with Copernicus, Kepler and other pioneers, led the development of the new sciences of astronomy and physics (i.e., "natural philosophy"). "Natural history" had been closely tied to the classical Greek philosophy of Socrates, Plato and Aristotle. Socrates left no writings when he died (399 B.C.) but he had taught Plato and Plato taught Aristotle. After being lost to Europe for over a thousand years, some of Aristotle's and Plato's writings were rediscovered in the Middle Ages, paving the way for the Renaissance of European thought. The medieval Christian version of Aristotle's philosophy became known as scholasticism, or as Thomism, for Thomas Aquinas (d. 1274).

Aristotle's study of living things had convinced him that everything in nature moved toward some final purpose or divine form. Plato, with a somewhat different take on the way divinity operated, also saw nature as basically organic. Long after Aristotelianism and neo-Platonism had been absorbed into theological understanding, along came the new astronomers and physicists, treating the heavens and earth not as a divinely driven organism but as a kind of divinely designed machine or clockwork. "Mechanism" quickly became the philosophical currency of natural scientists, who began to drop from their descriptions of nature any mention of divine influence. Galileo's seventeenth-century rivals were Aristotelian thinkers.

The classical Greek and medieval philosophers paid much attention to *deduction,* the logical steps of reasoning from axioms or first principles. Aristotle focused on that kind of logic, though he also understood *induction,* the opposite process of reasoning from sense perceptions to arrive at new general principles. Deduction played a recognizable role in the new sciences, but induction soon became the hallmark of scientific methodology.

From the seventeenth century onward, the energetic empirical spirit of science produced mechanistic explanations for one phenomenon after another, fostering a revolution in philosophy. French philosopher René Descartes (1596-1650) tried to stave off the encroachment of mechanistic thinking into the world of human experience. In Cartesian dualism, a kind of divine spark remained imbedded in human beings, enabling individuals to think rationally about their own existence and about the rest of the world.

With the mathematically persuasive successes of physical science, especially after the work of the great English physicist Isaac Newton (1642-1727), science became the foundation of philosophy, rather than the other way around. Enlightenment thinkers of the eighteenth century enthroned scientific rationalism as the only reliable source of knowledge and tried to apply it to human society as well as to physical phenomena. Deism became a sort of holding pattern, retaining a distant role for a divine Creator while embracing a mechanistic philosophy that excluded God from the actual workings of creation.

In 1859, publication of *The Origin of Species* by English biologist Charles Darwin brought naturalistic philosophy into the study of living things in a dramatic way. Organisms, including humans, could henceforth be envisioned as complex machines arising through a combination of inherited variability and a selection process that was totally natural and inherently mechanical.

Darwinism seemed to solidify and unify scientific rationalism, providing effective ammunition for the culture war kindled by Huxley and others. Philosophically, the concept of human evolution seemed to accomplish the final reduction of human biology (and hence of all human activity) to chemistry and physics. *Reductionism* has played a major role in scientific rationalism, positivism, naturalism, materialism and other forms of essentially atheistic scientism. Ironically, secular humanism reduces human beings to something like "the descendants of defective purple bacteria"—and then on down the scale to mere "matter in motion."

At the beginning of the twentieth century, physics was almost completely deterministic, giving the impression that everything in nature was predictable and potentially describable as an inevitable cause-and-effect sequence. As nature was probed more deeply, however, in particular down to the subatomic level, certain problems failed to yield to the old paradigm. A new kind of physics arose, sometimes dubbed "Einsteinian" to distinguish it from classical or Newtonian physics, and to honor the work of Albert Einstein (1879-1955). Einstein became known for proposing a special theory and later a general theory of relativity, and for his simple equation relating matter and energy to the square of the velocity of light.

A whole new theory of quantum or wave mechanics was required to describe the behavior of tiny packets of energy. Max Planck (1858-1947) coined the term *quanta* (singular, *quantum)* for those packets, and derived a simple relationship between the energy of a particle and its associated frequency of radiation, with a proportionality constant that has since borne his name. Among the first to make use of Planck's quantum theory, Einstein used it to explain various photoelectric phenomena. Then Niels Bohr (1885-1962) was successful in applying the theory to the structure of atoms. Physics, and eventually chemistry, would never be the same.

In 1927, Werner Heisenberg's mathematical explorations of quantum theory led him to conclude that the position and momentum of a particle cannot both be known simultaneously with precision. That is, if the value of one of those parameters is precisely determined, the value of the other must remain uncertain. The product of the two uncertainties came out to be essentially equivalent to the value of Planck's constant.

The new physics, and specifically Heisenberg's uncertainty principle, struck a blow to determinism to which philosophers are still trying to adjust. Theologians are gradually catching on that the physical world may be far more "open" than scientists and naturalistic philosophers had thought. This possibility has revived interest in formulating a "natural theology," some versions of which bear little resemblance to biblical theology.

Evolutionary biology was deterministic from its beginning and has essentially stayed that way despite the turbulence in physics. In the latter half of the twentieth century, the mechanistic outlook brought rapid growth in biochemistry, biophysics and molecular biology. Discovery of common patterns in the metabolic and genetic machinery of diverse organisms was as exciting as anything that had happened in astronomy or physics in the seventeenth century.

Successes from treating organisms as physico-chemical mechanisms have contributed to an impression of unity of all the sciences, and of nature itself. Yet that impression has also led to philosophical oversimplification, the same thing that happened in physics after the initial successes of the Newtonian approach.

When a particular approach succeeds in solving certain problems it is tempting to assume that the same approach will work for all future problems. It is said that military disasters occur when the generals who won the last war think themselves prepared to fight the next one with the same strategy and tactics. Although classical and modern physics have both been amazingly successful, it is an unwarranted extrapolation to expect all unsolved problems to be reducible to the kinds of problems already solved.

If for no other reason, the sheer "irreducible complexity" of biological systems may render some problems beyond the reach of physical science as we now know it. The inductive process does not tell us in advance what general principles to expect, nor how they will fit together with other principles already established.

For twenty critical years beginning in 1932, Warren Weaver (1894-1978) was the farsighted director of the Rockefeller Foundation's Division of Natural Sciences. He was the first person to channel substantial financial support into quantitative experimental biology in this country and abroad. Credited with launching modern biology, Weaver was a mathematician whose religious views, though quite liberal, made him aware of the severe limitations of science.

In a 1959 essay, Weaver argued that instead of homing in on a final picture of reality, scientific knowledge provides "a more and more sophisticated view of our own ignorance." Further, he wrote, scientific thought has a "texture of finality" less satisfying than that of religious thought—since science seems to require radical shifts in what is considered to be true every half-century or so.

As a practicing scientist in the 1920s, Weaver had observed the revolution in physics firsthand, but remained rather indifferent because quantum theory seemed so incomplete. He was not alone in thinking that sooner or later it would be surpassed. That has not yet happened, but relativistic quantum mechanics is today subject to a variety of competing interpretations.

Warren Weaver agreed that at first glance scientific truth seemed much more secure than religious truth, but saw that, at its core, science was actually far from solid. Although he had no doubts about scientific reasoning as a useful tool, to him it also had deep philosophical flaws. Deductive logic suffered from being "quite powerless to create truths—it can only reveal previously and unconsciously assumed truth."

As a mathematician, Weaver was convinced that the work of Karl Gödel had demonstrated inescapable flaws in deductive logic. Gödel showed that for any set of postulates rich enough to be of scientific interest, (1) it is impossible to prove their consistency and (2) it is always possible to ask questions that are undecidable within that system. Weaver was convinced that inductive reasoning had been found wanting as well, because of an intrinsic inability to distinguish between observations leading to "lawlike" statements and those leading to "unlawlike" statements. He felt that induction's ability to deal with future cases was thus compromised, but that was "the only useful aspect of induction."

If the philosophical underpinnings of the well-established physical sciences have come into question, what can be said about evolutionary biology, which serves as the "clincher" for the atheistic scientisms rampant today in American higher education? Christians who work in biology refuse to be classified as "metaphysical naturalists"; they argue that using the same scientific methods as an atheist does not obligate them to adopt the same philosophical outlook.

Acknowledging natural selection's explanatory power on a microscale (e.g., in the change of gene frequencies in peppered-moth populations) does not force one to conclude that the same mechanism will explain the origin of life or of human beings, or that God is thereby excluded from the workings of his creation.

In 1991 Phillip Johnson argued in *Darwin on Trial* that Darwinism is not merely totally naturalistic in the philosophical sense but basically *is* a philosophy rather than science. What attracted his interest was the way macroevolution was defended in many popular books attacking "scientific creationism" in the 1980s.

Sidestepping creationist arguments, Johnson observed that leading scientists were quick to label almost any skepticism toward grandscale evolution as unscientific nonsense based on religious belief. Johnson, a law professor at the University of California at Berkeley, saw such labeling as a strategy designed to permit the larger body of scientists to feel justified in ignoring even scientifically valid criticisms of macroevolution. Silencing effective criticism had turned "evolution" into an axiom of belief. If Darwinism had sufficient empirical support, Johnson reasoned, its proponents would not continue to prop it up by rhetorical labeling.

Johnson's targets were polemicists like the late Carl Sagan, Douglas Futuyma, and particularly Richard Dawkins, who had said that Darwinism "made it possible to be an intellectually fulfilled atheist." Exalting the status of Dawkins's "blind watchmaker" thesis had essentially excluded the theistic position from serious consideration in academic circles. Johnson, a Christian, sought to level the playing field for theistic philosophy.

At first *Darwin on Trial* was ignored, then put down in biting reviews by leading Darwinists as one more piece of "creationist propaganda." Johnson had had the audacity to question the empirical foundations of the whole macroevolutionary hypothesis (that all living things are descended from a common ancestor) as well as the "creative power" of neo-Darwinian mechanisms assumed to account for that alleged descent.

In a second book, Johnson pursued his case further, arguing that even the methodological variety of naturalism "limits the alternatives that may be taken seriously" and "is only superficially reconcilable with theism in religion." Calling on his own expertise, he analyzed court cases touching on education, religious freedom and "political correctness" in the academic world.

Johnson has vigorously responded to his critics and has had a lively interaction with other scholars via the lecture circuit, correspondence and the Internet. His position is reinforced when leaders in the scientific establishment state publicly that neo-Darwinism is incompatible with any meaningful theism. He says he is encouraged by the efforts of a number of young scientists and philosophers working from a theistic premise to develop an alternative research program based on "intelligent design."

As noted above, some Christian thinkers consider the philosophical underpinnings of science and theism so compatible that they seek a kind of harmony or even philosophical unity in natural theology. At the other extreme, some Christians regard naturalism as so inherent in traditional science that they see a need for a new kind of "theistic science."

For many other Christians, to decide between those two points of view may not be an easy choice to make.

Excursus into Politics

Many philosophical issues can be left simmering on the back burners of our minds until new arguments or circumstances turn up the heat again. Such ponderings can be kept to ourselves.

Political issues, on the other hand, are those that generally force us to take some kind of noticeable action. Voting in an election is a political act, and, for those eligible to vote, so is *not* voting. Voting (or declining to vote) is a public expression of a privately held conviction. In a democracy, the secret ballot protects private opinion in order to encourage public expression.

Political issues do grow out of philosophical issues but the linkage is not always obvious. Most people would like public policy to be based strictly on (their) philosophical convictions but, in practice, compromises are necessary. A philosophy on which a political system could be based is called an ideology. Ideologues promote their system as a logically consistent solution to a public problem. A common tactic for ideologically driven politicians is to instill fear of the consequences of competing philosophies. In the process, they have been known to conceal hidden agendas and to exploit inept media coverage of important issues.

The point of this excursus is that political choices can be even more difficult and more demanding than philosophical choices. For example, Christian thinkers have quietly dealt with competing theistic and naturalistic philosophies for centuries. The conflict generally makes the papers only when it enters the political arena. In the United States it has taken the form of legal battles over how biology should be taught in public schools.

Christians with scientific training will almost inevitably be drawn into those battles at one level or another. As with many other political issues, our sympathies may not rest entirely with one side or the other. The claims of protagonists in most public conflicts are reminiscent of the kid in the comic strip who claimed, "He started the fight when he hit me back."

Philosophical arguments are frequently multilayered and nuanced, but political activists try to boil everything down to simple yes-or-no propositions. To broaden their base they must enlist supporters not otherwise interested in their cause by forming ad hoc alliances with groups backing other causes. For example, the National Center for Science Education (NCSE), which promotes the teaching of evolution, considers itself an ally of almost any political group opposing the "religious right." (Few groups are likely to identify themselves as part of an "antireligious left.")

At the other extreme, some creationist groups do not hesitate to blame all or most of the world's ills (from abortion to communism to fascism to racism) on "evolution." Only occasionally are the issues in a political battle clear enough to take sides without reservations. Sadly, your own convictions are as likely to be compromised by your friends as challenged by your enemies. Another sad fact about politics is that taking a stand is likely to turn some friends into enemies.

In politics an allegedly "progressive" agenda is usually pitted against an agenda considered "reactionary" or "traditional," even though what constitutes progress is a disputed philosophical question. Anything linked to science tends to look progressive because of science's cumulative nature and its role in technological innovation. On the other hand, Christians accept a revelation from the past, the Bible, as a source of lasting truth. That tends to cast anything linked to Christianity in the role of traditionalism. No wonder some people are surprised when a Christian pursues scientific knowledge.

Labeling people and ideas is a part of politics that contributes little to understanding. Consider some of the labels Americans have applied to other countries: In less than a century, Japan has gone from a curiosity to deadly enemy to needy recipient of largess to one of our most important trading partners to an unfriendly competitor to whatever it is at the moment. Meanwhile, the Soviet Union went from noble ally to evil empire; then its credit ran out some years ahead of America's credit.

The collapse of the USSR actually reversed the meaning of certain political labels. Russian leaders who had been the communist enemies of American conservatism were soon being called "*conservative* hard-liners" by President George Bush, and Russia's new free market capitalists became "*liberal* reformers."

What does it mean to be labeled, or to call oneself, an "evangelical," when every U.S. president since Richard Nixon has publicly identified himself with evangelical Christianity? As someone has pointed out, that is enough to make any evangelical, whether Republican or Democrat, rethink the validity of labels.

Swings from one extreme to the other are common in political life. In philosophy, one hopes to home in on an eternal truth, or at least on a lasting truce. When philosophy and politics are intertwined, a truce can be hard to come by and truth even harder. In political disputes each side tends to define itself by what it opposes. Oddly, the one proposition on which diametrically opposing sides can generally agree is that there is no middle ground. Consequently, anyone who takes a moderating, middle-of-the-road position is likely to be seen as an enemy by both sides.

That happened to the American Scientific Affiliation when it tried to help teachers caught in the crossfire of the so-called creation/evolution controversy. ASA's *Teaching Science in a Climate of Controversy* basically urged both sides not to claim too much, yet was labeled as typical creationist propaganda by defenders of Darwinism and as typical evolutionist propaganda by their political opponents.

Although the controversy over teaching evolution in the public schools ended up in the courts, it may not have ended at all. Both "belief in creation" and "belief in evolution" have implications beyond science, producing convictions too strong to permit compromise. Neither side has been willing to accept adverse legal results as final. Since judges are elected, or appointed by elected officials, a group stung by a court decision can work politically to seat more favorable judges for the next round. By educating the public, both sides in this particular controversy still hope to obtain a final victory:

> That is precisely why they had fought so hard over the content of public biology teaching. But this point simply underscored the dilemma: a lasting legal victory on the issue of evolutionary teaching awaited a verdict of popular opinion on evolution while that verdict was at least partially dependent on the content of public instruction.

Public issues that make the newspapers are not the only political disputes a Christian in science will likely face. Of more immediate relevance to most of us are conflicts over laboratory policy, university regulations or simply departmental politics. In the real world, despite disagreements, policies must be put into place. Decisions have to be made, and the voting on many departmental issues will not be by secret ballot. Our colleagues are likely to know which side we take, and are likely to remember.

Politics has been called the art of compromise. Sometimes a consensus can be reached if enough people are willing to give a little. When consensus is not possible, "horse-trading" may be the next best thing; that is, being willing to accept a loss on one issue in order to win on another. When a university, department or other entity sets a policy that everyone in the group must abide by, the policy will affect some individuals more drastically than others, both positively and negatively. We are unlikely to get our way every time, so we must learn to be good losers. On the other hand, if we are *always* on the losing side, that may be an indication that we are not where we belong.

When should policies be changed? The policies in place were adopted to avoid having to repeat the same arguments over and over again. Policies have histories: they were set up because of a specific situation on the basis of past experience. Eventually new situations arise, more experience has accumulated, and a policy that once made sense now begins to seem arbitrary, at least to someone. Should an exception be allowed, or the whole policy changed? The traditionalists want to hold the line; the progressives want a "new deal."

One science professor said that on nearly every policy question that came up in his department over the years, faculty members were divided almost evenly. On curricular requirements, on the method of assigning graduate students, even on the wording of departmental brochures, roughly fifty percent of his colleagues would argue for doing things a certain way, and the other fifty percent would take an opposite position. Since there were no "party lines," the makeup of the two sides kept changing.

Certain issues cannot be put aside to think about at our leisure. They demand immediate attention, careful study of arguments on all sides, and our vote. The choices they force on us may not be easy.

Taking a Stand

As Christians in science, where do we take our stand? For that matter, *when* do we take a stand that distinguishes us from others? Should we always try to side with other Christians? The problem is that on many issues, thoughtful Christians can be found on both sides. There is even a problem in trying to behave as true scientists, because scientists are trained to be analytical, weighing all sides and suspending judgment. What we really want is to be open to new truth without hesitating to confess what we already know in our hearts to be true.

Some prefer to say that they are absolutely sure of the truth of Christ. Others make a lesser claim: that they are as sure of Christ as anyone can be about anything. Yet no matter how we speak of our faith, "sharing" it by opening ourselves to other thoughtful persons puts us at some risk. Making ourselves vulnerable is part of an effective witness. If we want the people we care about to take *our* faith seriously, we must engage in honest comparison with *their* faith. Our faith must be up to that kind of testing. We have to stand up and be counted.

Learning how and when to fly the flag as a Christian is an important part of belonging to the scientific community. Learning how to respond to conflicts is another. The Bible gives support to both peacemakers and warriors. The choice we make between those two modes must suit both our personality and the circumstances. Those who take up intellectual arms should remember that to react like one's enemy is to lose the battle. Those who seek to make peace should remember that to reconcile opposing forces requires us to stand between them.

With regard to the so called creation/evolution debate in particular:

The caricatures, the easy criticisms, the propaganda, the familiar commonplaces of the various sides are comfortable—but they have become costly both within and for the Christian community. So what should we do? On all sides we need to unhitch our egos and do some hard, maybe even painful work. And maybe the various sides should talk. Not debate—talk. It is just possible, neither side being omniscient, that both sides could gain something from serious contact with competent practitioners on the other.

It may be wise to step back from some issues even when people whom we admire are passionate about them. One advantage of being a scientist in some situations is that scientists are expected to be relatively impersonal and dispassionate. Christians who sidestep issues should remember not to treat as unimportant what may be of crucial importance to someone else. Why not simply listen to one position at a time and try to clarify it by asking questions that show we take it seriously? In fact, that should be our first step before either entering the fray or trying to reconcile opposing sides.

On many issues there are good arguments on more than one side, including the philosophical issue of "chance versus design," which is behind the political issue of how biology should be taught in public schools. Does today's biology require a new theoretical approach, treating the information-bearing DNA molecules as messages more akin to an encyclopedia or a complicated piece of software than to ordinary material objects?

Philosophical naturalists who cannot conceive of an unevolved intelligence are forced to keep reminding themselves that although biological phenomena "give the appearance of having been designed for a purpose," that cannot be true. They respond by capitalizing Evolution or Chance or Nature, in their minds if not on paper, thus deifying an abstraction and endowing it with creative power. The Bible condemns as idolatry the attributing of primal creative power to anything or anyone other than God.

As Phillip Johnson has written, "If God is real, then a naturalistic science that insists on explaining everything is out of touch with reality." Of course, if God is real, a theology that insisted on explaining everything without taking science into consideration would also be out of touch. Christians in science are not likely to make either mistake, though we may not always agree on how to express our most basic convictions.

Some issues are terribly important. Others result from semantic misunderstandings. Some Christians have expressed concern that Phillip Johnson's challenge to Darwinism may do theism more harm than good. They seem to feel that his argument in essence boils down to the old "God of the gaps" position, a position weakened every time a gap in our understanding is filled by scientific discovery. Physicist Howard Van Till of Calvin College, for example, thinks it better to champion a biblical view of a world possessing "seamless integrity," a world created by God with the capacity to do whatever God wants it to do.

To Johnson, Van Till's argument sounds too much like the old deistic position, in which God never intervenes in the workings of his creation. Besides, Johnson would say that he is addressing his challenge to atheistic naturalists who pay no attention to the Bible except to mock it. Is it necessary to side with one or the other of these two Christian scholars? One thing Christians can do is to pray that both will be effective witnesses for Christ in their own spheres of influence.

Fighting words cause needless fights. For example, "divine intervention" is a phrase that engenders conflict. To endorse the concept seems to reduce God's action in the world to sporadic tinkering. Yet to deny it seems to negate the whole theistic outlook. Perhaps some reconciliation could be achieved by substituting another phrase, such as "divine invention." When a breakthrough occurs in an innovative workshop, we call it an *in*vention, but not an *inter*vention, because we know that the inventor must have been working creatively even between "creations."

Putting It All Together

Once again I will end a chapter with some first-person comments. I have already described how I got into scientific work and I have written about what caused me to change careers. Here I will try to give an impression of what day-to-day life in the lab was like for me. The way I put science and faith together may not have been exemplary but my own experiences are the ones I know best.

Looking back on my scientific career, I see many points at which God guided me in a particular direction, kept me from making a big mistake, or rescued me from the worst consequences of many small-to-midsize mistakes. The details of those situations would not apply to anyone else, but maybe I can say something helpful about the way I sensed God's presence. I would not describe that perception as a conscious awareness (at least most of the time), certainly not as a mystical experience. It was more like the effect on a person's life of having signed an employment contract, or of receiving a research grant. I simply knew that I was connected—obligated to Someone who was counting on me and who wanted me to succeed.

When I entered graduate school I had been a Christian for a dozen years, with two of those years spent in the Navy, away from home and from the supportive environment of the church in which I had found Christ. That meant that I had already learned to pray on the run, as it were. Before I ever entered a lab I was carrying on a kind of running conversation with God about everything that happened to me.

That conversation was intermittent rather than constant, but the Lord always seemed to welcome its resumption. For all I know, he may have orchestrated certain events just to draw me back into the conversation, sometimes in perplexed need but often in the sheer joy of seeing "the dancing hand of God" in action. Beyond my own salvation in Christ, the two things I came to appreciate most were the Lord's exquisite sense of timing and his enduring sense of humor.

In biochemistry I had many satisfying experiences with my Senior Partner in the lab—which is one way I came to think of Christ, though never as flippantly as that might sound. It may have been the quality, if not the quantity, of those experiences that turned me into a "metaphysical minimalist." That is, the practice of discussing the day's work with my Lord probably kept me from feeling that I had to work out an explicit philosophical position, or worldview, to tie my faith and science together.

When I finally left biochemistry to enter a new profession, what I took with me was not a philosophy but the living memory of adventures with Christ in the lab and elsewhere. Now, over two decades later, I still think of myself as an apprentice to the Creator in a great experiment of living the rest of my life.

Would I now have a different attitude if my first career had not paralleled the golden age of science in America? That I cannot say, though I know that the Holy Spirit is available to all Christians who must cope with sudden emergencies, long-term disasters, even perpetual drought. What I *can* say is that God stayed with me through disappointing failures as well as satisfying accomplishments, for which I expect to be eternally grateful. Yes, I mean eternally. The Nobel Prize is not the only prize worth striving for.

The title of this section is taken from a book by Richard Bube, who has thought profoundly and written widely about relating science to Christian faith, both personally and philosophically. In *Putting It All Together* he described seven patterns of integration on the philosophical level. The pattern he recommended is one of "complementarity," drawing on insights from both authentic science and authentic theology. Without putting a name to my naive philosophical position, I suspect that I have followed the same pattern.

It was interesting to me that in a book discussing many philosophical and temporal issues, Bube's final paragraph stressed the significance for scientific work of our attitude toward eternity:

Christians do science recognizing that it does have a potential but that its potential is limited. They look to the future in order to do what needs to be done here and now in the present. They look to God in the face of what seems to be temporal pessimism so that the optimism generated from eternity may enable them to serve here and now in the way in which they are called. The realistic faith required to carry on science in spite of the ambivalence of its consequences requires trust in the ultimate control of God over all things.

5

Now the
Good News

A CHRISTIAN GOING INTO science faces problems common to scientists,
and scientists who become believers share the spiritual trials of fellow
Christians. Some special problems do arise from bearing allegiance to both
communities. Treated with care and prayer, they become opportunities to
experience and demonstrate the gospel's transforming power.

Divided Loyalty
For Christians, the New Testament ranks our priorities in a definite order.
First we are to serve God "with all our hearts and minds and souls," then to
care for our families (including our "family in Christ") and our neighbors.
Other things come in third. For some careers, that might not pose much of a
problem, but scientific work makes heavy demands on one's time, can
seldom be carried out on a prearranged schedule, and requires intense
concentration.

Graduate students in the sciences have traditionally been expected to put
in long hours, often late in the evenings and on weekends. Experiments can
last all night or might need to be watched for several days, or something that
goes wrong can force a cancellation of other plans at the last minute.

Anyone can put up with a few years of stress, but for most young scientists the pressure does not end with graduate school. Rather, getting a Ph.D. ushers one into a period of intense competition for a good position, then for tenure, research grants and recognition. For some, working under such high pressure becomes a lifelong habit, even if families suffer and other aspects of life are truncated. If in times of intense professional effort we are also drawn into serving in various church offices, our loyalty to Christ may seem to add an additional burden. How do we balance trying to be the best possible scientist against other demands?

Christians who become topnotch scientists must get there by essentially the same route taken by others. As urged in chapter three, thinking of our profession as a vocation or ministry is a way to overcome part of the pressure problem. A sense of mission enables us to feel that by doing our best in research and other aspects of professional life, we *are* serving God with all our being. Dedicating our lives to scientific work in the name of Christ is the best way to keep from compartmentalizing faith and work.

With practice, we can avoid designating certain aspects of our lives for thought while reserving others for prayer. The mark of an integrated Christian life is to think *and* pray about whatever is important. When we demonstrate our integrity that way we make a needed contribution to the church as a whole. Sometimes, though, a local church to which we belong may have a different concept of what we should be doing with our time. That is especially likely for a small congregation with few members capable of taking leadership roles.

If we sincerely dedicate our scientific career to the Lord, we can try to come to an understanding with the Christian community that we are serving as their missionary to the world of science. That still leaves us with the problem of reconciling the demands of professional and family life. Even if certain responsibilities in a local church can be put on hold for a few years, young children are growing up and will not wait. Inattention to one's children, spouse or aging parents can cause tension and later regret, a high price to pay for tenure or other professional recognition.

If we say we work long hours for the sake of family as well as for the Lord, we must be careful not to fool ourselves. If we see ourselves as laboring for the future of loved ones, we must not neglect them in the present. It is possible to fall into a trap, letting professional advancement take precedence over home responsibilities—all in the name of serving our family. Some are tempted by the appeal of orderly scientific investigation to draw away from the confusing complexity of sustained interaction with those closest to them.

A lab can be quiet and peaceful; families are often noisy and demanding.

It may seem unfair to have to compete professionally with others for whom science is their whole life. At times Christians may have to sacrifice some professional opportunities because of other demands on our time. If so, we should realize that the "winners" in science may be making another kind of sacrifice. Few people nearing the end of their lives, surrounded by families (or conscious of their absence), say, "I wish I had spent more time at work."

The NAS booklet *On Being a Scientist* devotes only a single page to the lives of scientists beyond their professional responsibilities. Yet its overall message is that scientists are (or should be) full human beings. Full human beings have families of origin and (eventually, for most) of commitment. Further, the basic human values seen by NAS as necessary for the good of science, such as honesty and fairness, are best nurtured in families.

Conflicting human loyalties trouble even young scientists who have had no religious training. The pace of modern society seems to war against many things Americans claim to have once valued, such as traditional family life and the welfare of young children. Children get their values from many sources, but parental influence seems to have declined drastically in many segments of our culture. For a variety of reasons, millions of aging parents are institutionalized, another disturbing trend in American society.

As pointed out in chapter four, Christians who try to live by biblical precepts are sometimes ridiculed as being bound by tradition. Secular humanists uphold science as a rational, progressive alternative, leading to an open-ended future. Of course, if the future is truly open-ended, there is no way to measure progress, so all we have is change. The current state of American culture is the result of change, and no one who cares about society should hesitate to question whether particular changes have been, or would be, desirable. Occasionally even the secular world seems to note that having roots in a religious tradition is not such a bad thing.

Science is not the only profession hard on family life. Grueling demands are traditionally made on medical career entrants, for example. The practice of overworking hospital interns and residents has been criticized as not only inhumane but even dangerous to patients in the care of those apprentice physicians. Intense careers in the business world can also be destructive to family life.

Christians who have adopted good family values from their own families and the church can help to humanize the profession of science. All those biblical images of God as "heavenly Father" and of the church as "the family of God" or "God's people" are not trivial. Scientists who deal constantly with highly technical abstractions need the positive counterbalance of belonging to some kind of family in which love is freely expressed. Exactly what role God plays in physical phenomena may not be clear, but a physicist who is "born again" can see clearly a role for God in his or her life. Knowing God in that intimate way does not necessarily put one at a disadvantage, even in the practice of physics.

Taking Care of Business

Circumstances will determine how to inject love and human concern unobtrusively into physics or whatever field you are in. The Holy Spirit stands by to guide you in making your specific contribution. Recognizing that your colleagues are as needy of human warmth as the rest of us, you can seek ways to provide it, even as a graduate student on a tight schedule and a low income.

In low-pressure times one can invite colleagues to meals, arrange social get-togethers, or find other ways to build trusting friendships. In difficult periods in our own lives, we can demonstrate our human vulnerability and how we cope with pressure. When others face personal pressures, we can then offer practical assistance and prayerful support. Professional and family responsibilities will place limits on what we can do for others, but with the Spirit's "renewable resources" we can probably do more than we think we can.

One way of exerting a quiet influence is through prayer, seeking the good of each colleague and of the specific lab or department where we work, perhaps of the whole branch of science to which we are committed. If we do not seek their good, who will? One young couple, sensing that other faculty members and spouses did not know each other well, began inviting pairs of faculty couples to dinner to begin building community in their department. Discovering that people would not open up under those circumstances, they changed tactics and invited one couple at a time. Some deep conversations led to changed lives and real friendships.

If your living situation does not permit much hospitality, there are ways to touch others with God's love even during the working day. Faculty or research group meetings sometimes drone on, for example, or important committee meetings are held up waiting for the perennial latecomer. Instead of writing off that time as a total loss, or isolating yourself in your own problems, why not think about each person in the room, one by one, bringing that individual's needs before God in prayer? Difficulty in praying for specific people may be a sign that you need to get to know them better. Once the committee gets down to business, make it the Lord's business, especially if "lives depend on it" (as in an oral examination).

There are many other ways to turn professional life into active ministry, beyond merely doing our work well. The knowledge that there is more to life than science has given many Christians a special incentive, even a special competence, to take the benefits of scientific understanding to others. In the long history of Christian missions to Third World countries, many have borne not only the gospel but also modern medicine, education and agricultural technology. Teaching science even in one's own culture requires skills not learned in a laboratory, plus a broad set of human values. If the future of science is left only to those who are "strictly scientists and nothing else," science may not have much of a future.

Moral Intensity

In many social environments, to introduce yourself as a scientist makes you sound like an interesting person; to introduce yourself as a Christian may have the opposite effect. There are probably many reasons for that, but the perceived connection between religious commitment and moral judgment is surely one of them. To the world at large, Christians are seen as moralists or moralizers, despite the cautions Jesus gave his followers to avoid being, or appearing to be, judgmental of others. *Ethics* and *morality* are frequently interchanged, but ethicists tend to be respected while moralists are looked down on as busybodies.

Moral or ethical standards pertain to any aspect of human behavior, though "immorality" often has a narrower connotation of sexual misconduct. Biblical exhortations to virtue or righteousness, beginning with the Ten Commandments, are likely to be ignored or even ridiculed in modern society. However, to consider any behaviors good and others bad, or even to rate some as better than others, is to engage in ethical or moral judgment. Ethics, sometimes thought of as the science of moral behavior, provides the philosophical basis for individual morality.

Discovering sin. The kind of moral intensity engendered by the personal dimension of religious commitment is easily caricatured as goody-goody. Meanwhile, the essentially impersonal character of scientific publication has encouraged a split between what it means to be a good scientist and a good person. Scientists who cheat on income taxes, or on their spouses, can be admired as good scientists, as long as their published data are considered trustworthy.

The National Academy of Sciences published *On Being a Scientist* as a discourse on ethical behavior, dealing with ethics in the limited sense of professional conduct. It used relatively mild terms like *ethos, values, responsibilities, professional obligations* and *misconduct.* Nevertheless, it made a case for what scientists should do, or *must* do, ethically speaking. At one point the 1989 edition even used the strong biblical word *sin,* saying that outright fraud "may be the gravest sin in science."

Having brought ethical issues to the attention of young scientists, the National Academy went on in 1992 to publish *Responsible Science: Ensuring the Integrity of the Research Process.* Although that report was immediately praised for publicly airing scientific misconduct as a serious issue, its way of defining misconduct brought some criticism.

Responsible Science named "fabrication, falsification, or plagiarism in proposing, performing, or reporting research" as its number one category of misconduct. Certain "questionable research practices" already outlined in *On Being a Scientist* formed a second, less serious category. A third category of "other misconduct" included sexual harassment, misuse of funds, coverups of misconduct in science, reprisals against whistle-blowers and malicious allegations of scientific misconduct.

Two of the twenty-two panel members responsible for producing *Responsible Science* objected to citing various levels of scientific wrongdoing. They felt that making such distinctions would blur the boundary between actionable misconduct and mere misjudgment. A member of a congressional committee complained that the report provided inadequate standards to help Congress oversee proper use of federal research funds.

Obviously it is difficult to produce a clearly stated moral code or set of agreed-upon rules covering all situations. Even the most basic moral imperatives (the Ten Commandments' "Do not kill. Do not commit adultery. Do not steal. Do not lie," and so on) force those who seek to obey them to ponder what is right in certain ambiguous situations. Jesus moved those imperatives from the realm of behavior to that of intention. He condemned lust as the precursor of adultery, anger as a deadly form of "murder in the heart." His followers therefore have to grapple with the subtleties of both wrongheadedness and wrongheartedness. The first step toward finding forgiveness in Christ is to acknowledge the moral inadequacies of our own hearts.

Resisting temptation. An appropriate Christian response to the NAS report on *Responsible Science* is found in the prayer Jesus taught his closest followers: "Lead us not into temptation, but deliver us from evil." Evil comes to us packaged attractively and with a false label. Perhaps a coworker suggests ignoring a troublesome bit of data in order to get an abstract in on time, so the lab can present a paper at a national meeting. What weight should be given to arguments that "Everybody does it" or "Everybody knows that abstracts are only tentative"? Temptation always sounds so reasonable.

Suppose it is not a peer but your graduate advisor who wants you to make your experiments look better than they really are. Suppose you could get by with a little trimming of the data this time. Even worse, suppose you are sharp enough to get by with it time after time. Suppose it is obvious that everybody understands the practice, so "it can't possibly hurt anybody." Suppose you discover that many of your peers are cutting corners. What do you do then?

To be true to our calling, Christians must uphold a standard higher than what others are doing, higher than our own self-interest or even what is best for science. We must do what is right because it is right and because we belong to God. Trying to uphold a Christian moral standard in the lab makes us acutely aware of the temptation to bend the rules to our own advantage, whether or not we actually do so (this time). If we begin to go against our conscience, it gradually tends to be a less reliable guide.

Drawing the line. The current searchlight on fabrication, falsification, and plagiarism may clean up scientific publication for the near future. Temptation in the shadowy areas of *Responsible Science*'s lesser categories will still be with us. Of course one would not steal a computer from the lab, but what about making personal use of it when it is not being used for research? Is there a clear rule against writing personal letters on laboratory stationery, or merely a tacit agreement that it should not get out of hand? When that fine line is hard to locate, the New Testament advises us to avoid even the "appearance of evil."

How to deal with possible misconduct by others can be perplexing. Sometimes one can exert an influence simply by example, or by asking others in a nonthreatening way how they manage to reconcile questionable behavior. At other times it may be appropriate to blow the whistle, at the risk of unpopularity or even reprisal for "bringing down the law" on behavior others have taken for granted.

Patterns of subtle sexual harassment or racial discrimination are particularly difficult to counter when everyone is doing it but no one else is seeing it, or so it may seem. Actually, others may see but lack the courage to oppose what goes on. Years ago a Christian graduate student, invited to join the campus chapter of a professional scientific fraternity, learned from a close Jewish friend that Jews were ineligible. He wrote a letter declining membership, stating as his reason that his otherwise qualified friend had been excluded. The following year things changed. His friend received an invitation and joined. The letter writer received no reply, nor was he again invited to join.

In situations not covered by *On Being a Scientist* or other appropriate sets of guidelines, it is particularly important to pray for wisdom to discern the biblical principles that apply. It may help to write out alternative courses of action and their possible consequences. Consider how each step would look to others, and how you would feel if someone else took that step. Give each potential move the test of universality: What would happen if everybody did it? Try to sort out what is most honorable in the long run, remembering that the "long run" is not merely the length of your career, but extends into eternity.

Although Christians should not be nitpicking pharisees, Jesus said we must be faithful in small details if we are to be trusted in larger matters. A slip-up, in large matters or small, makes us feel that we have let others down, including the Lord. Yet the New Testament gives us assurance that "If we confess our sins, he who is faithful and just will forgive us our sins and cleanse us from all unrighteousness." If we make a mistake, we must resolve not to make that same mistake again. To live as a Christian is to live in love, not fear. It means learning a lesson from each of our mistakes, while trusting God to keep us from making a fatal mistake.

Christians have assurance that our eternal security will not be in jeopardy because of careless mistakes or because of the residue of original sin within us. On the other hand, the promise that we will be cleansed from all unrighteousness does not mean that we can avoid the proximate consequences of any wrongdoing. The Bible is realistic about the inherent tendency of people to behave selfishly, and it is honest about the havoc such behavior can cause.

No one is sinless, and we do not escape the effects of sin on ourselves and others. A famous agnostic once observed that, in nature, there are consequences but no judgments. To a theist, human nature has a spiritual dimension that makes moral judgment an essential part of life. When people hurt other people, somebody pays, one way or another. A firm conviction that nothing, not even our sins, "can separate us from the love of God" should make it easier for Christians to own up to personal responsibility.

Sin should never be flaunted. Reputations are important, and Christians represent not only ourselves but the whole family of God. One's reputation for telling the truth can be ruined by being caught in a single lie, even if that is the only time one has ever "shaded the truth." The third chapter of Genesis makes it clear that lying is the primary corrupter of innocence. Falsification is not only a sin in itself but also comes into play in efforts to cover up every other kind of wrongdoing.

The "big lie" takes many forms. Under certain circumstances, gonado-trophic hormones seem to whisper almost audibly to people who other-wise think very clearly: "Look, the two of you are alone and you're sexual human beings. You're physically attracted to each other. Nothing else matters." It is a lie, of course, but particularly effective because it is built on a partial truth. Even though we *are* sexual human beings, other aspects of life, and other people, *always* matter. Habitually listening to lies tends to distort one's grasp of reality; some people actually come to believe outrageous falsehoods.

In *On Being a Scientist* and *Responsible Science,* the National Academy was thus b.c. ("biblically correct") to pinpoint falsification in its various forms as the basic evil. Tempted to fudge or plagiarize, a scientist may believe that no one will know. Caught in the act, he or she may say, "I didn't know it was wrong." Getting by with it may be even worse than getting caught, making it harder to recognize and honor truth in the future.

No wonder the Bible tells us to "flee from evil" before evil gets its hooks into us. To be tolerant toward wrongdoing is not only dangerous but, for a Christian, is itself a form of falsehood. We belong with those who yearn for righteousness and who desire to uphold it. Whatever the flaws in our own integrity, integrity is what we stand for.

Relations with Others in Science

Christians should be known not only for personal integrity, but also for helping others to be at their best. We can be different from those around us in style and even substance without being a killjoy or a moral drag. In matters of personal conduct, we can often avoid confrontation without at the same time going along with the crowd.

The idea is not to affirm everything that people do, but to affirm people as individuals, whatever they do. Jesus set the ultimate example, giving his life for those neither basically good nor even law-abiding, but actually dead set against him. He accepts us as we are but he did something to change us. We, too, should accept people and seek goodness in them and from them. Our concern for those with whom we work should make it easier, not harder, for them to love goodness too.

Some churches emphasize "separation from the world" to such an extent that their young people are unlikely to enter such a "worldly" profession as science. Christians who do go into science from socially conservative back-grounds handle crosscultural problems in different ways.

Take the simple matter of studying or working in the lab on Sundays, for example. For some it is not an issue. Others do it if everybody else in their group does it and the professor expects it, but they feel bad about dishonoring the Lord's day. Some regard working on Sunday as a concession they must make now, intending to stop as soon as they get their degree, or finish their postdoctoral years, or gain tenure. Others quietly avoid working on Sundays whenever possible, but do not complain when research demands it. Some consider Sunday observance as a distinct mark of a Christian and make an issue of it, possibly suffering for the stand they take.

Christian missionaries in crosscultural situations have learned to be cautious in opposing the cultural practices of any group of people with whom they hope to share the gospel. To stand in opposition to a long-accepted practice in your research group or department may convey an impression entirely different from what you intend. If it gets you labeled as a troublemaker or kook, you may have forfeited opportunities to witness in other ways. It could make your dedication to science suspect, stir up hard feelings, or lead to an ultimatum.

On the other hand, if you treat a specific situation as a genuine moral dilemma for you, you might earn the respect of others for standing up for what you believe. You might discover that others feel the same way but have hesitated to speak up. Done in the right spirit, standing up for a principle can be the right thing to do even if eventually you have to choose between giving in or leaving. Done in the wrong spirit, or for the wrong reasons, it can be disastrous even if you win that particular battle. Be cautious about turning a mission field into a battlefield.

Christians may feel insecure in certain social situations, especially if they have grown up in a relatively sheltered environment. For example, individuals opposed to drinking alcoholic beverages may find themselves at departmental parties where everyone else seems to be drinking, even to excess. When drinks are offered, a simple "No, thank you," should do the trick without making a scene.

If pressured further to drink, asking for coffee or a nonalcoholic soft drink may give you a cup or glass to hold without drawing attention to yourself. With today's awareness of the social costs of alcoholism, to say politely, "I've had plenty already," or "Thanks, but I'm driving," will usually get you off the hook. One graduate student found that he could compliment a host or hostess by saying, "Oh, I couldn't. I drink only at *dull* parties." To pull that off honestly, since he didn't drink at all, he had to be willing to help keep any party lively, or leave.

Certain traditions cause special problems. Suppose it is traditional in your department for each graduate student, on passing his or her qualifying exams, to buy drinks for the whole group at the local bar. If you do not drink, you can still go to such celebrations to congratulate your friends. Even when there is some drunkenness, you can probably find a way to participate without compromise. Perhaps you will actually be welcomed as the evening's "designated driver."

Now, though, what happens when it becomes your turn to supply the liquor? To back out might make you look not principled but merely cheap, especially if no one noticed that you did not drink at earlier parties. A creative alternative would be to host a different kind of party, with outstanding food instead of liquor, plus some merry entertainment to show that you want your friends to enjoy themselves, even if sober.

A postdoctoral researcher at an Ivy League school who was invited to a graduate student party turned it into a hilarious time by organizing games and songs. He was later profusely thanked by the hosts, who said, "We're so glad you came. We couldn't afford to buy booze." Many people drink or use other mind-altering drugs to "have a good time." Can we show them how to have a better time? If they are driven to anesthetize themselves, is there another way we can help them bear sorrow or pain? If they are being influenced by the crowd, can we become an alternative influence?

Behavioral differences fester when something that is trivial to one person is a matter of principle to another. Sometimes we must simply part company, as when ethnic jokes or stories demeaning to women are going around the lab, or when colleagues act "on the loose" at a national meeting. No matter how unobtrusively or politely we separate ourselves, we are likely to be pegged as self-righteous prudes, religious fanatics, or worse.

If we seem odd, or at odds with accepted mores, we may be dropped from social gatherings or, more serious, may find ourselves "out of the loop" when important discussions are going on in the lab. Even without provocation, Christians are sometimes regarded with suspicion or are judged on the basis of stereotypes. Who wants a rigid moralist or a flaming evangelist at the next bench?

If we find ourselves in disharmony with our colleagues, we should first examine ourselves to be sure that we are not simply being unpleasant. A student once described the Christians in her dorm as the ones who "always bow their heads before a meal and then always complain about the food." It may be that a colleague's dislike for us is based on personal traits rather than on our moral principles. The New Testament exhorts Christians to do our best to live in peace with those around us.

Positive Alternatives

As we have seen, recent publications on ethical behavior in science have tended to define misconduct, leaving proper conduct undefined. Christians should focus attention on positive qualities, exemplifying, to the best of our ability, the whole spiritual fruit basket listed in the New Testament: love, joy, peace, patience, kindness, goodness, faithfulness, gentleness and self-control. Our faithfulness in carrying out assignments or our kindness toward the lab's student dishwasher or janitor can offset many negative impressions.

Being positive tends to open more doors to substantive conversations about Christian faith than being negative. The best kind of evangelism can perhaps be defined as the positive things we do that lead others to ask why we seem to be different. If as believers we are repeatedly put to the test by colleagues, so much the better for our faith and our character, and perhaps for the lab as well.

The New Testament is also clear about what to do when a disagreement arises: first, try to straighten it out on a one-to-one basis before going public. Beware of assuming bad motives on anyone else's part; recognize that you may not know the whole story, and be willing to give the other party the benefit of the doubt. Ask for clarification and pray for wisdom before making any judgment. The habit of phrasing a judgment as "what seems right under the present circumstances" is often just as effective as making an absolute moral point, and may keep you from becoming a tyrant when you have gained more authority over others.

When a problem has been resolved, or even defined, it is a good idea to put in writing what was decided. Misunderstandings can flare up again if people later have widely different recollections. A dated "memorandum of understanding" spelling out a joint agreement, with a copy sent immediately to each party, may seem a waste of time, but it provides an excellent safeguard against future problems.

We usually have plenty of problems to occupy our minds and hearts without stirring up new ones. Christians should be "as wise as serpents, but as harmless as doves."

Conflict with Other Christians

As important as it is to maintain good relations with those with whom we work, it is also important to avoid getting out of synch with the rest of the Christian community. We are likely to seem as odd to some church members as we seem to scientific colleagues who have never before encountered a serious believer.

Despite a noble tradition of Christians in scientific work, few church leaders actively encourage young people to choose a research career. At great universities once set up as religious institutions, science is now seen in a strictly secular light. Even at colleges still flying the Christian flag, science professors may feel less appreciated than faculty in Bible or music departments, where instruction is less expensive and may seem more relevant to spiritual growth and propagation of the gospel. Only a few theological seminaries have begun to incorporate scientific matters into pastoral education.

Evangelical churches that send missionaries around the world seldom see the "world of science," or of scholarship in general, as a mission field. That lack of vision brought parachurch organizations like InterVarsity Christian Fellowship and Campus Crusade for Christ into existence as missionary organizations. Of course, churches would be glad to see Christians recognized as distinguished professors and Nobel Prize winners. Yet the church as a whole, and especially the conservative Protestant branch of the church, has not done much to set young Christians on the paths leading to such recognition.

Scientists with no religious background who hear the gospel as adults and respond to it may find themselves ill at ease in an evangelical subculture. Even young people who grew up in a conservative church and then took up the study of science may at times feel estranged from other Christians who have not had that kind of training.

Spiritual unity is important to the body of Christ, but sometimes that unity is more apparent than real. The members of a congregation or of a whole denomination can appear to be in agreement on some issue simply because questions are never raised about it. Scientists are accustomed to facing hard questions, so in a religious context a person with scientific training can be dismayed to discover that critical questions are not even being asked. If he or she asks such questions, the result may be an embarrassed silence rather than the open dialogue expected in a scientific context.

Unity that cannot withstand expression of contrary opinion is hardly true spiritual unity. On the other hand, in a religious context, the stakes are high and eternal destinies are at risk.

The impersonal character of scientific thinking makes it less inhibited than religious thinking. In the game of science one can ask almost anything or propose almost anything as a possibility, simply because one is playing with abstract ideas. Churches, on the other hand, deal directly with real human lives and deep human needs. Biblical terms like *sacred, holy, salvation* and *eternity* indicate that Christians are not playing around in seeking to meet human needs. Devotion to God is not a game—nor, for that matter, is serious devotion to science.

Scientists who care about the church have a special responsibility to help it change for the better. With patience, we can help the church recover the empirical spirit Jesus modeled in telling his hearers to "Come and see for yourselves." He called himself "the way, the truth, and the life." Truth is never diminished by asking questions. In science as well as religion, faith requires going beyond the evidence at hand, but too many people, in and out of the church, falsely see religious faith as accepting doctrines in spite of the evidence.

Not all questions are equally helpful, in Christian circles or elsewhere. Few scientists would tolerate a barrage of questions that slowed the pace of a lecture by demanding of every statement made, "How do you know *that?*" Sooner or later, an exasperated scientist pushed on some basic point would say, "I looked it up, I trusted the literature, I see no reason to doubt it. Now, let's move on." The persistent doubter would earn a reputation as a troublemaker or misfit, even if such questions occasionally turned up a shaky assumption.

Religious dialogue carries additional emotional freight, so to be helpful, questions need to be asked thoughtfully and prayerfully. What should one do when ministers or other speakers say something about science and get it wrong? To point out an error in a public meeting will embarrass the person who made it and will probably push that person into a defensive posture. It is generally better to make one's point in private and let any public correction be made later by the speaker who originally made the error.

A typical church group encompasses a far wider range of formal education than any group of scientists or students. That puts a further restraint on the way questions should be raised. In an open discussion the temptation to show up blatant ignorance, or simply to show off, is at times palpable. The urge to speak up as an authority can be almost overwhelming when other Christians put down science or scientists, especially if they do not know what they are talking about.

In taking the gospel to our scientific colleagues we would be careful not to alienate them unnecessarily. We should be equally sensitive when we try to counter ignorance or deep suspicion about science among people who honor the Bible. Our call to witness faithfully goes in both directions.

Within theologically conservative churches, the whole Bible is often interpreted quite rigidly, despite a general awareness that it is a library containing various types of literature. Sometimes considerable selectivity is employed in choosing which parts to take literally. What does the Bible mean to say about the age of the earth, if anything? Can a Christian who comes to accept the geological conclusion of an age of billions of years remain in fellowship with a narrower creationist convinced by biblical interpretation that the earth is only a few thousand years old? It is not easy, and it requires abundant good will on both sides.

The good will necessary in such hard cases must come from joint recognition of spiritual unity in Christ and from a high regard for the Bible. Two forgiven sinners who uphold Scripture as God's word should be able to "cut each other some slack." A superior knowledge of geology or a better command of logic can win an argument but lose us a friend. It might be better to table the argument and strengthen the friendship. In the long run, a friend who trusts us about other matters is more likely to trust us about geology. And we ourselves might learn something in the process.

Isolation and Loneliness

For some of the reasons cited above, Christians who go into science as a career frequently feel like strangers both in their laboratories and at church. They may begin to doubt that they belong in one or the other. A string of experimental failures or a spiritual dry spell can trigger intense loneliness. Long periods of sparring with skeptics at work, or with hyper-orthodox supporters of pseudoscience at church, can make one weary of "duel" citizenship.

Christianity and science are both social enterprises, though an occasional loner can survive or flourish in either. For most of us, a lonely time is a dangerous time. If we are forced to find strength through prayer and reading the Bible, a time of personal crisis can become a time of personal growth. Without access to spiritual resources, however, loneliness can be overwhelming. It can lead to spiritual or professional decline or even to despair and clinical depression.

To break out of lonely isolation, we need to be reminded that if God has truly called us into science, the Holy Spirit is available to us for whatever comes our way. Jesus said, "I am with you always." He did *not* say that his followers would never know doubt or fear or trouble or even tragedy. He said that he would be with us when we face such trials. We need not hide our worst moments or innermost fears from him. The cross and Christ's resurrection may not mean anything to our colleagues, but to us they bring assurance that all our failures are already forgiven. Jesus wants to be our closest friend.

Despite depressing feelings, we are not alone. Nor are we the first to have such feelings. All Christians in scientific work have probably felt isolated at one time or another. Yet there are thousands of us, and, for many, finding each other has helped us break out of isolation and has become a joy in itself. Members of a vast "unseen college" of intelligent believers can easily be found in the books they have written, if in no other way.

It is always encouraging to pray with other followers of Jesus in small groups dedicated to him. Two or three like-minded believers gathered together to share each other's problems are all it takes. We are in good shape if we have even one other person to pray with at home or at work or at church. With several of those bases covered, we are unlikely to feel lonely at all. Locating other Christians in the institution and in the field in which we work is not only a joy but a responsibility. They, too, may be feeling isolated. Our job is to find them.

One of the best ways to maintain balance is to associate with as many other Christians in science as we can discover. The American Scientific Affiliation (ASA) has offered that kind of contact for over fifty years, and now Christian groups or informal networks exist in various scientific specialties. Chapter six offers some concrete suggestions for making connections with your peers.

On the other hand, a good argument can be made that a spiritual connection with people who are *not* our professional peers is both an obligation and a source of support when we need it. The fellowship of "kindred spirits" whose minds are on something other than science is important. It can lift us from the doldrums and send us back to the lab with a song in our hearts or at least with a less-knotted chain of thought. Sometimes simply getting away from research problems is a way to get a fresh perspective needed to break a mental logjam.

Each member of a group of Christians can find therapeutic value in freely sharing sorrows and joys totally unrelated to their work. The theory of Christian fellowship, one might say, is that since only part of a group will be "down" at any one time, God's inspiration will be transmitted through some positive outlooks in the group as well as through more negative ones.

Another possibility, if one takes seriously the concept of being called to scientific work, is to enlist the prayers of a church group whose members pray regularly for missionaries. Such prayer warriors need not understand the technical aspects of laboratory research any more than they understand the intricacies of translating the Bible into the language of a distant tribe. Their petitions are for a "prayee's" welfare and for God's will to be done, whatever the complex circumstances. Christians in science would benefit from being accountable to a regular prayer group and from writing an occasional "spiritual progress report" to those who pray for our particular mission.

Any of these procedures for solving the problem of isolation can turn into an unexpected opportunity for growth. The hitch is that they require initiative. Shy persons, as *Prairie Home Companion* host Garrison Keillor says, need the courage to "get up and do what needs to be done."

Pray for that courage and act on it. Your action may be the answer to someone else's loneliness. We are all in this (i.e., in God's kingdom) together.

Crosscultural Communication

How to bridge the "communications gap" is a day-to-day problem for anyone trying to be both a Christian and a scientist, not just for someone writing a book. Perhaps a first-person account of some of the author's efforts will encourage you.

Most of us witness quietly to our scientific peers and some are also publicly outspoken as believers. Others seem to "fly below the radar" to avoid calling public attention to their faith, perhaps until their scholarly accomplishments give them a feeling of security. I suspect that my evangelistic style was somewhere between. Before turning to evangelism, though, let me recount a few efforts to communicate in the other direction, to the Christian community.

Early in my career I wrote a short piece for a student magazine, published under the title, "Christ and the Day's Work." I wrote about doing one's daily tasks with care as a form of worship. I have forgotten exactly what I said but I do recall the incident behind it. It was then common to do by mouth much of the pipetting now done with rubber suction bulbs. Transferring samples of a concentrated ammonia solution, I got distracted and for a second aliquot stupidly used the same pipet, by then full of ammonia vapors that I sucked into my mouth. The "burn" lasted long enough for me to reflect on my folly and to write about keeping our minds focused on doing the Lord's business of each day.

A letter to the magazine criticized my article for belittling the concept of worship. I guessed that the critic was a preministerial or seminary student, in training to lead public worship in a church setting. It began to dawn on me: Christian leaders who can hardly imagine worshiping in a lab may not be the most helpful guides about how to be a Christian there. I think that is when I began seriously turning for spiritual guidance to those traveling the same path.

A lesson on how easily one can be misunderstood lingered long after a lecture I gave at a small Christian college. At one point I described the impersonal objectivity of scientific publication as a legitimate rule of the game, saying that I did not expect my research papers to indicate that I was a committed Christian. The audience included a philosophy professor who misconstrued my remark. Years later I learned that he began using me (by name) as a bad example of a scientist who "leaves his faith at the door when he enters his laboratory."

I would never have said what he evidently thought I had said. I knew I needed guidance and forgiveness in the lab as much as anywhere else, especially in my interactions with students, technicians and colleagues. The philosophy professor did not understand that what gets into the refereed literature does not tell the whole story of what goes on in science. Evidently I had not made that clear.

Christians in writing and publishing recognize a difference between the "Christian market" and the "secular market." The two are so distinct that lists of bestsellers seen in newspapers seldom contain books from Christian publishers, even if they are outselling everything else. In the past, secular bookstores would not carry Christian books, so now we have Christian bookstores that seldom stock works by secular authors, even those of lasting value. The point is that trying to communicate requires keeping in mind the specific "filters" through which our words must pass.

What we say or write can come across with an entirely different meaning to different groups of people. Consider my experience, over a period of decades, in writing about life's origins. With my first Ph.D. student I wrote a chapter on that subject for an ASA symposium volume published in 1959, the Darwin centennial year.

Several technical papers had appeared on the formation of amino acids in gaseous atmospheres supposedly resembling prebiotic conditions on the primitive earth. It looked as if more experimental work might turn a lot of speculative "paper chemistry" into something tangible. We wanted to put that research into theological perspective, alerting readers that discussions of evolution were about to enter a new (molecular) phase.

Our chapter urged caution about concluding that the gap between nonliving matter and life must remain forever unbridgeable. We pointed to a danger in assuming "sudden supernatural intervention as the only possible interpretation," while asserting that no description of mechanisms by which life came into existence could ever be a complete answer to theological questions about life's origin.

Molecular evolution did indeed become a hot topic, stimulated by the "DNA revolution." Some thirty years later, however, when I again wrote on the origin of life, the experimental work had been far less fruitful than I had anticipated. In ASA's *Teaching Science in a Climate of Controversy,* I explained to teachers that "At this stage of our scientific knowledge, it would be irresponsible to give students the impression that 'life arose by chance.' Scientists do not know how life arose."

Many conservative Christians who read the earlier chapter strongly objected to the suggestion that the chemical origin of life might eventually be put on a firm empirical foundation. Three decades later, another kind of reader seemed outraged at the claim that the origin of life and other key questions about evolution remained unanswered.

What I *said* had not changed, but *Teaching Science* was written for secular rather than Christian readers, and appeared in the aftermath of legal and political battles over "scientific creationism." Noting the two responses, one historian called it "a strange world" that could make me, disdained as an evolutionist by one group, seem to diehard Darwinists to be "a dangerous crypto-creationist."

It *is* a strange world. Or rather, a Christian working in science lives in two worlds that often seem strange to each other. Bringing our two worlds together requires us to express what is important in one of those worlds in language appreciated by the other. With each world suspiciously guarding its borders, finding appropriate ways to communicate keeps us on our toes—and on our knees.

I have great respect for Christian writers who try to bridge the gap, and for publishers who give them the opportunity. One publication I know well is *Radix* magazine, published by Christians but with non-Christian readers also in mind. In 1979, to celebrate the magazine's tenth anniversary, the editor asked me to put together an issue devoted to science.

The lead story, "God and the Scientists: Reflections on the Big Bang," described the scientific evidence for what astronomer Robert Jastrow called "hard creation." The article was based largely on Jastrow's remarkable address at the 1978 AAAS meeting, which sent reporters scurrying to pound out front-page stories on implications of the "big bang," a creation event forever beyond the grasp of science. My coauthor was physicist Paul Arveson, who had attended the lecture. Paul had publicly asked the speaker how, in the light of the evidence of creation and his willingness to take it at face value, he could remain an agnostic.

In front of a thousand people, Jastrow replied that his feeling went beyond

Einstein's cold concept of God but stopped short of personal faith, to which he could not yet bring himself. He said, quite openly, "I keep coming close to the edge of faith, but I never quite make it over." At the end of our article we expressed hope that some faithful Christian colleague might take him aside, perhaps at a scientific meeting, to suggest prayer as a new line of investigation. That way he might discover "compelling new evidence" that Jesus Christ was God's message-bearer to earth. Jastrow had already published a popular paperback on evolution of the universe and of life, *Until the Sun Dies*. Our *Radix* article ended this way:

> What Robert Jastrow needs is our prayers, with thanksgiving that he has come so far. What he doesn't need is condemnation for holding "materialistic presuppositions" that allegedly keep scientists from being objective. He is one scientist who understands how "scientism" works. He is trying to cope with evidence that flies in the face of his presuppositions. Christians seldom face up to their own inconsistencies with such detachment.

> Who knows? Perhaps in Robert Jastrow the Son of God will live—before the sun dies.

Radix has published other serious pieces on the physical and social sciences from a Christian perspective, on environmental stewardship, health care and other subjects. One of my contributions was a sonnet contrasting the biblical story with a story told by an atheistic biologist:

> *Reprise*
> (on Richard Dawkins's *The Blind Watchmaker*)
> In the beginning, Genesis begins
> With purpose, love, and power intertwined
> Combatting mythic amateurs. God wins,
> To set the future stage for humankind:
> Seeking power to boast of, Adam sins.
> That ancient urge, extensively refined,
> Recurs as Dawkins gazes through his lens,
> Sees no purpose, calls his Maker blind.
> With "lucky stars" again controlling men's
> Contingence—in at least poor Richard's mind—
> The Logos who dwelt among us surely grins,
> A Watchman over creatures he designed.
> All science depends, when push has come to shove,
> On human persons, born through acts of love.

In a 1988 issue of *Radix* devoted to the nature of truth, I recounted some of my interactions with non-Christian faculty colleagues, including hard-nosed positivists who held that "any question that cannot in principle be answered by the methods of science is an exercise in nonsense." It was good for me to "go to the mat" with "some great mind-wrestlers of my generation," I wrote, because "twenty years of that puts spiritual muscle on a guy."

Witnessing in Public and in Private

This discussion has begun to shift to evangelistic discourse. As times change, so do opportunities to make known both our true selves and our Savior. Today, much lively interaction between Christians and non-Christians about science and religion takes place on the Internet.

During my academic tenure, many secular campuses designated an occasional or even an annual week for consideration of ultimate questions. I spoke at a number of those "focus weeks" or "religious emphasis weeks" in the United States and also at several "missions" sponsored by InterVarsity chapters at provincial universities in Canada. At the missions, I gave lectures openly advertised as evangelistic, sometimes to a general audience, sometimes to science students and faculty.

In the early 1960s I lectured at a "science emphasis week" at a small Christian university, which led to an invitation to become a "Visiting Biologist to Colleges." That program of the American Institute of Biological Sciences was designed to get a message to undergraduates about new incentives to do graduate work in biology, but only for students adequately prepared in chemistry, physics and math. For a booklet sent to college science departments, the Visiting Biologists were asked to describe ourselves and list ten "catchy" titles for lectures, including (if a speaker was willing) "one or two titles suitable for chapel talks."

As one of only two or three self-described Christians on the list, I received invitations from Christian colleges as well as secular ones. Wherever I spoke, I tried to use analogies ("models," to a scientist) from my own field to illustrate my understanding of biblical concepts. For example, I might say that being spiritually alive is like being in a state of dynamic metabolic equilibrium, but being spiritually dead is more like reaching thermodynamic equilibrium.

In 1971 I had a chance to put some of those biochemical analogies into a chapter in E. M. Blaiklock's *Why I Am Still a Christian,* a response to Bertrand Russell's famous *Why I Am Not a Christian.* I also explained that though I had become a Christian as a young boy, I did not apologize for a childlike faith, because

> it was my own decision when it was made, and it opened up a satisfying life for me. Years later I became a biochemist in about the same way that I became a Christian. I was influenced by my parents and teachers. I made a firm decision when I had an imperfect knowledge of the alternatives. If the process of choosing my professional career was ill-informed and subject to haphazard influences, that in itself does not cause me to repudiate the choice. Rather, it causes me to rejoice in God's wisdom rather than my own, and to seek His guidance in my biochemical work as well as in all other aspects of my life.

I am grateful for those special opportunities to represent Christ in a public way. For most of us most of the time, private speaking and writing are the primary ways of doing what Jesus called "fishing for people." There are good ways to fish other than casting a wide net in public. My favorite style of evangelism is more like trolling.

In talking to friends or strangers, or in writing to almost anyone about almost anything, I like to draw along in front of them some hint of who I am as a follower of Jesus Christ. Will they take the bait and want to know more? One never knows which individuals the Holy Spirit has prepared. If they do not want to pursue the matter, we are still friends. If they express even a nibble of interest, we may be entering into something lasting—maybe into eternity.

That is one reason why our home in Berkeley is called the Troll House.

6

Living a
Whole Life

THIS CHAPTER IS ABOUT PUTTING science and faith together as a lifelong process. Living a Christian life is more of an art than a science, and many scientists have spoken of "the art of doing science." The two art forms have certain similarities, but are not necessarily linked together. Hence a Christian could level off after reaching a certain point in his or her professional career, or remain a "babe in Christ" while continuing to develop as a scientist.

The most challenging art of all is to integrate the practice of faith and the practice of science over the years, or at least to maintain them at equivalent stages of development. To live a whole or balanced life, one needs to grow in each area in a way that stimulates growth in the other.

Using Spiritual Resources

The concept of spiritual life or spiritual growth is foreign to science itself, which deals only with measurable physical properties. Yet, as seen in chapter three, the values that scientists must bring to their work are rooted in the spiritual realm. Because the appropriate data are internal and hence available only for our own lives, we cannot measure our spiritual growth by comparison with other lives.

We can, though, in a sense, plot our spiritual development over time. Is our love for Christ and desire to follow him greater than it was a year ago? Do we see moral issues more clearly, do what is right with less hesitation, treat our colleagues with greater respect, care less about self-centered ambition?

The temptation to trim such personal data to make ourselves look good in our own eyes is as real as the temptation to "fudge" in scientific publication, but here we lack the safeguard of objective evaluation. Although it seems to run counter to our intuition, the best safeguard against spiritual self-deception is to open our inmost being to God, sacrificing or giving up ultimate control of our ego. It is a risky process and, for most of us, a gradual one.

The process is not at all external or objective, but it is both fiducial and empirical. We trust God with a bit of ourselves and see what happens. We let Scripture examine our hearts as we explore the Bible. We converse with God about more of our actions and attitudes. And we check for distortion in our own channel of communication by seeing what other believers are receiving.

Basing Our Lives on Scripture

As scientists we learn the literature of our field; as Christians we need to base our lives on Scripture to be sure we are following God's directives. A Bible (preferably in a modern translation) kept next to our other reference sources at the lab makes a statement about who we are, or at least about the person we want to be.

Showing that we take the Bible seriously may elicit from some colleagues a derisive response, which can be shrugged off or countered by asking what *their* lives are based on. That question may not have occurred to them. Besides serving as a catalyst to start conversations that go beyond the confines of science, the Bible has an important role to play in our daily lives as scientists. If we use it properly, the Bible can provide direction for charting our course into the unknown. The unknown is what scientists are trying to explore.

The Bible is not a textbook or laboratory cookbook, but a library of books varying in content and intent. To get at their wisdom, it helps to pick up some appreciation of the cultures prevailing when each was written. Like the scientific literature, the Bible is addressed primarily to thinking adults. Unlike that literature, it is not at all impersonal or impartial. It provides spiritual impetus, not just information.

Making the Bible part of our lives can help us mature as scientists. It can restore our incentive for doing science through its strong focus on God's creative work. To study how the universe is put together and to care for the earth are two ways of honoring the Creator. The Bible makes it clear that we are not to deify natural phenomena like the sun or moon or to attribute to them astrological control of human destiny. Beginning with the opening chapters of Genesis, our debt to the Creator can be traced through Old Testament books of the law, the prophets, and the Psalms; several New Testament books open with the same theme.

The Bible can remind us that our imperatives for moral conduct begin with the Ten Commandments, sharpened by Jesus' comments in the Gospels and applied in specific situations in other New Testament books (almost like the "Results and Conclusions" section of a research paper). As we move up the professional ladder, it is good to go back to Jesus' Sermon on the Mount; to the apostle Paul's advice on dedicating our lives to Christ, caring for people and doing the Lord's business; and to the strong words of James on doing what is right without bragging about it.

At times we may need to turn to the Bible to renew hope, an element seldom found in scientific writing. For Christians, the Bible is primarily the message of good news. Fallible scientists are part of the world God loves. A moral slip-up, even one that might ruin a scientific career, is not the end of the road when life has an eternal dimension. Biblical standards of conduct are demanding, but they are imbedded in a context of encouragement. We are offered a "change of heart" to help us *want* to do what is right.

To experience God as a "lab partner" throughout life we need to respond to the message of Scripture in a life-changing way. Although Christians from different traditions differ strongly on the means, all consider some kind of "communion with God" essential to spiritual growth.

For some, a guided liturgical exercise in a worshiping congregation is the most powerful way of practicing God's presence. Others cultivate an intimate, free-flowing, informal style of sharing their lives with God. Some keep a kind of "lab notebook" or journal of spiritual discoveries and prayer concerns. Today, some Christians address personal responses to God the same way they write letters: on a word processor.

Devotional Bible reading is easily ignored by educated Christians even if they do a certain amount of analytical Bible study, the two differing as much as experimental work from theoretical work. The concept of gaining inspiration from Scripture does have a certain parallel in science because fresh ideas for research can come from many sources (e.g., from reading accounts of other work). Ideas come when we are open to them. Many prominent scientists have echoed Louis Pasteur's famous dictum about discovery: "In the field of observation, chance favors only the prepared mind."

Reading the Bible for inspiration requires us to prepare our hearts as well as our minds. In prayer, we open ourselves to whatever God wants us to receive, asking for wisdom and the courage to follow it, thanking God for offering it. To keep repeating that process over the years is like preparing the "Materials and Methods" section of a report on living one's life. Who knows? We may find guidance for some less comprehensive experiments as well.

God's Word can be powerful in its impact (like a double-edged sword, the Bible says). It is a more risky avenue of inspiration than standard ways of planning research, such as reading the technical literature with an open mind. The risk in reading Scripture with an open heart is that God is not limited to our present concerns. An open heart implies a search for truth combined with willingness to obey it. To discover that God has some greater plan for our lives may disrupt our own plans.

Identifying Ourselves with God's People
Even if the intensity of scientific work at the beginning of a career keeps us from participating in certain church activities, it should never be allowed to sweep aside close contact with other Christians. As we mature professionally, the need for such fellowship increases. Many seek the mutual support and counsel of a small group of Christian scholars gathered for Bible study and prayer.

The more homogeneous the group, the more spiritually efficient it will be. That is, less time has to be spent breaking down barriers between people in the group. On the other hand, intellectual pride is likely to creep up on us if not held in check by interaction with a whole body of believers from diverse backgrounds. Identifying ourselves with the whole family of God and holding ourselves accountable to it becomes more and more important as we climb the ladder of success.

If scientific work is the calling in which we invest our mind and heart, we must not use that calling as an excuse to remain aloof from the rest of Christ's body. To maintain a proper balance it may be wise to sing in a choir, teach a Sunday school class, tutor disadvantaged kids, volunteer in a clinic, or do something else totally different from our daily work. Professional arrogance has a way of melting away as we perform some humble task for people who have little comprehension of science, but for whom Christ died.

One very sharp physics student found himself beset by intellectual doubts arising from a running theological debate carried on with militant skeptics. He confessed his doubts to a Christian professor, hoping for recommendations of good books on apologetics to straighten him out and help him win the arguments. Instead, the professor put him to work on weekends, shepherding a group of ghetto kids drawn to a struggling mission in a housing project.

It worked. The student's faith was strengthened, partly by seeing a few miracles, but mostly by operating at the edge of his abilities. Physics and metaphysics did not help much in that neighborhood; he needed the Holy Spirit. Laying one's life on the line for others in Christ's name frequently puts more reality into our theology than engaging in heavy-duty theological debate.

Using Professional Resources

Surveys show that scientific illiteracy exists even among scientists. For those interested only in their own research, the breadth of a good education can gradually be left behind by learning more and more about less and less. The kind of professional growth emphasized in this chapter goes beyond keeping up with the literature of one's specialty and continuing to publish in that field.

Growing into professional maturity should enhance, not diminish, a scientist's humanity, especially for a Christian already alert to a world beyond science. Of course it is our technical knowledge in a specialized area that pays the rent. No one would argue that a scientist should try to learn everything, even about science. The trick is to begin where we are and try to locate ourselves on a larger map of the whole scientific enterprise.

One way to do that is to browse more or less regularly in an interdisciplinary publication like *Science* or *The Scientist.* Besides flipping through *Science* for the occasional research report to help you in your work, take time to sample the review articles, editorials, news articles, book reviews and letters. Week by week they present a broad picture of science and of its role in society.

The Scientist also reports current research news but is better known for its coverage of ethical, legal and political issues related to science. Its op-ed pages provide a forum for scientists to discuss such topics as science education, employment prospects or government policies. Experienced scientists also offer guidance in professional matters: how to be a good referee, apply for a patent, be an expert witness in court, deal with political activists, publish a textbook, choose computer software, or seek alternative funding when grants run out.

Science and *The Scientist* are written for professional scientists. Mind-stretching articles by prominent scientists also appear in *Scientific American* and from time to time in more general magazines.

Breadth need not dull one's concentration, just as narrowness does not necessarily sharpen one's intellect.

Christians in science also should not allow ourselves to be squeezed into a narrow technical mold, a process that can begin with an undergraduate math and science curriculum with many lab courses but few electives. After broadening our grasp of issues of importance to the scientific community, we need to move on to a better grasp of the human situation as a whole.

Again, we should begin where we are, and with what we already know. For example, with the current focus on ethical issues, one could well begin with a study of *On Being a Scientist* from NAS or *Honor in Science* from Sigma Xi. Reading books listed in their bibliographies would start any scientist on a path toward general cultural literacy. A focus on ethical issues engages us in philosophy, religion, history and politics, just by letting one thing lead to another.

Of course there are many other ways to begin. The history of science can lead to a fascination with history in general. The important thing is to begin, and to keep going. In a sense, to grow as a scientist means to grow beyond science.

The kind of professional growth urged here has less to do with one's expertise than with the context in which that expertise is exercised. Practitioners in any field become more expert with practice. Today, though, we know that the narrower an "expert system," the more readily programmable it is. Computers are catching up, doing with greater precision and efficiency many of the things scientists have done in the past.

What cannot be replaced by computer programs is the vast complexity of human knowledge and the wisdom based on that knowledge that enables us to choose among goals. The Bible recognizes the value of both knowledge and wisdom. Neither spiritual growth, which adds depth to life, nor professional growth, which adds breadth, is primarily a matter of learning facts or having them at our fingertips. Growth requires us to immerse ourselves in human experiences that enrich and shape us as human beings.

Christians are not alone in desiring that technical work be humanized. One way to do it is to tell the human stories behind technical work. The American Chemical Society has begun to publish, for a general audience, the autobiographies of notable chemists in a series called *Profiles, Pathways, and Dreams.* Major scientific societies and the National Academy are obviously concerned to present science with a "human face."

The human face presented by American science has generally been male and Anglo-Saxon, but the roles of women and members of ethnic minorities are no longer being neglected. Some of their stories were featured in a 1996 PBS series called *Breakthrough: The Changing Face of American Science.* The camera followed each individual as he or she grappled with a technical problem, but also showed the same person in the setting of family, church or other off-duty activities. The twenty problem solvers were depicted as whole human beings, an aspect of scientists' lives frequently neglected in telling the story of science.

Using Integrative Resources

To sort out all that has been written on bringing science and faith together requires considerable discernment. Like scientists who tend to cite work published in their own language more frequently than foreign work, writers on science/faith issues have their own biases.

Many works by evangelicals are cited in this book. One reason is that such works have been helpful in the author's life. Another reason is simply to call attention to them, since many theologically liberal authors feel scant obligation to explore the work of competent evangelical scholars. For some reason, evangelical authors, despite their relatively conservative point of view, seem more likely to cite works from a broad theological base.

Of course one expects to encounter works with a stated viewpoint: Catholic or Protestant, theologically liberal or conservative, or on behalf of one side or the other of some theological controversy (abortion, creationism, economics, environmentalism, war, etc.). Works with unstated biases are the ones that require discernment.

A comprehensive general bibliography on science and faith is difficult to compile and keep updated. Books that merely repeat what has been said before can easily clutter a list. Another problem is that truly valuable works may not stay in print very long because the market for books on science and faith is relatively small. Books that have had a small press run without going into additional printings can be hard to find. As finances permit, it is advisable to begin building up a library of one's own.

Finally, even books of enduring value that attempt to integrate Christian faith and science can be scattered throughout a library because of classification problems. A book on Christian faith by a physicist (or a book on religious implications of physics) may end up next to books on science, theology, or the philosophy of science or religion. (Where will *this* book be classified, for instance?)

Almost any evangelical scientist can name one or two integrative authors who have already touched his or her life. One way to initiate a program of lifelong reading is to start with works cited by such authors as having been helpful to *them.* To that list one can add new books as they appear and books that are recommended by others. As their professional lives develop, many Christians begin to read more widely in philosophy and theology. Even scientists without personal religious convictions often find their theoretical interests expanding in those directions.

Beyond our personal interest, however, Christians in science must respond to theological questions asked by earnest seekers or aggressive skeptics. We want our responses to make sense and to be true to God's Word. Essentially all of the important questions have already been explored in a scholarly way by contemporary theologians and by scientists versed in theology. We need not reinvent good answers to hard questions.

Keeping Current

The wise but cynical sage of the book of Ecclesiastes, known for the saying, "There is nothing new under the sun," concluded that, "Of making many books there is no end, and much study is a weariness of the flesh." Those observations were recorded on a scroll thousands of years ago, before printing had been invented. Today we can walk into a library or major bookstore and wonder what we are missing in those thousands of books whose pages we have never opened. We will never know, because we do not have time to read them.

Only in a highly specialized bookstore or library would science be the largest category, but still, to read everything important in science became impossible long ago. No matter how good our intentions, it is hard to keep up in even the relatively narrow field in which we work. We find ourselves reading fewer books, relying instead on book reviews, eventually settling for annotated bibliographies. We hope that some capsule description will indicate whether reading a certain book would be worth our time, if we had the time to devote to it.

In compiling the "References" or "Literature Cited" section of a dissertation or research paper, one technique is to let other authors assist us. That is, we start with the one or two most relevant papers, track down each reference cited there, look up the references in those cited papers, and so on. We gain confidence that we have not overlooked anything of vital importance when we encounter no further works being cited in any new papers that turn up in the wider and wider net being cast.

Two wide-ranging bibliographical guides are now available to help Christians in science find books on a wide variety of pertinent topics. As new books continue to appear in print, bibliographies quickly go out of date, but these two have appeared relatively recently, with the promise of future updates. One is an inexpensive paperback available from ASA, *Contemporary Issues in Science and Christian Faith: An Annotated Bibliography,* which offers capsule descriptions of hundreds of books listed alphabetically by author, plus a categorical listing and a separate listing of still valuable books that are out of print.

The other useful guide is *Who's Who in Theology and Science,* a 1996 reference work underwritten by the Templeton Foundation. Its major alphabetical directory is of authors in the field, with biographical information plus citations of representative books and articles. A subject index with thirty-two categories leads back to those authors. Other directories in the volume describe over seventy organizations throughout the world and a dozen periodicals devoted to integrating science and religion.

To keep absolutely current, of course, one must turn to periodicals. For decades, pertinent book reviews as well as scholarly articles have appeared in two major U.S. journals: an evangelical quarterly, *Perspectives on Science and Christian Faith* (formerly *Journal of the American Scientific Affiliation,* established 1949), and a theologically more inclusive bimonthly, *Zygon: Journal of Religion and Science* (est. 1965). A new biennial evangelical journal from the United Kingdom, *Science and Christian Belief* (est. 1989), has arisen from a merger of *Faith and Thought* (published by the Victoria Institute) and *Science and Faith* (published by Christians in Science, formerly known as the Research Scientists' Christian Fellowship).

Useful periodicals have begun to appear from some of the other organizations listed in *Who's Who in Theology and Science.* For example, *CTNS Bulletin* (est. 1980) is becoming a full-fledged journal from the Center for Theology and the Natural Sciences in Berkeley, California. *Pascal Centre Notebook* is a newsletter from the Pascal Centre for Advanced Studies in Faith and Science in Ancaster, Ontario. *Science and Religion News* is a sort of bulletin board for a growing network of organizations, conferences and publications; it is published by the Institute on Religion in an Age of Science, one of three organizational sponsors of the journal *Zygon.*

In recent years Christians concerned about environmental stewardship have founded organizations to integrate scientific information with a biblical perspective. For example, the biblically based Christian Society of the Green Cross has begun publishing *Green Cross,* an environmental quarterly (est. 1995).

Today computers have revolutionized the way bibliographies (or any other databases) are compiled and kept up to date. Everything about information is undergoing change. (See Close-Up 4: On to the Internet.)

Discovering Our Closest Colleagues

Through various associations we can come to know other Christians in science in person and not merely through their writings. The American Scientific Affiliation (ASA) has been mentioned in this book as a primary resource for such comradeship. Since 1941 it has provided spiritual and intellectual nourishment for thousands of Christian believers, interacting with each other through ASA's annual meetings, local sections, quarterly journal, bimonthly newsletter and other publications.

ASA does not have campus chapters, but welcomes student members. Of course science students and young science faculty are welcomed by national and local Christian ministries on university campuses. At some major research universities, one or two large departments will have enough Christian students, faculty or staff to meet for prayer or Bible study, usually over a brown-bag lunch in a lab or office.

If your career takes you away from academic life, it need not take you away from Christian fellowship with your peers. ASA has encouraged the formation of disciplinary groups, and tries to keep track of Christian groups that meet at national scientific meetings. Many such groups are small and hard to find; some have no formal membership or permanent address, but function with a rotating chairperson or volunteer coordinator who maintains a mailing list and mails meeting notices from his or her own address.

Two groups now meet with ASA in its annual meeting, usually in July or early August: the Affiliation of Christian Geologists (ACG) and the Affiliation of Christian Biologists (ACB). Both publish newsletters and at ASA meetings sponsor field trips and arrange sessions on teaching and research in their disciplines. ACG members also meet during national meetings of the Geological Society of America.

For decades Christians in the six preclinical medical sciences comprising the Federation of American Societies for Experimental Biology (FASEB) have met at the annual Federation meetings. The Federation Christian Fellowship (FCF) meeting is listed in the official FASEB program along with other subsidiary groups, of alumni from major graduate schools or of research specialists (e.g., the "Liver Dinner," for researchers on hepatic function, which never has liver on the menu).

When the American Society of Biological Chemists began meeting separately from the Federation, Christian biochemists from FCF quickly formed a new group to gather at meetings of what is now named the American Society for Biochemistry and Molecular Biology. A still newer Federation of Christian Biophysicists meets at annual meetings of the Biophysical Society. Other Christian fellowships gather at annual meetings of mathematicians, neuroscientists, nuclear engineers, social scientists, and so on.

Someday a federation or council of Christian professional societies may be organized. Meanwhile, disciplinary and interdisciplinary symposia organized by the Coalition for Christian Colleges and Universities (CCCU) keep faculty on nearly ninety evangelical campuses in touch with each other and produce some valuable resources for other Christian faculty. The Coalition has sponsored production of a series of supplemental textbooks and administers the Harvey Fellows Program, supporting "Christian graduate students preparing for leadership in culturally-influential vocations in which evangelical Christians appear to be underrepresented."

Attending even one national gathering of Christians in a familiar area of science can make a world of difference in your morale. To meet others already doing good work in the name of Christ is a great source of encouragement to do outstanding work ourselves. Because we are scattered, not all of us have regular opportunities to meet in local gatherings. Of ASA's two dozen local sections (including three of CSCA, the Canadian Scientific and Christian Affiliation), the active ones tend to have one or two meetings a year; others exist primarily as a mailing list awaiting the arrival of someone with time and energy to spark things into activity again. Of course, you could be that person.

Coteries of committed Christians may also cluster at one of the think tanks set up to study science and religion, such as the Center for Theology and the Natural Sciences (CTNS) in Berkeley. A new phenomenon is the formation of task forces, study groups or consultations on science within mainline Protestant denominations. Check out what is going on in your own denomination; you may find other like-minded scientists as well as opportunities to serve the church directly. If you discover that no denomination-wide fellowship of scientists exists, your persistent inquiries might help get something started.

Since 1986 a group of professional theologians, a working group called the Theology and Science Group, has met at annual meetings of the American Academy of Religion. A Society of Ordained Scientists, begun in the Anglican Communion in the United Kingdom in 1987, includes Episcopal priests in North America with scientific training.

Quite distinct from groups interested in theological discussion are mission-oriented or service-oriented groups concerned with putting technical skills to work for the needy. Several evangelical referral services can put you in touch with opportunities to serve Christ at home and abroad.

A Life of Adventure

We have come to the end of another chapter and to the end of the Big Picture, so it is time for me to shift to first-person singular once again.

Writing this chapter in particular has made me realize how much the situation has changed since I began my career in biochemistry. Back then there were so few worthwhile books on science and faith that I knew of only one or two I could recommend to others. Now there are so many good ones that I would not be able to list them all. Instead of recommending my own "top ten," I have suggested ways to locate your own resources, including those yet to come.

Annual meetings of the ASA became a high point of each year for me. With our common allegiances to Christ and to science, participants could discuss science and theology earnestly, argue vigorously, and pray sincerely. These truest colleagues formed for me an intimate community, even though scattered in various disciplines across the country and around the world. For each reader of this book, I wish that kind of close, supportive fellowship, beginning in graduate school if possible.

As a graduate student excited by Fred Sanger's determination of the amino acid sequence of insulin, I gave a seminar on his papers as they appeared. I ended my talk with a look toward the future, when the primary structures of hundreds, perhaps thousands, of proteins would be unraveled. My fellow students saw my comments as a foreboding prediction of how much the next generation would be expected to know.

What we did not foresee was the ability of computers to store vast amounts of information for easy retrieval, though efforts to cope with the literature crisis were already being made. I remember how hard I struggled to master the pertinent literature of biochemistry and organic chemistry. When *Current Contents* made its appearance, I could scan the tables of contents of current journals without leaving my desk. Soon, though, I was overwhelmed by those little weekly digests piling up unscanned. For a while *Chemical Titles,* with its KWIC (Keyword in Context) index, seemed to be the answer. Today, desktop computers and on-line databases allow one to keep up more efficiently, though not without their own drawbacks.

"Labor-saving" and "time-saving" innovations do not necessarily save either time or labor. Mechanization of certain tasks can shift us from drudgery to work that enables us to be more creative, but it also introduces higher expectations of productivity. We are expected to use the time a computer saves to accomplish more than we could have done before. The fact is that each of us has about the same amount of time as the great pioneers of science who wrote their papers with quill pens.

The inexorable fact that we live in "real time" and not in some abstract concept of time is why priorities are so important. The apostle Paul named the three greatest things in life: faith, hope and love. I think by faith he meant our capacity to look back at life and see God's hand at work, leading us to where we are now and shaping our character. By hope he meant our capacity to trust God's willingness to stay beside us and see us through the future. Love is the greatest of the three, he said. I think he prioritized love because it functions in the present, and the present is the only time in which we can act. The past is frozen and the future has not yet arrived.

It may sound naive to speak of *love* as the key to a satisfying scientific career, but that is the essential message of this book. Try substituting *care,* if that word sounds less sentimental to you. (*Caritas* was the usual Latin translation for the Greek *agapē,* the highest form of love described in the New Testament.) To love God with "heart and mind and soul," to care for the creation on which God has bestowed so much care, to love science for what it can tell us about that creation and for the good it can do for people whom God loves, to exercise care in the way we go about our daily work—all *that* is what we have been called to do.

This book has been over five years and hundreds of conversations in the making. While working on a final draft, I received a letter from a Christian professor who wanted to encourage me in my task. He had been pondering the same question with which this book began: Why is it that evangelical Christians have given so little thought to serving Christ wholeheartedly (and wholemindedly) in the practice of science?

After reading a collection of testimonies of Christian students about their time in graduate school, he wrote:

The overwhelming impression that I retained after reading these personal experiences was that these were a very unhappy group of students. They didn't have enough time for Bible studies, they didn't have enough time to disciple students, they had to spend too much time in the library or the laboratory. In other words, they weren't interested in their academic work. *They* thought that their Christian testimony was weak because they did not have time for "Christian" things. *The world* sees unhappy Christians who do not know how to "enjoy the day that the Lord has made." I'm afraid the evangelical community has so brainwashed its citizens that they do not know how to live joyfully in an academic environment.

I thought that was pretty strong, but his letter got worse. He went on to say that he had been meeting weekly with a group of Christian faculty. A discussion within that group about the Christian's attitude toward work left him with the same impression:

One faculty member thought it was wrong ever to take any work home; one's professional work should be limited to forty hours a week. Almost all were concerned about overlooking opportunities to talk with students or to "witness" in class. Of course, these are proper things to do. But no one felt guilty about not thinking long enough or deeply enough about the challenges associated with professional work. Their professional work clearly did not have the same value in God's sight as their Christian "witness." These were not joyful Christians but guilt-ridden Christians. What astonished this professor was the contrast with Christians in professional sports. He had heard some coach in the NFL say what his life had been like: "You work seven days in a row, sleep at the office three nights a week, work twenty-seven weekends in a row. You don't see anybody, hardly read anything. Football is all you know." Such "winning" coaches are highly respected in the evangelical community, even sought after to appear with Billy Graham at his evangelistic crusades. Why should football be considered a more worthy pursuit to which to dedicate one's life than academic pursuits?

My friend concluded that evangelical Christians must feel threatened by the academic environment. Evangelicals can commit themselves to football unreservedly, he thought, because football poses not even a potential threat to the Bible or to our evangelical interpretations of it.

That is quite a challenge for Christians of the generation now entering professional life. Are you ready to accept it? Are you prepared to follow Christ into the laboratory, to be his representative there? If so, I wish you the best.

May most of your experiments go well, and at least a few give conclusive results.

May most of your theoretical ideas be sound, and may you detect any flaws before others point them out.

May your best research ideas be funded, and fruitless lines of investigation be abandoned quickly.

May your scientific work be creative and productive, your witness faithful to both the world and the church.

May your integrity be solid as a rock, even when pounded by waves of temptation.

May you bring out the best in those who work around you, from the janitor to the director of the laboratory.

May your cup of joy run over and splash on your colleagues, leading them to ponder the Source of your joy.

Finally, in case your work goes *extremely* well, I am told that the proper thing to say when receiving the Nobel Prize is *Tack så mycket,* Swedish for "thank you very much."

Close-Up 1

The Core
of Christian
Faith

THE CHRISTIAN WAY OF LOOKING at the world differs from the scientific way, but the two perspectives can be seen as having a similar structure.

The similarity holds whether scientific thinking is depicted in the old way, as an edifice of theory resting on a foundation of fact, or in the postmodern way, as a theoretical network or web. At the web's center, a core of essentially stable empirical content extends out in all directions to increasingly negotiable aspects of a reasonably unified theoretical system. A scientific system of thought might be called a paradigm (Thomas Kuhn), a research program (Imre Lakatos), a research tradition (Larry Laudan) or something else.

Christian faith (or *the* Christian faith) has at its core the shared experiences and basic beliefs of a community, extending out to more and more negotiable theologies. Philosopher/theologian Nancey Murphy has called theology "a rational reconstruction of the beliefs of a Christian community." *Theology* is roughly equivalent to *theory* in science; another term is *doctrine* (or "teaching," from the same Latin root as *doctorate*).

The core experience is usually described as one of encountering God by placing unreserved trust in Jesus Christ. The good news of God's forgiveness, dependent on Jesus' incarnation, crucifixion and resurrection, opens for believers access to a depth of spiritual awareness otherwise unknown. Despite variations in theological explanation, the Bible remains a record of, and resource for, that core experience. (See Close-Up 2.) From time to time, Christian communities, reflecting on the "theory" of their faith and understanding, have produced a brief outline called a creed (from *credo,* Latin for "I believe").

Although professional theologians have written thousands of books on doctrinal questions, probably no one has done a better job of describing the core of Christian faith than C. S. Lewis. His *Mere Christianity* (1956), still in print, is a collection of talks previously given on Great Britain's BBC radio. In the preface of the published version Lewis responded to criticisms of the way he defined Christianity. He said that readers should draw no conclusions at all from his silence on disputed points, either that he thought them important or that he thought them unimportant.

Lewis noted that the severest critics of his efforts to boil Christianity down to its essentials tended to be "borderline people," whereas people deeply committed to a particular expression of Christian faith tended to agree with him. He took that as a confirmation that at the center of each communion, "there is something, or a Someone, who against all divergences of belief, all differences of temperament, all memories of mutual persecution, speaks with the same voice."

Some listeners objected to Lewis's definition on grounds that an individual who could not believe the doctrines of the faith might be much closer to Christ's spirit than an orthodox believer. Lewis's reply was that their objection, though admirably sensitive and charitable, contributed little to the question of definition. The term *Christian* was originally used to designate early disciples who accepted what the apostles taught about Jesus. Christians differ profoundly from others because of their particular beliefs, even if they *seem* to be like everyone else. If their behavior is inappropriate, it would be more accurate to say they are not good Christians than to say they are not Christians. "We already have the word *good,*" Lewis wrote.

Almost everyone expects Christian commitment to produce distinctive behavior. Even people who think of themselves as having no religious convictions of their own are quick to label Christians who fail to meet their standards as hypocrites (from the Greek for "play actors"). For the purposes of this book, being a Christian means pretty much what C. S. Lewis said it means: a commitment to certain beliefs, not adherence to a code of conduct. Because beliefs are more private than conduct, no one is given license to say that anyone else is or is not a Christian. People have a right to identify themselves as being inside or outside the bounds of any confession, statement of faith or creed.

One question that has been a major source of dispute and division concerns final spiritual authority. Many Protestant communions follow the Reformers' historic lead, proclaiming as ultimate authority *sola scriptura* (Latin, "Scripture alone"). Roman Catholics have historically regarded the church (specifically, the hierarchy of the Roman Catholic Church, headed by the pope) as having ultimate authority in spiritual matters.

In fact, to most Catholics the words of the Bible hold an exalted place, and to most Protestants it is clear that without the historic church the Bible would not have been preserved. Further, most Christians credit the activity of God's Holy Spirit in individual hearts and minds as a third important voice for discerning spiritual truth.

Thus despite many differences in doctrine, practice and emphasis, essential Christian unity across many cultures is remarkable, as C. S. Lewis said. By moving away from peripheral issues and toward the core of Christian faith, we demonstrate that unity to the scientific world.

Close-Up 2

The Bible & Science

THE SCIENTIFIC STORY IS TOLD in thousands of books of many different types. In a good science library one can find laboratory results written up in bound volumes of primary journals, secondary sources of abstracts or reviews, annual reviews of research in various fields, conference proceedings, handbooks of data, lab manuals, textbooks, histories and biographies, philosophical treatises, science news magazines, popular books for non-scientists, even children's books explaining science.

Likewise, the Judeo-Christian story fills many volumes, though in contrast to science, one book is the basis for all the rest. The Bible is essentially a whole religious library, containing books of history, poetry, prophecy, ethical instruction, even personal correspondence, set down in different centuries by different writers and later collected to form the biblical canon.

Although to an atheist there can be no Word of God, that is what the Bible represents to most believers. It is held to be authoritative because of its ultimate Author, who revealed his identity and purposes to a few inspired writers. Their individual styles and literary genres are generally evident, though it is not always clear exactly how to read some parts of the Bible. It takes some experience to interpret the Bible wisely, just as training is necessary to make sense of much of the literature of science.

Primarily the Bible is a straightforward account of God's people, bracketed at its beginning and end by references to prehistory and posthistory in more dramatic language. Where truth is truncated or conveyed in a unique literary style, questions of interpretation arise. The term *parabolic* could be applied to passages where the point is more important than the details, as in the parables Jesus told to his disciples. *Story* is itself an adequately descriptive term for the early chapters of Genesis, provided we recognize that modern scientific accounts of origins are also stories, though told for other purposes.

What all can agree on is that throughout, from the first verse of Genesis, the Bible praises God for wondrous works of creation and redemption. The Old Testament weaves an ornate tapestry, telling of God's care for the earth and for the people of Israel over centuries of time. The New Testament continues that story, picking up a messianic thread as a central theme leading to the incarnation of Jesus, the "anointed one" (*Messiah* from the Hebrew, *Christ* from the Greek).

The universe really exists, the Bible says, because the Creator has brought it into existence and continually maintains it through his power and love. No wonder modern science arose and prospered in a culture that accepted that biblical view. In a sense, the Bible demythologized the natural world, treating it as the product of a rational mind rather than as some ineffably haunted realm. The logical conclusion was that to gain a true understanding of the world, it must be studied with God-given rational faculties.

The Bible makes its case in prescientific language, of course, but in language clear enough to be understood in as technologically advanced a culture as our own. Biblical language is generally far more powerful than anything found in a science textbook. Many biblical passages about God's relation to the created world, and our own relation to that world, are cast in poetic form, memorable even in translation from the original language.

For Christians, Jesus Christ is not only the exemplar of true wisdom but the incarnate Creator of the universe. The apostle John began his Gospel with a sweeping affirmation about Christ as the *logos,* or living Word, from "the beginning." The apostle Paul began a letter to Christians at Colossae by describing his own "rescue from darkness" and transference "into the kingdom of his beloved Son," through whom and by whom "all things have been created." Other passages echo the same theme.

The four Gospel accounts of Jesus' life, which emphasize his spiritual and moral teaching, point out that he taught "with authority." Jesus demonstrated authority even over natural phenomena by healing sick people and by other actions that left eyewitnesses astonished. Christians in science appreciate the empirical spirit Jesus seemed to impart, as when he said "Follow me" when gathering his closest associates. After his resurrection, as a way of settling their doubts, he encouraged their investigation of the data at hand: "Look at my hands and my feet; see that it is I myself. Touch me and see; for a ghost does not have flesh and bones as you see that I have."

The Bible has a down-to-earth quality despite its focus on the spiritual and eternal. From the Ten Commandments of the Old Testament to the Sermon on the Mount and pastoral admonitions of the New, its understanding of wisdom is couched not in philosophical abstractions but in the practical consequences of "knowing God." Jesus offered no shortcuts to help Judean shepherds or Roman soldiers get ahead in their occupations. What they could learn from him was how to live their whole lives in faith, hope and love, which today's scientists also need to learn.

Scientists pride themselves on "not taking anybody's word for it." Researchers do cite prior sources, but in the scientific literature there is no ultimate prior source. In contrast, biblical authority to some extent parallels the authority of the U.S. Constitution in that all our laws are derived from it or at least must be in harmony with it. It is the lack of such a document in scientific practice that makes it difficult to establish ethical norms and pass them on to each new generation of scientists.

For Christians, including those in science, the Bible has a prior claim on one's life.

Close-Up 3

The American
Scientific
Affiliation

THE AMERICAN SCIENTIFIC Affiliation (ASA) was founded in 1941 with an electrical engineer, F. Alton Everest, as its first president. The idea of establishing a society of evangelical Christians trained in science is credited to an evangelist and amateur scientist, Irwin A. Moon, associated with Moody Bible Institute of Chicago. As he traveled across the country delivering his "Sermons from Science," Moon was troubled by "the many students he encountered who were learning un-Christian science—and the many Christian workers who were teaching unscientific Christianity."

A 1995 informational brochure of the American Scientific Affiliation stated the reasons for ASA's existence:

Science has brought about enormous changes in our world. Christians have often reacted as though science threatened the very foundations of Christian faith. ASA's unique mission is to integrate, communicate, and facilitate properly researched science and biblical theology in service to the Church and the scientific community. ASA members have confidence that such integration is not only possible but necessary to an adequate understanding of God and His creation. Our total allegiance is to our Creator. We acknowledge our debt to Him for the whole natural order and for the development of science as a way of knowing that order in detail. We also acknowledge our debt to Him for the Scriptures, which give us "the wisdom that leads to salvation through faith in Jesus Christ." We believe that honest and open study of God's dual revelation, in nature and in the Bible, must eventually lead to understanding of its inherent harmony.

The ASA is also committed to the equally important task of providing advice and direction to the Church and society in how best to use the results of science and technology while preserving the integrity of God's creation. It is the only organization where scientists, social scientists, philosophers, and theologians can interact together and help shape Christian views of science. The vision of the ASA is to have science and theology interacting and affecting one another in a positive light.

The ASA Constitution includes this Statement of Faith:

1. We accept the divine inspiration, trustworthiness and authority of the Bible in matters of faith and conduct.

2. We confess the Triune God affirmed in the Nicene and Apostles' creeds which we accept as brief, faithful statements of Christian doctrine based upon Scripture.

3. We believe that in creating and preserving the universe God has endowed it with contingent order and intelligibility, the basis of scientific investigation.

4. We recognize our responsibility, as stewards of God's creation, to use science and technology for the good of humanity and the whole world.

Anyone interested in the objectives of the Affiliation may join. Full Members (with at least a bachelor's degree in science), Student Members (science majors), Associates (interested nonscientists) and Student Associates must all give assent to the ASA Statement of Faith. Any interested individual may become a Friend of the ASA without subscribing to the Statement of Faith. Members with a doctorate in some branch of science or the equivalent in experience may become Fellows and thus be eligible for election to the five-person executive council. All classes of members receive ASA's quarterly journal, *Perspectives on Science and Christian Faith,* to which others may also subscribe.

The American Scientific Affiliation was almost entirely Protestant until its Statement of Faith was revised in 1989 to eliminate easily misunderstood phrases and to add a commitment to responsible stewardship of science and technology. With its statement now resting on the ancient Apostles' and Nicene creeds of the catholic (i.e., universal) church, ASA has begun to attract

Roman Catholic scientists as well.

ASA's address is P.O. Box 668, Ipswich, MA 01938
Telephone: (508) 356-5656
Fax: (508) 356-4375
E-mail: asa@newl.com

The Canadian Scientific & Christian Affiliation (CSCA) is a sister organization with a distinctly Canadian orientation (P.O. Box 386, Fergus, Ontario N1M 3E2 Canada).

ASA's Web page on the Internet:
http://www.calvin.edu/chemistry/ASA/

Close-Up 4

On to the Internet

AS WE STEP INTO THE twenty-first century, the printed page is still with us, but perhaps not for long. No one knows where speeding down the information superhighway will take us.

Some thirty years ago a computer network for the exchange of data among research groups was set up by the Advanced Research Projects Agency (ARPA) of the U.S. Department of Defense. It allowed researchers to share their data without going through all the steps required to print it in a report or a journal mailed to subscribers. Information distributed electronically became known as e-mail.

Few scientists in that original ARPA network could have guessed that their relatively private publishing shortcut would lead to a global cultural transformation. Now, with inexpensive desktop computers and modems connected via ordinary telephone lines, computer users everywhere have access to vast amounts of information on the Internet.

By mid-1995 perhaps fifty million people were using "the Net," and over five million host computers were adding to the information already out there. The fastest growing aspect of the Internet is called the World Wide Web, with over thirty-five million people already browsing "sites" or "home pages" established by organizations, publications, businesses, even individuals. The number of Web sites has been growing at the rate of more than a thousand a day.

Since most Web sites are interconnected, merely by clicking on a phrase or icon on one site users can easily move to another to search for more information of interest to them. This giant interactive directory more or less resembles the familiar yellow pages. Nobody needs all the information available but one can usually find what is needed by dialing a few numbers.

To many, the Internet is a symbol of political freedom because it does not belong to a government, corporation or anyone else. Communications addressed with the proper Universal Resource Locator (URL) wend their own electronic way without anyone running the system. That feature and its transnational character render the Internet essentially out of control. Calls for its regulation are heard because it makes accessible to anyone anywhere, including children, information deemed dangerous, from pornography to racist propaganda to step-by-step directions for building bombs. Questions have been raised about the effects of its widespread use on the fabric of society.

Doomsayers argue with optimists over the import of such issues as (a) ownership of information and responsibility for its reliability and security, (b) criminal misuses, from spreading data-destroying viruses to e-mail fraud to theft of proprietary information, and (c) inequities between computerized countries and the rest of the world. Costs are another concern, but many individual users do not pay them. Corporations, universities and many undergraduate colleges have institutional accounts providing on-line services without billing individual users.

Scientific societies have embraced the Internet, partly because of the rising cost of scientific publication. As journals have increased in number and price, libraries have had to drop subscriptions, decreasing journal revenue to the societies that publish them. Yet scientific societies with refereed research publications feel responsible for the reliability of what they publish. Is material posted on the Internet "published"? Should it have archival integrity or is it intended to be ephemeral? The Internet represents a kind of "virtual library" where the holdings are on call instantaneously without having to be stored in a single institution.

Publication of certain types of information on paper for distribution by "snail mail" is already coming to an end. In 1995 a veteran scientist was dismayed to read: "This is the last hard copy of this publication you will receive. To receive further issues, place your name on our electronic mailing list by registering on our home page." Then came one of those strange new addresses beginning "http://www" and followed by over forty other letters and symbols, separated in places by a period or "dot."

The first four letters stand for HyperText Transfer Protocol (computerese for the way the information is compressed and linked); the three letters after the double slash marks identify the World Wide Web. E-mail addresses must be exact and should not run past the end of a line, lest a hyphen or space be taken as part of the "string."

Both computational chemistry and "bioinformatics" (dealing with genomic data) are producing an explosion of chemical information, which may explain why the 150,000-member American Chemical Society seems to have led the way onto the Internet. The ACS Chemical Abstracts Service now provides a number of on-line services.

Certain kinds of information are particularly well suited for e-mail distribution. From an ACS Internet address one can check out job openings or register in an employment data bank, read a newsletter for chemical educators or "hot articles" about to appear in ACS journals, obtain meeting information such as advanced programs or forms for submitting abstracts (preferably by e-mail or floppy disk), or order specialized software or ACS symposia or other books.

The end is not in sight. "Virtual seminars" already enable participants to "attend" by downloading the papers for study and then interacting with the presenters in a "global chat room." Even "virtual laboratories" are on the horizon, enabling a scientist to submit samples to a distant laboratory and then electronically to direct experiments using a major instrument at that lab, all the while electronically interacting with collaborators there.

Other societies, such as Sigma Xi and AAAS, have followed the lead of ACS. AAAS continues to explore new ways to make the Internet scientist-friendly after introducing in 1995 an on-line version of its weekly journal *Science. Science* has expanded its Web site to offer Enhanced Perspectives (linking researchers to important databases), Next Wave (discussing topics of interest to young scientists), and EurekAlert (supplying prepublication articles to science journalists).

Educational uses of the Internet go far beyond the world of science. Internet access is provided to faculty and students at over three-fourths of American colleges and universities. "Intranets" connecting everyone on a campus have changed the way courses are taught, assignments are handled, and announcements are made. An important component of a college education today is learning to navigate through oceans of information on the global Net.

Christian higher education has not lagged behind. To keep Christian colleges from getting lost in cyberspace, the Coalition for Christian Colleges and Universities (CCCU) established a Web page to provide information about Christian higher education and its more than eighty member institutions, many of which were fully "wired" by early 1995.

The CCCU Web page was established with the assistance of Gospel Communications Network (GCN), organized in 1995 as a strategic alliance of national and international Christian organizations. GCN's Web site links such ministries as the Association of Christian Schools International, International Bible Society, the Navigators, and InterVarsity Christian Fellowship, with "hotlinks" to some 4,500 Christian sites.

By now many Christian organizations, periodicals and publishing houses have established their own pages on the Web to let people know what they have to offer, changing the information as frequently as necessary. For example, InterVarsity Press can constantly update its entire catalog, provide full descriptions of new and forthcoming books, and let browsers sample a chapter of a new book or read an interview with its author or find out what reviewers have said about it—all at the touch of a mouse.

Bulletin boards, chat rooms, or SIGs (special interest groups) on subjects relating to science, religion or both, some hosted by evangelical Christians, are an enduring, if ever-changing, feature of the Internet. Individual e-mail users log on to participate in such colloquia, addressing the whole group of subscribers or using the group to discover like-minded individuals with whom to carry on further e-mail discussion. The "list serve" manager chairing the group has generally been someone vitally interested in the topic and willing to devote the time necessary to tidy up communication when necessary. Terry Gray, chemistry professor at Calvin College in Michigan, is the American Scientific Affiliation's "list servant."

At the end of 1995, the impact on the university of these new communications technologies was weighed in *The Real Issue,* a publication of Christian Leadership Ministries. Wesley Baker, professor of communication arts at Cedarville College in Ohio, urged Christians to take advantage of the new technology, opposing only its "utopian promotion." The technology is here to stay, though changing so fast that anything written about it is quickly out of date. The Internet can aid Christian scholars in doing truly interdisciplinary work and in demonstrating true collegiality to the secular world.

By 1996, Christian Leadership Ministries was pioneering the establishment of a Christian version of a virtual campus, "Leadership U," accessible from CLM's Web site.

Close-Up 5

Good Company

THIS FINAL CLOSE-UP presents some heroes and role models who have been faithful witnesses to Jesus Christ in professional life. It is appropriate to introduce them in first-person style because I have known all of them well enough to have written about them before.

I began this book with a call to evangelical scholarship from physics professor John A. McIntyre of Texas A&M University. Jack went from a B.S. in electrical engineering to a Ph.D. in high-energy physics at Princeton (under Robert Hofstadter, who later won the Nobel Prize in physics). Jack worked with particle accelerators at Stanford, Yale and Texas A&M before moving into applied medical physics. He has designed and improved positron-emission tomography (PET) instruments to measure biochemical activities in the living human brain, work that may help clinicians study such brain disorders as schizophrenia, epilepsy and Alzheimer's disease. He holds eight patents.

(Although Jack could think of no committed Christian who had won a Nobel Prize in science, he missed at least one: Professor Charles H. Townes of the University of California at Berkeley. I once heard Professor Townes say in a lecture on his experiences as a physicist that to him "God is personal, yet omnipresent—a great source of strength, who has made an enormous difference to me.")

Mention of the Nobel Prize brings to mind a Christian who has at least been nominated: Henry F. Schaefer III, a pioneer in computational quantum chemistry. In 1984, as a forty-year-old professor at Berkeley, Fritz became the youngest member ever elected to the International Academy of Quantum Molecular Sciences. In 1987 he became Graham Perdue Professor of Chemistry at the University of Georgia and director of the university's Center for Computational Quantum Chemistry. At that time he was the author of over 350 scientific publications and one of the "most frequently cited" scientists in the lists compiled by the Institute for Scientific Information (ISI).

A Christian actually invited to Stockholm for the Nobel ceremony was the late Roger C. Burgus, a biochemist who determined the structure of TRF (thyrotropin releasing factor) and several other "brain hormones." Roger did that work with physiologist Roger Guillemin, moving with him in 1970 to the Salk Institute in La Jolla, California. Roger Burgus saw the 1977 Nobel Prize in Physiology or Medicine awarded to Guillemin and his archrival Andrew Schally. For a number of years Roger Burgus was on ISI's list of the thousand most frequently cited scientists. He died in 1995.

A prominent medical scientist whose work on mapping the human genome may yet earn him a Nobel Prize is Francis S. Collins, who has both a Ph.D. and an M.D. As director of the National Center for Human Genome Research at the National Institutes of Health since 1993, he is frequently quoted in both the scientific and popular press. Before that he led a group at the University of Michigan in codiscovering the genes for cystic fibrosis in 1989 and for neurofibromatosis in 1990. In interviews, Francis frequently identifies himself as a Christian who takes the Bible as seriously as his scientific calling.

High-energy physics, quantum chemistry, brain hormones and the human genome are not exactly the backwaters of scientific investigation. Christians have been quietly at work in some of the most newsworthy fields of science and technology. For example, physical chemist Kenneth A. Lincoln of NASA used high-temperature mass spectrometry to develop heat shields for the Galileo space probe, which in 1995 finally began sending back information on Jupiter after a six-year flight to the outer reaches of our solar system. Ken's work on heat shield materials had already contributed to the success of NASA's space shuttle.

Materials scientist Jack C. Swearengen worked for years at Sandia Corporation in Livermore, California. With his knowledge of nuclear weapons, he served in 1988-90 as scientific advisor for arms control in the office of the secretary of defense. By helping to develop technical means to verify arms control treaties, he contributed to U.S. negotiations with the Soviet Union in the Strategic Arms Reduction Treaty (START) talks in Geneva. He is now a professor and coordinator of manufacturing engineering at a new Washington State University branch campus in Vancouver, Washington.

Physicist Robert Kaita has spent eighteen years at Princeton University's Plasma Physics Laboratory, working on the Tokamak Fusion Test Reactor (which has momentarily produced 10.7 megawatts of power by nuclear fusion, a world record). Bob now heads the diagnostic effort on the Princeton Beta Experiment-Modification (PBX-M), a smaller, newer-generation fusion reactor.

Physicist Francis Everitt, originally from England, has for many years directed Stanford University's role in the multimillion-dollar Gravity B Space Mission, designed to test aspects of Einstein's general theory of relativity. Francis has said that what kept him going on that project since 1962 was "love of the chase" and the "almost architectural quality" of thinking through a difficult experiment and seeing all the bits fit together.

Ghillean T. Prance, head of the Royal Botanic Gardens in Kew, near London, is an international authority on the plant life of Amazonian Brazil, having collected nearly thirty thousand specimens himself. When we met at one of the early conferences on Christian environmental stewardship at the Au Sable Institute in Michigan, "Iain" was directing the Institute for Economic Botany at the New York Botanical Institute. Now he is back in his native England and has been knighted.

Another field biologist is Laurence C. Walker, Lacy Hunt Professor Emeritus of Forestry of Stephen F. Austin State University in Texas, who has consulted on the management of dwindling forest reserves on every continent except treeless Antarctica. Larry's books on forestry show his great love for God's creation and his concern for stewardship in harvesting forest products.

A Christian who played a critical role in the development of radar (acronym for "radio detection and ranging") in World War II was the late Robert M. Page. He joined the staff of the Naval Research Laboratory (NRL) near Washington, D.C., as a physicist in 1927 and led a move to use pulsed waves instead of continuous waves in radar. When he left NRL in 1967, Bob held sixty-five patents, including some for postwar innovations such as over-the-horizon radar.

Sonar was another World War II development to which a Christian made fundamental contributions. Electrical engineer F. Alton Everest did fundamental research on undersea sound transmission for the University of California Division of War Research at San Diego. Alton later used his technical skills in the production of Christian films for the Moody Institute of Science, for teaching communications in Hong Kong, and as a consultant on the design of recording and broadcasting studios. At age eighty-six he has continued to write how-to books on audio engineering based on his consulting experience. DEC is the acronym of Digital Equipment Corporation, of which Kenneth H. Olsen was a founder and long-time CEO. Under his leadership DEC carved out a niche supplying reliable computing systems intermediate between huge mainframes and the now-common desktop machines. An issue of *Computerworld* magazine devoted to the 1986 DEXPO exposition (of some three hundred vendors of products for DEC users) profiled Ken and quoted him as saying that "the scientist and the Christian must believe in searching for the truth and being humble." At the centennial meeting of Sigma Xi, Ken was given the 1986 Common Wealth Award of Distinguished Service in Invention.

At Motorola Corporation in Phoenix, Arizona, Fred S. Hickernell works on state-of-the-art wireless communications systems that could someday link up not just every address but every person on the globe. Fred won the 1995 Achievement Award of the Ultrasonics, Ferroelectrics and Frequency Control Society of the Institute of Electrical and Electronic Engineers (IEEE), for outstanding contributions on dielectric and piezoelectric films for acoustical and optical microelectronic devices.

Hundreds of Christians have been recognized for outstanding work in their fields. A few have been elected to the prestigious National Academy of Sciences (NAS), including linguist Kenneth L. Pike. Everyone in the field of linguistics seems to know Ken's name because of the widespread influence of his tagmemic theory of the structure of living languages. After retiring as a full professor from the University of Michigan, Ken has devoted his time to serving the Summer Institute of Linguistics and Wycliffe Bible Translators.

In the biological sciences, John E. Halver, now professor emeritus in nutrition at the School of Fisheries of the University of Washington, was elected to NAS in 1978. As a member of both NAS and ASA, John contributed the preface to the 1986 ASA publication *Teaching Science in a Climate of Controversy.*

In the natural sciences, Robert B. Griffiths, Otto Stern Professor of Physics at Carnegie-Mellon University, was one of sixty-one new U.S. members elected to the National Academy in 1987. He had already received many other honors, such as the U.S. Senior-Scientist Award of the Alexander von Humboldt Foundation, the A. Cressy Morrison Award of the New York Academy of Sciences, and the Dannie Heineman Prize for mathematical physics. Bob has been recognized as one of the four originators of the "consistent histories" approach to our understanding of quantum reality.

The late Aldert van der Ziel of the University of Minnesota, who earned his doctorate in physics, was elected to the National Academy of Engineering (NAE). He received many other honors, including two honorary doctorates. Born in the Netherlands, he managed to survive the Nazi occupation and emigrate to Canada in 1947. He joined the faculty of the Department of Electrical Engineering at the University of Minnesota in 1950. At the time of his death in 1991, he was one of the world's authorities on noise in electronic devices and had supervised the doctoral work of over eighty students. In addition to fifteen books on electronic noise, solid state electronics, and semiconductor devices, he had also written two books on theology and science.

A scientist who has won wide recognition in two different fields is Owen Gingerich, professor of astronomy at Harvard University and a senior astronomer at the Smithsonian Astrophysical Observatory. In 1992 he also became chair of Harvard's History of Science Department. He is a leading authority on the early astronomers Nicolaus Copernicus (b. 1473), who proposed the heliocentric system, and Johannes Kepler (b. 1571), who played a major role in bringing about acceptance of the Copernican system. Owen has brought science and faith together in lectures at many universities.

Many Christians have chaired departments in secular institutions or held office in scientific societies. R. David Cole chaired the department of biochemistry at the University of California at Berkeley, then played a lead role in reorganizing all the biology departments at the university. In the process, his own department became the department of molecular and cell biology.

Professor Tomuo Hoshiko, now retired from the department of physiology and biophysics at Case Western Reserve University in Cleveland, served as president of the Society of General Physiologists in 1981. He had been a visiting professor in Japan and Belgium and served on the professional advisory committee of his university's Center for Biomedical Ethics.

Geneticist V. Elving Anderson has investigated inherited mental disorders, done genetic counseling at the Dight Institute of Human Genetics in Minnesota and been an exemplary "statesman of science." In 1982-1983 he was national president of Sigma Xi, the Scientific Research Society. For Sigma Xi's hundredth anniversary in 1986, he chaired its centennial planning committee. After retiring from the University of Minnesota, Elving coauthored a book on bioethics.

A major influence in the field of communications theory was the late Donald M. MacKay, a Scot with a degree in natural philosophy (physics) from St. Andrews University. Donald developed an interest in analog computers from doing wartime research on radar for the British Admiralty. After teaching physics at King's College, London, he established and chaired the research department of communications and neuroscience at Keele University in Staffordshire, England. His department brought together researchers in physiology and machine communication to investigate similarities and differences between computers and the human brain.

There are many Christian professors in major research universities. Among those in engineering departments is Richard H. Bube, recently retired from Stanford's department of materials science and electrical engineering. A solid-state physicist, Bube managed a research group investigating photoelectric materials at the RCA Laboratories in Princeton before moving to Stanford, where he chaired his department for over ten years. Dick is known both for his work on photoelectric phenomena (six books, over 280 research publications) and for his writings on Christian faith and science, including four books and over 125 articles.

Another engineering professor is mechanical engineer Walter Bradley of Texas A&M University, a specialist in material properties that cause structural failures in such applications as rotors whirling at high speeds. He has presented calculations of the thermodynamic requirements for abiogenesis at meetings of the International Society for the Study of the Origin of Life (ISSOL). Walt is known for combining serious intellectual pursuits with a vibrant Christian witness on university campuses, having lectured under the auspices of Probe Ministries and Campus Crusade's Christian Leadership Ministries.

Mechanical engineer David H. Offner is now professor emeritus at the University of Illinois and an authority on the design and analysis of mechanical systems and components. Offner, whose Ph.D. is in theoretical and applied mechanics, taught an elective course on creativity in engineering design and in 1976 developed an introductory course in bionics (technology in living systems).

In the medical sciences, I fondly recall the late A. Kurt Weiss, a physiologist at the University of Oklahoma Medical Center. In 1956 at the Twentieth International Physiological Congress in Brussels, we met on a bus from the airport, and by the end of the ride to where the meetings were held we had discovered each other as brothers in Christ. Born a Jew in Graz, Austria, Kurt lost most of his family to the Holocaust. Eventually I heard the dramatic story of his escape to America as a teenager, his conversion to Christian faith, and his career in medical teaching and research in gerontology and endocrinology. In the 1960s he was one of the founders of the Federation Christian Fellowship. Kurt Weiss died in 1987.

Kurt's colleague in the same department, Kenneth J. Dormer, began his professional life as a cardiac physiologist but has recently been developing a cochlear implant prosthesis to aid people who suffer from a particular kind of hearing loss. He helped set up the A. Kurt Weiss Memorial Lectureships at the Oklahoma Medical Center. In 1985 Ken went with several other professors to the University of Nairobi, Kenya, to give scientific lectures and seminars and to offer a Christian witness under the auspices of Christian Leadership Ministries.

D. Gareth Jones is a professor of anatomy and structural biology at the University of Otago in New Zealand. He has written many books to help Christians grapple with advances in medicine that affect ethical debates over matters of life and death.

In agricultural science, Martin L. Price is an entrepreneur in "appropriate technology." After receiving his Ph.D. and teaching biochemistry at the college level, Martin took up agronomy and founded the Educational Concerns for Hunger Organization (ECHO) in Florida. A Christian "experiment station," ECHO produces seeds from underutilized food plants with potential for subsistence farmers. In exchange for the seeds, missionaries and Peace Corps workers report the results of their plantings. ECHO has promoted rooftop gardening for urban dwellers in St. Petersburg and Moscow, where high food prices have brought misery to thousands.

Gordon C. Mills is professor emeritus of human biochemistry and genetics at the University of Texas Medical Branch in Galveston. Before retiring in 1989 he had published some seventy research papers (mostly on erythrocyte enzymology and human blood disorders), taught biochemistry to thousands of medical students and mentored graduate students. Gordon won the annual John C. Sinclair Award of the medical branch's Sigma Xi chapter for his contributions to "humanity, scholarship, and research." He has served God despite physical limitations: a back injury as a boy left his legs paralyzed.

In graduate school I met physical chemist Robert L. Bohon. After working at a small commercial laboratory in Champaign, he moved to the 3M Company, where he held many posts before his recent retirement. For over a decade Bob ran a division at 3M's corporate research laboratories providing analytical support for the environmental engineering and pollution control division.

Biochemist Chi-Hang Lee, born in Vietnam of Chinese parents, studied in the United States and earned his Ph.D. at Rutgers. He worked for the same food company through several changes of ownership, retiring recently as director of a laboratory of Del Monte Foods Corporation in Walnut Creek, California. Chi-Hang has done much writing and speaking about science and Christian faith for Chinese Christians in the United States and abroad.

Chemist Ann H. Hunt, a senior scientist at Eli Lilly pharmaceutical company, is a specialist in the use of nuclear magnetic resonance (NMR) spectroscopy to solve problems of intricate chemical structures. She was the first woman to be elected to ASA's executive council and in 1986 became its first woman president.

Another woman in chemistry is Marie Berg, developer of a science curriculum for Minnesota firefighters that equips them to deal with hazardous materials. Marie grew up in Germany, receiving her Ph.D. at Heidelberg in 1934. After many hardships, in 1940 she barely got out with her husband and son to come to America. Even then she often went to bed hungry, until she landed a job at a university dental school doing unpleasant research on human saliva. Marie joked, "Better halitosis than no breath at all," but her four publications from that work launched a long career.

Women in the social sciences include social psychologist Mary Stewart Van Leeuwen, now at Eastern College after serving on the faculties of York University in Canada and Calvin College. Mary became a Christian while doing field work in Africa, after meeting a missionary couple who made the gospel clear to her for the first time.

Like Mary Stewart Van Leeuwen, anthropologist Miriam Adeney of Seattle Pacific University has managed to live a full professional life despite heavy family responsibilities. Miriam has lived in the Philippines and continues to study the cultural differences of ethnic groups. At Regent College in Vancouver, British Columbia, she has set up a Bookwriting Program to help Christian writers from developing countries produce literature authentic to their own cultures.

Christian fellowship has put me in contact with many social scientists I might not have known otherwise. Social psychologist David G. Myers of Hope College, Michigan, is known for his investigations of factors contributing to human happiness. Besides three widely used psychology textbooks, Dave has written half a dozen popular works on psychology and coauthored a supplemental text with Malcolm Jeeves.

Experimental psychologist Malcolm A. Jeeves was at the University of Adelaide in South Australia when I met him at the same 1965 Oxford conference on a Christian philosophy of science where I met Donald MacKay. Author of a number of books on psychology and Christianity, Jeeves has since been Foundation Professor of Psychology at St. Andrews University, Scotland.

Psychologist Stanley E. Lindquist earned his Ph.D. at the University of Chicago with majors in both physiological and clinical psychology. While teaching at the university level he developed a private clinical practice, then established the Link Care Center in Fresno, California, to make psychological testing and therapeutic services available to new and returning foreign missionaries.

Sociologist David O. Moberg, professor emeritus at Marquette University, held Fulbright professorships in the Netherlands and West Germany. As a participant in the 1971 White House Conference on Aging, he wrote a background report on *Spiritual Well-Being*. He is coeditor of the annual *Research in the Social Scientific Study of Religion*. From 1968 to 1977, Moberg, an evangelical Protestant, chaired his department at Marquette, a Roman Catholic university in Milwaukee.

Biochemist Michael J. Behe, a practicing Catholic, is a professor at Lehigh University. Behe is a bench chemist who is convinced that despite much talk, Darwinists have yet to demonstrate how any real-life biochemical system could have arisen by stepwise molecular evolution.

Michael Epstein has been an analytical chemist at the National Institute of Standards and Technology for the past twenty-five years. A short leave to teach as a sabbatical replacement at Mount Saint Mary's College in Emmitsburg, Maryland, gave Mike greater respect for the hard work of teaching. He edits a newsletter for the Society for Applied Spectroscopy, does computer consulting and has his own Web page.

Father Enrico Cantore is a physicist and philosopher who founded the World Institute for Scientific Humanism. By humanism Cantore meant "human dignity"; he regards naturalistic scientism in all its forms as a deceptive pseudohumanism. To pray with this Jesuit priest and speak of our mutual love for Jesus and science have been highlights for me at several ASA meetings.

Many scientists serve Christ as professors in Christian colleges. Hard rock geologist Davis A. Young of Calvin College in Michigan has published in the *Geological Society of America Bulletin* and *Journal of Petrology* besides writing books on the bearing of geology on biblical interpretation. Daniel E. Wonderly has done graduate work in geology, on sedimentology in particular. In the course of a long teaching career, Dan has written winsome books pointing theologically conservative Christians to the evidence for an ancient earth.

In biology, Russell L. Mixter taught thousands of students over his long career at Wheaton College in Illinois and has influenced many other evangelical Christians with his good sense about scientific questions. Raymond H. Brand also taught at Wheaton. An animal ecologist, Ray has studied insect life in native and restored prairies and has been very active in the Christian environmental movement. Population geneticist David Wilcox of Eastern

College in Pennsylvania has made contributions to studies of "mitochondrial Eve" and written about the strengths and weaknesses of evolutionary theory.

Others come to mind because of their writings on science and faith, such as physicist Howard Van Till of Calvin College and chemist Russell Maatman of Dordt College in Iowa. Some professors who have gained less recognition have nevertheless seen their students go on to accomplish great things. One was the late H. Harold Hartzler, who taught physics to Harvard's Owen Gingerich when Owen was an undergraduate at Goshen College in Indiana. Harold retired from Mankato State University in Minnesota in 1976.

What about teachers in secondary schools? Marilyne S. Flora has taught biology at both high-school and college levels. In 1984 she extended her influence beyond her own classrooms by helping to set up Intellitool, a family-run business designing and manufacturing low-cost computer-based equipment for teaching physiology. Helen E. Martin began teaching at Unionville High School in Pennsylvania in 1967. After guiding students in building and operating their own weather satellite tracking station, she reported on their work at meetings of the National Science Teachers Association (NSTA) and AAAS. She was the 1987 international lecturer for NSTA and its British counterpart, the Association for Science Education (ASE).

Editorial work? Elizabeth Zipf left embryological research for Biosciences Information Service (BIOSIS) soon after receiving her Ph.D. BIOSIS produces publications for biologists, especially *Biological Abstracts,* covering more than ten thousand scientific journals. Betty began as an associate editor but rose to become head of the editorial department, acting director and technical consultant to the president. Wil Lepkowski has been an editor of the American Chemical Society's weekly *Chemical and Engineering News* and is now a special correspondent for that publication, often bringing a humane perspective to issues of industrial technology in feature articles and interviews.

Elective office? Former Calvin College physics professor Vernon J. Ehlers began bringing his scientific thinking to local citizens' groups concerned about environmental problems. Soon he found himself running successfully for the Michigan legislature. He is now in the U.S. Congress representing the district where former president Gerald Ford got his start.

Some Christians have stepped from science into a more conventional kind of ministry. One of my friends to do so was the late Robert C. Frost, a young assistant professor of anatomy at Baylor's College of Medicine when I taught biochemistry there. Bob eventually took up a ministry of writing and speaking among charismatic Christians. Chemist Charles Thaxton, who received his Ph.D. for X-ray crystallographic studies, did a postdoctoral year at

Harvard in the history and philosophy of science. Putting his scientific background to use in apologetics and evangelism, Charlie eventually moved his family to the Czech Republic, to be a sort of "visiting professor" to Eastern European universities. He has begun teaching a course on science and spirituality at Charles University in Prague.

Neurophysiologist Gary I. Allen became director of the laboratory of neurobiology at the State University of New York at Buffalo when Nobelist Sir John Eccles left. Gary had published some thirty research papers before he stepped out of scientific work in 1976 to form the Christian Mission to the United Nations Community in New York.

Astrophysicist Hugh Ross directs Reasons to Believe, an evangelistic ministry based in Pasadena, California. Hugh's writing and speaking have helped to demonstrate to conservative Christians that big bang cosmology and an ancient earth are compatible with a faithful reading of the Bible.

Physicist Robert J. Russell is one of a number of scientists who have become professional theologians in an effort to build bridges at a scholarly level. After earning a degree in theology, in 1981 Bob founded the Center for Theology and the Natural Sciences (CTNS) in Berkeley. CTNS is an affiliate of the Graduate Theological Union, at which he is now professor of theology and science in residence. In 1994-1995 he was one of the ASA/Templeton lecturers on science and faith.

Another physicist trained in theology is Robert C. Newman, director of the Interdisciplinary Biblical Research Institute (IBRI). IBRI, founded in 1979, is informally associated with Biblical Theological Seminary, Hatfield, Pennsylvania, where Bob is a professor of New Testament. Bob brings both his scientific and theological training to questions of origins.

William A. Dembski, holder of Ph.D.s in math and philosophy, more recently received an M.Div. at Princeton Theological Seminary. While at Princeton he directed the Center for Interdisciplinary Studies and was managing editor of the *Princeton Theological Review*. He is now a visiting scholar at Notre Dame's Center for the Philosophy of Religion.

The late W. Jim Neidhardt, who taught physics at New Jersey Institute of Technology in Newark, was an avid amateur theologian. Jim spent part of his 1985-1986 sabbatical as a visiting scholar at Louisville Presbyterian Seminary in Kentucky.

A number of Ph.D.s in science now serve churches or denominations directly in some capacity. Organic chemist Barbara Pursey teaches at the University of Dubuque Theological Seminary in Iowa and serves on her presbytery's committee on ministry. Theoretical physicist George L. Murphy pastors a Lutheran church in Tallmadge, Ohio. Others have led parachurch ministries, including former ASA executive director Robert L. Herrmann, (a biochemist), and his successor at ASA, physiologist Don Munro. In Great Britain, zoologist Oliver R. Barclay has headed Christians in Science and edited its journal, *Science and Christian Belief.*

Chemical engineer Charles E. Hummel had a long career with InterVarsity Christian Fellowship before retiring as its first director of faculty ministries. As a civilian discharged from the U.S. Army in Japan while serving in the occupation force there after World War II, Charlie worked at taking inventory of Japanese research facilities; on his travels he helped begin Christian work among Japanese university students. In 1987 he was invited back to Japan by the KGK (Japanese affiliate of the International Fellowship of Evangelical Students) to help celebrate KGK's fortieth anniversary and see some fruits of his labors in the Lord's name.

Charlie Hummel's successor as IVCF faculty ministry director is inorganic chemist J. Terence Morrison, who stepped out of a teaching and research career at Butler University for more direct Christian service.

Finally, financier John M. Templeton has had an abiding interest in science and has long been an ASA member. He got his start in geophysical prospecting and after striking oil began investing. Now he is the name behind a respected group of mutual funds. Since 1973 his Templeton Foundation has awarded the annual Templeton Prize for Progress in Religion, intended to parallel in prestige (and slightly exceed in amount) the Nobel Prizes. A Yale graduate and former Rhodes scholar, John Templeton is a Presbyterian layperson who has served on the board of Princeton Theological Seminary.

Each person I have named has reminded me of another, working in the same field or in a similar setting. While compiling and pruning this list to fit the space, I learned that another ASA member, John Suppe, professor of geology at Princeton University, had just been elected to membership in the National Academy of Sciences.

Out of space, I am embarrassed that I have had to skip over many worthy people who have been exemplars to me. What I am *not* worried about is embarrassing anyone above by naming him or her as a follower of Jesus. Most have made a point of telling publicly of their Christian motivations for going into science, or of finding Christ after they took up the profession. All have contributed to science in one way or another while clearly identifying themselves as Christian believers.

We are in very good company indeed.

Notes

Chapter 1: Jesus in the Laboratory?

Initial quotations are from McIntyre (1992). The inset endorsement of astronomy is from Calvin (1948, p. 86).

On the influence of Puritanism on the founding of the Royal Society of London for Improving Natural Knowledge, and on the rise of science in general, see C. Russell (1985, chap. 5). The Royal Society, one of the first scientific societies in Europe, had its roots in several informal groups in Oxford and London, including an "Invisible College" mentioned by chemist Robert Boyle in the 1640s. The Society received its first Royal Charter in 1662.

On secularity, one aspect of work is who pays for it, so a legitimate contrast is "secular vs. ecclesiastic." By that criterion, ordained clergy and others employed by a church or church agency are the only persons *not* engaged in secular employment. Because of the separation of church and state, controversy exists in the United States over whether schools and hospitals operated by tax-exempt religious bodies should be taxed because of their secular functions. Some church leaders decry the "secularizing of culture" while urging Christians not to separate the secular from the *sacred* (though *sacred* means "separated" or "set apart" for God). Theologian Harvey Cox (1965, p. 18) distinguished between *secularization* ("basically a liberating development") and *secularism* ("a new closed world view which functions very much like a new religion"). See also Capon (1967), Wuthnow (1985) and Pannenberg (1996).

Creator and Redeemer: The passage on the wisdom of God's foolishness is 1 Corinthians 1:18-31.

Being a Christian: C. S. Lewis's words are from the Preface of Lewis (1956). For Lewis's views on science and especially on evolution, see Ferngren and Numbers (1996). Those unfamiliar with Lewis can get a fictionalized glimpse of him from the 1993 film *Shadowlands*. See Lindskoog (1994) on the dubious authenticity of some writings alleged to be Lewis's that have turned up since his death in 1963.

Being a Scientist: For texts of the Arkansas Creation Science Statute (Act 590 of 1981) and of the Overton decision in *McLean v. Arkansas Board of Education,* see Hanson (1986). Both texts are also included in Gilkey (1985). On the controversy over the expert testimony of philosopher Michael Ruse, on which Judge Overton relied heavily, see Numbers (1992, pp. 249-51). For a critique of attempts by Ruse and others to define the boundaries of science, see Laudan (1988).

The inset paragraph on realism is from Rescher (1984, p. 159). The cautious words are from Laudan (1984, p. 104).

The tale of the three scientists in Scotland has been handed down orally without citation in many labs; sometimes the three are a chemist, physicist and mathematician, with the mathematician being the most precise.

On the difference between human thought and computation, see Penrose (1994). An essay review of Penrose's book distinguished between "intelligence" (ability to solve problems and perform certain kinds of tasks) and "intellect" (capacity for understanding and insight). Humans possess both, but computers lack intellect; designing a chess-playing machine requires intellect, but the machine itself has none (Barr, 1995, p. 53).

On operation science versus origin science, see Thaxton, et al. (1984, epilogue) and Geisler and Anderson (1987).

The inset paragraph on the increase of scientific knowledge is from Hull (1988, p. 26). Hull's book touches on the history and philosophy of science but belongs to the growing field of the sociology of science ("the science of science"). For a classic collection of essays in that field, see Merton (1973).

Being a Christian and a Scientist: Actually there have been plenty of Christian role models and heroes in science, though the Christian commitment of many scientific pioneers (e.g., Copernicus, Galileo, Kepler, Pascal, Boyle, Newton, Linnaeus, Dalton, Cuvier, Faraday, Mendel, Joule, Pasteur, Kelvin, Maxwell) has been ignored, treated as a curiosity, or dismissed as a mere cultural influence by many non-Christian writers. For some contemporaries, see Stafford (1987) and "Close-Up 5: Good Company."

The Publisher(s): On ASA: From 1949 through 1986, *Perspectives on Science and Christian Faith* was known as the *Journal of the American Scientific Affiliation.* On IVP: The fall 1996 academic catalog listed seven titles under the heading, "Science and Technology."

The Book Itself: Teaching Science in a Climate of Controversy was written by David Price, John Wiester and Walter Hearn, who from 1984 to 1995 comprised ASA's Committee for Integrity in Science Education (ASA-CISE, 1986). For their comparison of the ASA booklet for teachers with *Science and Creationism* (NAS-COSAC, 1984; 2nd ed. 1995) see D. Price, et al. (1990).

On gender issues in speaking of scientists: *American Men and Women of Science,* published by R. R. Bowker (17th ed., 1995-96), gives biographical data on American scientists, listed alphabetically, in eight volumes. Before the phenomenal expansion of science after World War II, all American scientists could be listed in a single volume; the 8th edition (1949) contained some 50,000 biographies. The 90,000 biographies in the 9th edition (1955) required three volumes, one each for physical sciences, biological sciences, and social sciences; biochemists and biophysicists could choose which of the first two volumes they wanted to appear in. Only with the 14th edition (1971) was the name changed from *American Men of Science.* A cumulation of the first fourteen editions was published in 1979, presenting the biographies in seven alphabetical volumes plus a separate index by discipline.

For a discussion of using generic language when speaking of humans but male pronouns when speaking of God, see V. Hearn (1989).

The Author: Walter R. Hearn has a B.A. in chemistry from Rice and a Ph.D. in biochemistry from the University of Illinois. After a year of postdoctoral research at Yale University School of Medicine and three years on the Baylor University College of Medicine faculty, he moved to Iowa State University in Ames for the next seventeen years. His writings on science and Christian faith include chapters in Mixter's *Evolution and Christian Thought Today* (1959), Bube's *The Encounter between Christianity and Science* (1968), Blaiklock's *Why I Am Still a Christian* (1971), R. W. Smith's *Christ and the Modern Mind* (1972), Hatfield's *The Scientist and Ethical Decision* (1973) and Templeton's *Evidence of Purpose* (1994). Walt Hearn has described his childhood and early Christian experience in a chapter in Virginia Hearn's *What They Did Right* (1974, pp. 97-107) and their move to Berkeley after leaving academic life in Sider's *Living More Simply* (1980, pp. 73-96).

Chapter 2: Science Inside Out

A 1996 study showed that some twenty percent of Americans understand the term *DNA,* twice the number who understand *molecule.* Public interest in DNA, fanned by fears of possible hazards of genetic engineering and by DNA's forensic use (e.g., in the O. J. Simpson trials), dates back to a precedent-setting, intimate account of James Watson's Nobel Prize-winning work with Francis Crick, *The Double Helix* (Watson, 1968). For other versions, see Olby

(1974), Sayre (1975) and Judson (1979).

For a sense of how recent and profound the impact of computers has been, see Newell and Sproull (1982), plus other reports in the February 12, 1982, issue of *Science* on the revolution in computers and electronics. Electronic mail, bulletin boards and file transfers were then being pioneered on the ARPANET of the Advanced Research Projects Agency of the Department of Defense, established in 1966. (Note that news stories in that same issue—on alleged fraud, nuclear reactor emergencies, scientists' efforts to end the arms race, and environmental controversy—illustrate the institutional upheaval depicted in this chapter.)

A Troubled Institution: The title of Lederman's 1991 report played on *Science, the Endless Frontier,* an earlier, optimistic report by Vannevar Bush (1945). As an electrical engineering professor at the Massachusetts Institute of Technology, Bush built the first analog computer and continued to improve it. That led to his appointment as head of the National Defense Research Committee in 1940, one year before the United States entered World War II; a 1942 report by Bush resulted in the Manhattan Project, which developed the world's first atomic bomb.

Although the August 26, 1991, *Time* cover blazoned "tight money, blunders, and scandal," the article by Jaroff (1991) ended on an upbeat note. He wrote that Vannevar Bush's "clarion call" had "launched America into its Golden Age of science and helped transform society," adding that Bush's 1945 words "still ring true today." Yet in the same issue, a story on "The Double Take on Dioxin" concluded: "There was a time when most scientific knowledge was considered objective and unassailable. These days, however, it is often hard to tell where science stops and economics and politics take over" (Gorman, 1991).

The inset quote on the Lederman report is from Lepkowski (1991). The quotes from R. G. White and Rustum Roy are from that *Chemical & Engineering News* story. The long inset quote, employment statistics, quote from Daniel Kleppner and career recommendations for young scientists are from Holden (1991). Other articles in the *Science Careers* pullout section covered "hot fields" likely to employ larger numbers of scientists, "hot" research tools likely to be important in the future, and personal experiences of scientists at various stages of their careers. On careers in the physical sciences, see also Tobias et al. (1995).

On international effects of the inevitable leveling off of research support in industrialized countries, see Ziman (1994). British physicist John Ziman pinpointed the mid-1970s as the time when the growth of worldwide science slowed to a steady state.

For Medawar's optimistic advice to young scientists, see Medawar (1979). Perutz's caution was expressed in a 1981 review of Medawar's book reprinted in a collection of essays (Perutz, 1989, pp. 193-201). How universities should adapt to the present employment situation was discussed by physicist Sidney Perkowitz (1996). For a consideration of whether or not we are in the "twilight of science" based on interviews with leading scientists, see Horgan (1996), negatively reviewed by Hayes (1996).

Science May Need You: President Kennedy's famous challenge came from a passage in an 1884 address by Justice Oliver Wendell Holmes to a post of the Grand Army of the Republic. Jesus' comments to his disciples about serving others are in Mark 10:35-45. The admonition to trust God completely is from Proverbs 3, which also contains sound ethical principles.

Questions of Value: On values in science, see Rolston (1988, 1989). Philosopher/theologian Holmes Rolston III has tried to restore "value vocabulary" to science to counter the reductionism of biologists like E. O. Wilson (1971) and Richard Dawkins (1976). Rolston's ecological ethic is based on the concept that "genes essentially are information, and information is of value." See also Rolston (1991) and accompanying responses.

The Value of Science: The utilitarian basis on which science is often sold to the public is well illustrated by the final words of the preface to *Science and Creationism* (NAS-COSAC, 1984, p. 6), by NAS president Frank Press:

In a nation whose people depend on scientific progress for their health, economic gains, and national security, it is of utmost importance that our students understand science as a system of study, so that by building on past achievements they can maintain the pace of scientific progress and ensure the continued emergence of results that can benefit mankind.

Unbridled optimism for science and science-based technology tended to fade during the cold war, when U.S. nuclear policy was MAD (Mutually Assured Destruction). For one theologian's balanced but hopeful assessment of problems and possibilities from that period, see Cox (1968). Cox's chapter was included in a book edited by scholar of science and religion, Ian Barbour.

In a later book, Barbour (1980) turned his attention to such concerns as environmental degradation, resource use and appropriate technology. Barbour outlined three public attitudes toward technology (as liberator, threat and instrument of power), with a thoughtful section on human values (Barbour, 1980, pp. 59-80). See also Monsma (1986), a positive view of technology as a means of carrying out the biblical "cultural mandate" from the Calvin Center for Christian Scholarship, with recommendations of twenty significant books on technology from the 1970s and 1980s.

Some educators think that the best way of generating interest in science among students is to link science, technology and society ("STS"). The National Association for Science, Technology and Society (NASTS) held its eleventh annual "technological literacy" conference in 1996. For a Christian view of STS curricula, see Cobern (1988). On the selling of science to the American public, see Nelkin (1988).

The public is divided on whether the environment as a whole faces an immediate crisis, and on how to deal with perceived long-range threats to the environment. Four Christian biologists review the situation in Van Dyke et al. (1996). See also Wilkinson (1980, 1995). For a vigorous exchange, see Wright (1995) and Olson (1996).

Values from *Science:* A prolific critic of the effects of the scientific mindset on society was French lay theologian and law professor Jacques Ellul (d. 1994). In *The Technological Society* (1964), Ellul pinpointed *la technique* ("the totality of methods rationally arrived at and having absolute efficiency in every field of human activity") as an inevitable concomitant of a scientific, problem-solving ethos. *The Technological System* (1980) elaborated on technology as "discourse on technique," warning that technological systems get out of control. *The Technological Bluff* (1990) argued that politicians, the media and technologists overstate the possibilities and radically conceal the negative aspects of "progress"—an immense bluff that "finally sucks us into this world by banishing all our ancient reservations and fears" (p. xvi).

After writing two hundred pages on the impact of computers on society, Ellul abandoned the project, begun in 1978, because things were already changing so fast that he was "always two years behind" (p. xiv). (See Close-Up 4: On to the Internet.)

Another critic of the scientific ethos from the humanities side of the curriculum has been Huston Smith, featured in a 1996 PBS series, *Wisdom of Faith,* hosted by Bill Moyers. Before joining the faculty at the University of California at Berkeley, Smith was a professor of philosophy at Washington University, the Massachusetts Institute of Technology and Syracuse University. Best known as a scholar of world religions (H. Smith, 1958) he has celebrated important truths by which people lived before the rise of modern science (H. Smith, 1976). In a collection of essays (H. Smith, 1982), he argued that those truths had not been refuted but merely displaced by a new scientistic epistemology.

Citing Page Smith (P. Smith, 1990) on what scientific dominance has done to the universities, Huston Smith credited a scientist for encouraging him to "drop innuendo, come into the open, and say right out that [not in principle, but in practice] science *is* scientism" (H. Smith, 1994).

For a negative view of academic "anti-science" critiques, see Gross and Levitt (1994). For a positive attempt to integrate "the spirit of science into an authentic humanism" by a Jesuit physicist, see Cantore (1977).

Charles Darwin's concern about losing certain aesthetic tastes as a result of intense focus on scientific work is from his autobiography (1892, pp. 53-54).

The tale of the single-minded physicist is from the author's memory of different versions heard on various occasions. For other caricatures of scientists, see cartoonist Sidney Harris's work in one of his collections (1989, 1990, 1992).

For the text of "Science: Our Common Heritage," see Boulding (1980). For an account of politics in Soviet genetics in the period 1937-1964 ("the Lysenko tragedy"), perhaps "the most bizarre chapter in the history of modern science," see Medvedev (1969).

Values in Science: On the love of money as "a root of all kinds of evil," see 1 Timothy 6:10. Specifics of priority disputes (Robert Gallo), hasty press conferences (Stanley Pons and Martin Fleischmann), stonewalling over alleged fraud (David Baltimore), misusing grant funds (Donald Kennedy) and other troubling incidents were reported in *Science* and *The Scientist* throughout the 1980s and 1990s. For an overview by a journalist who dubbed Representative John Dingell the chief "watchdog" of science, see Jaroff (1991).

The quote about scientists failing to conform to the standard model is from Broad and Wade (1982, p. 8); rejoinder from Hull (1988, pp. 313-17). The phrase about "ordinary human passions" is from Broad and Wade (p. 223), as is the description of the two goals of science (p. 212). The "competitive cooperation" phrase is from Hull (1988, p. 319), as well as the comment about effects of dishonesty on "opponents" and "allies" (p. 321).

For responses from the National Academy to the perceived ethical situation in science, see NAS-COSEPUP (1989, 1992); from Sigma Xi, see Jackson (1992) and Sigma Xi (1993); from AAAS, see Chalk (1988) and Teich and Frankel (1991), the latter a collaborative effort with the American Bar Association. For a Christian response to the ethical situation, see Haas (1986).

Where Do Values Come From? The quotes on the religious basis of the scientific ethos are from an AAAS presidential address (Boulding, 1980, p. 832). For the Ten Commandments, see Exodus 20; for Jesus' expansion on them, see Matthew 5; for his summary of "all the law and the prophets," see Matthew 22:34-40. On sorting out the roots of modern science, see Lindberg (1992); on the biblical soil in which science took root, see Hooykaas (1972) and C. Russell (1985, chap. 4).

Lessons from History: On playing the scientific game by the rules, see an exchange between Dickerson (1992) and W. R. Hearn (1992a). For a crash course in church history, see, for example, Dowley (1977). On the erosion of religious belief in public culture, see Pannenberg (1996).

On scientists' relation to government, Galileo's demonstration to the Venetian senate and his reward from the doge of Venice is mentioned in Hummel (1986, p. 88), drawing on Drake (1978). When the U.S. Congress chartered the National Academy of Sciences at the request of a group of Harvard professors and government scientists, "the ostensible purpose of the academy was to mobilize science for the Union war effort" (Van Tassell and Hall, 1966, p. 30). For over fifty years, the War Department seldom sought advice from the Academy. In July 1916, however, members of NAS prompted organization of the National Research Council, both to "help in the war and to advance the cause of science" (Lasby, 1966, p. 260).

For an overview of the development of science and how it became institutionalized in Europe and America, see the introduction to Van Tassel and Hall (1966). For case histories of government entanglement, see Lakoff (1966); the introductory essay on "The Third Culture: Science in Social Thought" was a response to Snow (1961) by a political scientist (Lakoff, pp. 1-86). Lakoff's book was dedicated to Don K. Price, then dean of Harvard's J. F. Kennedy School of Government, possibly the first person to speak of a "scientific establishment." See D. K. Price (1954, 1965).

The dismal legacy of communist regimes, despite the high value they placed on science, has been noted by many observers: "The Soviet Union was officially dead, but its corpse would rot for decades, confounding attempts at civil, political, and environmental renewal" (Kaplan, 1996, p. 275). On communism's environmental legacy, see Feshbach and Friendly (1992) and Peterson (1993). On its human costs, see Rosenberg (1995).

On scientists' insistent demands for "scientific literacy," one physicist doubts that more than about six percent of American adults will ever be able to make independent judgments on science-based issues (Shamos, 1995).

The inset paragraph on science as secular religion (NAS-COSEPUP, 1965) is quoted in Salomon (1973, p. 68). On the same theme, see also Lapp (1965) and Klaw (1968).

On the waning of public confidence in science, the quoted sentence and inset paragraph are from Nisbet (1980, pp. 347-8). Robert Nisbet was formerly Albert Schweitzer Professor of Humanities at Columbia University.

A Personal Testimony: This section is based on two works by the author: a chapter in Hatfield (1973) and a 1977 article in *Radix* magazine reprinted under a different title in Sider (1980). The first two inset quotes are from Hatfield (1973, pp. 95, 96); the last two are from Sider (1980, p. 85, 86-7). On "the Golden Rule," see Matthew 7:12 and Luke 6:31.

Chapter 3: Science as a Christian Calling
On the relation of scientific thinking to detective work and detective fiction, see Haddam (1996, p. 59).

What Scientists Do: The first inset paragraph is from Bube (1991, pp. 110-11).

For over two hundred samples of writing about scientists, see Gratzer (1989). Gratzer excluded science fiction works (defined as "the exploration of imagined worlds") and expositions of "the nature or the substance of science," though a few books explaining science to nonscientists have been very popular. *A Brief History of Time* (Hawking, 1988) was a recent bestseller, though it may not have been as widely *read* as its sales indicated (White and Gribbin, 1992, pp. 220-51). Hawking was already a television personality, and television probably has more influence than print media on the public perception of scientists. *Cosmos* (Sagan, 1980) stayed on bestseller lists for months after being introduced as a well-publicized TV series. Many *Nova* episodes on PBS have made scientific investigations seem as gripping as stories of criminal detection.

For samples of six stereotypes of scientists (the demonic, the amoral truth-seeker, the moral idealist, etc.) in literature from the eighteenth century to the present, see Haynes (1994).

The inset quote on investigative styles is from Peter Medawar (1979, p. 3). It appears in *On Being a Scientist* (2nd ed., 1995), referred to as an NAS publication although it was authorized by the Governing Board of the National Research Council (NRC), whose members are drawn not only from NAS but also from the National Academy of Engineering and the Institute of Medicine. The NRC Committee on Science, Engineering, and Public Policy which produced it is often abbreviated (and pronounced) COSEPUP. The text of *On Being a Scientist* is available on the World Wide Web page of NAS hosted by Gopher: http://www.nas.edu via gopher.nas.edu or via FTP at ftp.nas.edu

The inset quote on scientists acting in their own self-interest is from Hull (1988, p. 394). Hull portrayed science as "a matter of curiosity, credit, and checking."

The quoted sentence about truth is from Polanyi (1958, p. 305), a book considered a key break with positivistic reductionism (Templeton and Herrmann, 1989, p. 11). His earlier *Science, Faith and Society* related truth and freedom in response to Marxist and Stalinist influences on science. A preface written by Polanyi after the USSR crushed the 1956 Hungarian revolt was added later to Polanyi's 1946 text (Polanyi, 1964). See also Polanyi (1969).

Should I Be a Scientist? On God as spirit, see John 4:24. English cognates of the New Testament word for "spirit" (Greek, *pneuma*) also show its relation to gas or air, as in *pneumatic* and *pneumonia.*

"Spiritual increment" has been proposed as the primary criterion of scientific creativity (Ghiselin, 1963a, p. 37). See also Ghiselin (1955). Taylor and Barron (1963) is a collection of papers on scientific creativity. Christian physicist Charles Townes described the "sudden discovery of understanding" that led to his invention of the maser as kin to a "religious revelation" (quoted in Berland, 1962, pp. 71-3). Other scientists have described the "moment of discovery" in similar terms. For examples see Ghiselin (1963b) on Poincaré, and "Intuition" in Beveridge (1957, pp. 91-108).

Although some key words used in this chapter (e.g., *spirit, mystery*) are not used in the practice of science, some thoroughly naturalistic scientists (e.g., Carl Sagan, 1980) have spoken of their "awe" at the immensity or some other aspect of the universe. Awe is a response to mystery not far removed from reverence or devotion—although as the Bible warns, it can be misdirected. Awe is a strong emotion, for which the Bible sometimes uses the word *fear,* as in Psalm 111:10.

The catalogs of Christian publishers list many books on the methodologies of Bible study and prayer, of discipleship, and of giving and receiving spiritual guidance (sometimes under the heading of "spiritual formation"). Because secular humanists constantly equate science with rationality and religion with irrationality, it is important for Christians not to confuse spirituality with emotionality, despite the strong emotional impact of sensing God's guidance. Books like J. I. Packer's *Knowing God* (20th ed., 1993) exert a corrective influence by emphasizing the cognitive as well as emotive aspects of finding and following God's will. For a study guide on career choices for Christians, see Bernbaum and Steer (1986).

What It Takes To Be a Scientist: On the "variety of gifts," see Romans 12 and 1 Corinthians 12; on using one's gifts, see 1 Timothy 4:14 and 2 Timothy 1:6; on the greater gifts, see 1 Corinthians 13:13.

An early study of the personal characteristics of scientists was carried out by Harvard psychologist Anne Roe (wife of paleontologist George Gaylord Simpson). She interviewed sixty-four leading research scientists and gave them psychological tests revealing, among other things, their intellectual flexibility (Roe, 1953).

Lifestyles and Role Models: On science as community, see Pollard (1961). On being "salt" and "light," see Matthew 5:13-16.

Chapter 4: What to Expect
According to sociologist Robert Wuthnow, although scientists are less religious than other people, "irreligiosity is far more pronounced among the least scientific disciplines—the social sciences and humanities" than in the natural sciences (Wuthnow, 1985).

On scientists and secular fundamentalists: Among the Humanist Laureates honored in the Academy of Humanism by the Council for Secular Humanism (CSH), scientists (e.g., Francis Crick, Stephen Jay Gould, Carl Sagan, E. O. Wilson) have actually been a minority. Of course CSH, which publishes *Free Inquiry* and *The Secular Humanist Bulletin,* welcomes support from scientists, especially in its Committee for the Scientific Examination of Religion. For the philosophy of CSH's founder, see Kurtz (1986). CSH began as the Council for Democratic and Secular Humanism; the title was shortened in 1996, partly because its acronym, CODESH, sounded too much like the Hebrew word for holiness *(qodesh).*

On abuses of academic freedom: The potential entanglement of personalities and philosophies was depicted in a novel (McCarthy, 1951) long before "political correctness" dominated American campuses. On one kind of roadblock a Christian professor may encounter, see Bube (1989b). Academics with religious beliefs have at times been marginalized, but few clear-cut cases of discrimination have gone to court (Johnson, 1995, pp. 173-92). In 1989, *Scientific American* refused employment to veteran science writer Forrest Mims III because he was not a "believer" in Darwinism, though his conservative Christian beliefs had no bearing on his technical articles for the magazine (Bergman, 1993).

For Jesus' caution about judging others, see Matthew 7:1-5, part of Jesus' Sermon on the Mount.

Living Crossculturally: An excellent depiction of a scientist at work appears in one of the novels of C. P. Snow (1958). In response to Snow (1961), literary agent John Brockman dubbed some of his prominent scientist clients (plus a few others) the "emerging third culture." He organized *The Third Culture* (Brockman, 1995) as a series of secular sermons and commentaries by his "trend-setters," for whom science is definitely the only game in town. They disparage the humanities, and religion in particular.

For helpful discussions on whether science and the practice of Christian faith are basically different or basically similar, see especially Barbour (1968a), Bube (1968, 1995) and Polkinghorne (1986, 1991, 1992).

On the crosscultural challenge to Christians, see for example Hopler and Hopler (1993), Elmer (1994), B. Adeney (1995) and Lingenfelter (1996).

The inset quote is from C. S. Lewis (1956, p. 61). On the two types of knowledge, see Polanyi (1958, 1969); the "I-Thou" phrase is from Buber (1970). See also Schideler (1966).

Nobody Said It Would Be Easy: On differences between men's and women's opportunities in science, see Sonnert and Holton (1996) and Brennan (1996). On the possibility of a gender-neutral science, see Keller (1985). Only ten women were among the 1,195 scientists cited in a popular biographical encyclopedia (Asimov, 1976). Women in ten branches of science tried to "set the record straight" by chronicling women's contributions (Kass-Simon and Farnes, 1990). Accounts of gifted women in an essentially male profession include the life stories of crystallographer Rosalind Franklin, who almost won the Nobel Prize (Sayre, 1975), and of geneticist Barbara McClintock (Keller, 1983) and nuclear physicist Lise Meitner (Sime, 1996), who did.

Making Hard Choices: With each branch of science having its own methods, there have been few practical how-to books for beginning scientists. Beveridge (1957) was more general than E. B. Wilson (1952), who emphasized statistical methods. The first Nobel lecture in chemistry (van't Hoff, 1901) was translated into English in 1967 as a guide for beginners. The lore of science is passed on to some extent by such authors as Medawar (1979), Oliver (1991), Carr (1992) and Braben (1994). In science, guidebooks are rare but handbooks are huge, even multivolume, reference works.

Advice on being a Christian in science was offered by Barbour (1960). On fitting into academic life, see discussions of the rationality of Christian faith by such writers as Gill (1989), Sire (1990, 1994) and Kennedy (1995). For a comparison of a Christian worldview with some alternatives, see Holmes (1983, 1985), Walsh and Middleton (1984) and Sire (1988).

Excursus into Philosophy: The best place to dig into the historical encounter between Christianity and science is the symposium volume edited by Lindberg and Numbers (1986). For a crash course, see C. Russell (1985); for a brief outline, see Kalthoff (1993). For a philosophically oriented historical treatment, see Pearcey and Thaxton (1994). The first inset quote is from Pearcey and Thaxton (1994, p. 19); the second from David Lindberg's "Introduction" (Lindberg and Numbers, 1986, p. 7).

The historical overview in this section is based largely on Pearcey and Thaxton (1994). On many of the philosophical issues see Ratzsch (1986) or Moreland (1989). For a readable account of Galileo's struggles, see Hummel (1986). On the revolution in physics, see Polkinghorne (1984).

John C. Polkinghorne is professor of mathematical physics at Cambridge University, a Fellow of the Royal Society, an Anglican priest and President of Queens' College, Cambridge. Besides the popular exposition of modern physics just cited, he has written many useful books on science and Christian faith (Polkinghorne, 1986, 1988, 1989, 1991). *The Way the World Is* (Polkinghorne, 1992) was originally published in 1983 as the first of a series. His 1993 Gifford Lectures (Polkinghorne, 1994) are a formal theological treatise following the outline of the Nicene Creed.

The Gifford Lectures in Scotland are devoted to "natural theology"; lecturers are required by the will of the founder "to treat their subject as a strictly natural science," without reference to or reliance upon "any special exceptional or so-called miraculous revelation" (quoted in Polkinghorne, 1994, p. 3). (Imagine lecturing on "physical chemistry" without being able to refer to chemistry.) Theists seem to get around these restrictions, but they raise questions about the meaning of *natural* and *theology.*

Whatever they think about "natural theology," mainstream Protestant theologians seeking to accommodate modern science into theology include Wolfhart Pannenberg (1988), Thomas Torrance (1989), Robert Russell (1988, 1989), Ian Barbour (1990), Nancey Murphy (1990) and Arthur Peacocke (1993). For a Catholic view, see Clarke (1988), a paper from conferences commemorating the tricentennial of Isaac Newton's *Principia* organized by the Vatican Observatory but including Protestants.

The work of such serious theologians is to be distinguished from that of scientists (physicists, mostly) who speak of God in an impersonal way, such as Stephen Hawking (1988), Paul Davies (1992) and Frank Tipler (1994). Tipler's bizarre but mathematically derived Omega-point theory is reminiscent of the vague evolutionary theology of the prolific Jesuit anthropologist Pierre Teilhard de Chardin (1959).

On the irreducible complexity of biochemical systems, see Behe (1996). For more on Warren Weaver's life and views, see his autobiography (Weaver, 1970). The arguments on the weaknesses of deductive and inductive logic are from Weaver (1959); the quotes on induction are taken from Clareson (1961, p. 300).

On alternatives to metaphysical naturalism, McMullin (1993, p. 327) sides with those who prefer an evolutionary account on scientific grounds but "are perfectly willing to allow that it was within the Creator's power to speed up the story by special creation of ancestral kinds of plants and animals, even though (in their view) this was not what God did." McMullin argues that this position is not deistic or semideistic.

Attention paid here to *Darwin on Trial* (Johnson, 1991) is not intended to imply that it has been the only scholarly critique of macroevolution or Darwinism. Other examples are Greene (1961), Denton (1985), Plantinga (1991) and Behe (1996). Alvin Plantinga's paper appeared in a special issue of *Christian Scholar's Review* on "Creation/Evolution and Faith," which included responses by biologist Pattle Pun, philosopher-theologian Ernan McMullin and physicist Howard Van Till, plus Plantinga's reply to his critics. For another symposium of critiques of Darwinism, with responses, see Buell and Hearn (1994). See also a collection edited by Moreland (1994).

The quote on Darwin and atheism is from Dawkins (1986, p. 6). For Johnson's direct response to Dawkins's blind watchmaker thesis, see Johnson (1991, 1993b). For negative reviews of *Darwin on Trial,* see Gould (1992) and Hull (1992); for a more balanced review, see W. R. Hearn (1992b). Johnson replied to critics of *Darwin on Trial* in an addendum to the second edition.

The quotes critical of methodological naturalism are from Johnson (1995, pp. 207-8). Besides Dawkins (1986, 1996), biologist William Provine (1988) and philosopher Daniel Dennett (1995) blatantly equate Darwinism with atheism. For examples of works cited by Johnson as encouraging to his thesis, see Behe (1996) and various papers in Moreland (1994). See also Denton (1985). Ludwig (1993) responded empirically to claims of the significance of computer programs like Blind Watchmaker (Dawkins, 1986) and Blind Shellmaker (Dawkins, 1996).

Some young scholars allied with Phil Johnson are editing a new quarterly journal, *Origins & Design,* published by Access Research Network (ARN, P.O. Box 38069, Colorado Springs, CO 80937; formerly *Origins Research,* currently $15/yr.). Audio and video tapes of some of Johnson's lectures are also available from ARN.

Excursus into Politics: On ad hoc alliances: Assertions that evolution is a fact appear in the National Center for Science Education's *Voices for Evolution* (Matsumura, 1995) from African Americans for Humanism, the American Civil Liberties Union, the Council on Democratic and Secular Humanism, the Freedom from Religion Foundation, and People for the American Way. Statements by the American Scientific Affiliation and the Center for Theology and the Natural Sciences are also included, though they warn against evolutionary naturalism as well as "scientific creationism."

On the meaning of the "evangelical" label, see Marsden (1991), Dayton and Johnston (1992) and McGrath (1996). On responses to ASA's *Teaching Science* booklet, see Numbers (1992, pp.

321-2) and Johnson (1991, pp. 126-8). For replies to some of those responses, see Bullock (1988) and Wiester (1988). The inset quote on political versus legal battles is from Larson (1985, p. 171).

Taking a Stand: On "warrior" and "peacemaker" roles, opponents of Christianity are likely to bring up biblical accounts of battles fought in God's name but ignore science's role in military research and development. The Bible is quite candid about conflict. On appropriate armor for *spiritual* warfare, see Ephesians 6:10-18; on "the good fight," see 1 Timothy 6:11-16 and 2 Timothy 4:6-8; on enduring hard struggles, see Hebrews 10:32-33.

More abundant and more challenging are encouragements to love peace and actively seek it. Jesus blessed peacemakers (Matthew 5:9), urged his disciples to "be at peace with one another" (Mark 9:50), sent them "like lambs into the midst of wolves" to spread a message of peace (Luke 10:1-12), and gave them peace (John 14:25-31). On living peaceably and reconciling enemies, see Romans 12:14-21, 2 Timothy 2:22-26, Hebrews 12:14-16 and James 3:13-18.

On maintaining civility, see Mouw (1992). The inset quote on "listening" is from a recent book on why the creation/evolution debate goes on and on (Ratzsch, 1996, p. 198). See also Ratzsch (1986).

The quote on biological phenomena merely giving the appearance of purposeful design is from Dawkins (1986, p. 1). A response by Howard Van Till to a Phillip Johnson article (1993a) from *First Things,* plus Johnson's reply to Van Till, was reprinted from the June/July 1993 issue of *First Things* as "God and Evolution: An Exchange" in Bauman (1993, pp. 269-93). A response by Nancey Murphy (1993) also drew a reply from Johnson (1995, pp. 229-30). Among many efforts to clarify such debates are those of Frey (1986) and Wilcox (1986).

Putting It All Together: I picked up the phrase "the dancing hand of God" from my friend John Wiester. I may have picked up "metaphysical minimalist" from chemist George Schweitzer many years ago, but I have used it of myself in print at least once (1991d). For a discussion of the idea of complementarity in science and in religion, see Haas (1983a, 1983b). The final inset quote is from Bube (1995, p. 196).

Chapter 5: Now the Good News

Since much material in this chapter comes from personal experience or personal correspondence, documentation is minimal. The situations referred to are mostly those of moving up the academic ladder; in that regard see especially Bube (1989a).

Divided Loyalty: On "the tyranny of time" see Banks (1984). On competing claims on a scientist's time, see Bube (1989a) and the chapter on "The Scientist as a Person" in Barbour (1960, pp. 99-118).

Today, being a spouse in a two-career marriage is less of a change from being single than it used to be—until the birth of a child turns a marriage into a family. Postponement of childbearing has its own consequences. On problems of young married couples and especially of young families, the various publications of Focus on the Family (P.O. Box 35500, Colorado Springs, CO 80935-3550) offer helpful advice.

Moral Intensity: On making moral judgments, recall Jesus' warning in Matthew 7:1-5. With regard to outright fraud, the phrase, "the gravest sin in science," seems to have been dropped from the 1995 edition of *On Being a Scientist* (NAS-COSEPUP, 1989, p. 16). In *Responsible Science* the minority statement of panel members Howard Schachman and Keith Yamomoto appears at the end of the report (NAS-COSEPUP, 1992, pp. 180-81). On defining ethical conduct in science, see also Woodward and Goodstein (1996).

For "the Lord's prayer" for deliverance from temptation and protection from evil, see Matthew 6:7-15. The "appearance of evil" Christians are warned to avoid (1 Thessalonians 5:20-22, KJV) is also translated "every kind of evil" (NIV). On the importance of being faithful in small matters, see Luke 16:10-13. The quote on confession and forgiveness is from 1 John 1:5-10.

On consequences, it was agnostic Robert Ingersoll who said, "In nature there are neither rewards nor punishments—there are consequences" (in *Some Reasons Why*, 1896). On what cannot separate us from God's love, see Romans 8:31-39. On the sexual form of the big lie, see the chapter on "Sexual Morality" in C. S. Lewis (1956, pp. 74-80). The New Testament says to "avoid" evil, sometimes using the stronger word *flee* or *shun*, as in 1 Corinthians 6:18-20, 10:12-14, 1 Timothy 6:9-11 and 2 Timothy 2:20-22.

Relations with Others in Science: The ultimate example in affirming people, no matter what they do, is Romans 5:8: "But God proves his love for us in that while we still were sinners Christ died for us." The New Testament is realistic about efforts to get along with people: "Do not repay anyone evil for evil, but take thought for what is noble in the sight of all. *If it is possible, so far as it depends on you,* live peaceably with all" (Romans 12:17-18, emphasis added).

The catalog of spiritual fruit is from Galatians 5:22, following a catalog of worldly behavior. The model for settling disputes—first by yourselves, then by bringing in others—was laid down by Jesus in Matthew 18:15-17. His exhortation to be wise and harmless is from Matthew 10:16.

Conflict with Other Christians: On the church and higher education, note that colleges in colonial America were established primarily to train ministers of the gospel; some of those early colleges became Harvard, Yale, Princeton, Brown, Columbia and Rutgers universities (see Marsden, 1994). For the history of InterVarsity Christian Fellowship in America, see Hunt and Hunt (1991). For the history of Campus Crusade for Christ, see Quebedeaux (1979).

On spiritual unity, besides Jesus' description of his disciples and himself as branches and vine (John 15:1-17), and his prayer that his disciples "may all be one" (John 17:20-26), see such exhortations as Ephesians 4:1-6. Jesus called himself "the way, and the truth, and the life" in John 14:1-7; Paul urged Christians to "test everything; hold fast to what is good" (1 Thessalonians 5:21).

On controversy among Christians, note Donald MacKay's comments on the value of criticism:

> I do my best to think and write in obedience to God's revelation in one particular area of apologetics. I *need* my brother who sees me as running dangerously close to heresy or incoherence to tell me when he has misgivings—not as a censor or pope, but as a comrade who fears for my health and that of those who read what I write. I need to weigh questions offered in this spirit, not as "attacks" but as helpful feedback to be evaluated as realistically as possible before God. If I find misunderstandings in what he describes as my position or its implications, I should point them out not just to defend myself but as part of my service to *him,* taking it for granted that he does not wish to cherish any false caricature of my position, because he too claims to serve the God of truth and will be glad to be corrected. Any idea of scoring points in a debate should be utterly abhorrent (MacKay, 1986d, p. 265).

MacKay was writing from experience, having defended his book *The Clockwork Image* after a critic had called its publication a disservice to Christian students (Cramer and MacKay, 1976). Beginning his reply by citing points on which he and his critic agreed, MacKay ended by saying:

> I am sure that with Cramer's help I could have made *The Clockwork Image* a better book. As it stands it is evidently open to even greater misunderstandings than I had thought possible. I hope that this exchange may help fend off at least a few of these (Cramer and MacKay, 1976, p. 125).

That did not end the controversy between these two Christians, however: see Cramer (1985) and MacKay (1986a).

Another evangelical attacked for a book he wrote for the general Christian public, *Brave New People,* was biologist Gareth Jones; for that story see Jones (1985, 1994). On coping with controversy, see also Menninga (1988). On how far forgiveness should go, see Jesus' words to Peter in Matthew 18:21-35.

Isolation and Loneliness: The term "hyper-orthodox" was used by theologian Bernard Ramm to refer to fundamentalists who demonstrated closed-mindedness. Jesus' words, "I am with you always," were among his last to his disciples, recorded in Matthew 28:16-20. On gathering with other believers for mutual encouragement, see Hebrews 10:23-25.

Crosscultural Communication: The author's short article on "Christ and the Day's Work" appeared in the February 1956 issue of *His* magazine (p. 15).

On Christian bookstores: the sad fact is that few stock serious books even by Christian authors. Store managers will tell you that pastors buy books of sermons rather than solid theological works; other customers want devotional or self-help books. In some Christian bookstores, which seem to survive on sales of greeting cards, jewelry and doo-dads, it is a relief to find any books at all—on a few shelves way in the back. This situation is part of the "scandal of the evangelical mind" (Noll, 1994). Logos Bookstores near universities have been a happy exception; some even carry a good selection of books on science and faith.

The two chapters on the origin of life referred to are Hearn and Hendry (1959) and "Did Life on Earth Arise by Chance?" (ASA-CISE, 1986, pp. 29-33). The "strange world" comment is from Numbers (1992, p. 322).

Radix magazine (P.O. Box 4307, Berkeley, CA 94704) advertises itself as "where Christian faith meets American culture." From its tenth anniversary science issue the Jastrow quote and the inset quote are from Arveson and Hearn (1979).

The sonnet "Reprise" is by W. R. Hearn (1993); the quotes in the paragraph following are from W. R. Hearn (1988a). On my stint as a Visiting Biologist for the American Institute of Biological Sciences, I recall that one of my chapel-talk titles was "Confessions of a Christian Biochemist." The last inset paragraph is from W. R. Hearn (1971, pp. 72-3).

Chapter 6: Living a Whole Life

The definition of art implied here is not that of fine art or "high" art but the "application of skill," as in *The Art of Scientific Investigation* (Beveridge, 1957).

Using Spiritual Resources: Helpful how-to books on Christian living appear every year, but among the classics are Lewis (1956), Packer (1973; new ed., 1993) and Stott (1975). On identifying with God's people, "personal involvement" should be as characteristic of the religious life of a scientist as "reflective detachment" (Barbour, 1960, p. 113). On the effectiveness of small groups for spiritual growth, see Nicholas (1985).

For incentives to study God's creation, see Deuteronomy 4:19, Isaiah 44:23, 45:18-19, Nehemiah 9:6, Psalm 8:1-9, 19:1-14, 104:1-35, 136:1-9, 148:1-14, John 1:1-10, Romans 1:18-20, Colossians 1:15-19, Hebrews 1:1-4. For encouragement to do what is right, see Exodus 20:1-17, Matthew 5—7, Romans 12, 1 Corinthians 13, Ephesians 4:1—5:19 and James 3. For hope, see John 3:16-17, among many other passages. On the power of God's Word, see Hebrews 4:12-13. The Pasteur quote is from Beveridge (1957, p. 46).

Using Professional Resources: Most resources for professional growth will be available in academic libraries or large public libraries. Scientific journals are too expensive for an individual to subscribe to more than one or two, but membership in AAAS (and ASA) provide breadth.

On the human face of science, there are of course many biographies and autobiographies of individual scientists. The *Profiles, Pathways, and Dreams* series now numbers about twenty titles; you may obtain a catalog from ACS Publications (1155 Sixteenth St., NW, Washington, DC 20036). For many years each volume of *Annual Reviews of Physiology* and other *Annual Reviews* (Annual Reviews, Inc., 4139 El Camino Way, Palo Alto, CA 94306) has begun with a prefatory autobiographical essay; some collective volumes have appeared. Opinions of famous scientists have been captured in such collections as Berland (1962), Brockman (1995) and Horgan (1996). Some accounts of the lives of contemporary Christians in science are in Hefley (1967), Barrett and Fisher (1984), Berry (1991) and Bube (1994).

The role of women in science is at last receiving attention. *Graduate School and Beyond,* women's stories from a 1989 conference (free from Division of Educational Programs, Argonne National Laboratory, 9700 South Cass Ave., Argonne, IL 60439), has a four-page list of resources for women in science. A not-very-encouraging study by Brush (1991) contained 102 references on women in science and engineering. A special section on "Women in Science" in the March 13, 1992, issue of *Science* drew so much favorable comment that it was expected to become an annual feature.

An equivalent special section in the March 29, 1996, issue of *Science* ("Maintaining Diversity in Science," pp. 1901-21) was devoted to women and minorities. Ethnic minorities in science are slowly gaining recognition. The showing of *Breakthrough* on public television happened to coincide with the twenty-third annual meeting of the National Organization of Black Chemists and Chemical Engineers. The 1996 meeting drew some eight hundred registrants, of whom almost half were students.

Using Integrative Resources: On biases, note that almost all works cited in this book are not only in English but published in the United States. One cannot "judge a book by its cover," but the theological position of an otherwise unknown author can to some extent be guessed by noting who published the book. Books from such publishers as Baker, Eerdmans, Zondervan, InterVarsity Press and Lion are almost always evangelical in outlook, but evangelical writers often seek publication elsewhere to try to reach a wider audience. At the opposite extreme is Prometheus Books of Amherst, New York, publisher of many profoundly anti-Christian works.

On where to begin, try a classic: Ramm (1954), Barbour (1960, 1968a, 1974) or Bube (1968), if you can find them. Or choose a recent evangelical contribution, such as Poole (1990), Pearcey and Thaxton (1994), or Bube (1995). The notes for Close-Up 5 will suggest others. Catholics can begin with Cantore (1977), Jaki (1978, 1992) or McMullin (1988, 1993); all are physicists, though McMullin frequently writes on evolutionary biology.

Delve into some topics beyond your technical range. Nonbiologists should keep abreast of the so-called creation/evolution question, because feelings run high and because you are sure to be asked for an opinion. The Appendix in ASA's *Teaching Science in a Climate of Controversy* lists several basic books, a few controversial ones, mixed collections by scientists and religionists, plus a half-dozen books by scientists committed to a biblical faith—a good "short list."

On that particular topic, two Christian quarterly journals are worthy of attention: *Origins* (est. 1973, $8/yr.) from the Geoscience Research Institute (Loma Linda University, Loma Linda, CA 92350); and *Origins & Design* (est. 1996; $15/yr.) from Access Research Network (ARN, P.O. Box 38069, Colorado Springs, CO 80937). They provide a balance for both the young-earth *Acts & Facts* (monthly newsletter free on request) from the Institute for Creation Research (ICR, P.O. Box 2667, El Cajon, CA 92021) and the semi-annual journal *Creation/Evolution* and quarterly newsletter *NCSE Reports,* both with membership in the anti-creationist National Center for Science Education (NCSE, P.O. Box 9477, Berkeley, CA 94709; $25/yr.). Beginning in 1997 the two NCSE publications will be combined into a bimonthly *Reports of the National Center for Science Education.* Other publications are available from ARN, ICR and NCSE.

On making your own contribution to the dialogue: Interact first with Christians in other fields, and do not hesitate to start small; a letter to the editor of a newspaper or magazine may be read by far more people than a book.

Keeping Current: The two biblical quotes are from Ecclesiastes 1:9 and 12:12. Roger Bacon (d. 1292) tried to write a universal encyclopedia of knowledge, but the task had already become impossible (Asimov, 1976, p. 45). The ASA annotated bibliography (ASA, 1992) has twenty-five subject categories. The *Who's Who* work (John Templeton Foundation, 1996) is available from Winthrop Publishing Co. (P.O. Box 2881, Framingham, MA 01710).

Subscription to *Perspectives on Science and Christian Faith* comes with ASA membership or can be ordered from ASA (P.O. Box 668, Ipswich, MA 01938; $30/yr.; students, $20). *Zygon* comes with membership in the Institute on Religion in an Age of Science (IRAS, 1100 E. 55th St. Chicago, IL 60615) or can be ordered from Blackwell Publishers (238 Main Street, Cambridge, MA 02142; $43/yr.; students, $32). *Science and Christian Belief* comes with membership in either Christians in Science (CiS, 102 Midhurst Road, Kings Norton, Birmingham B30 3RD, U.K.) or The Victoria Institute (Latchett Hall, Latchett Road, London E18 1DL, U.K.) or can be ordered from Paternoster Periodicals (P.O. Box 300, Carlisle, Cumbria CA3 0QS, U.K.; $45/yr.). CiS is related to the Universities and Colleges Christian Fellowship (UCCF, 38 De Monfort St., Leicester LE1 7GP, U.K.), of which it was a member professional group until becoming independent in 1996.

CTNS Bulletin comes with membership in the Center for Theology and the Natural Sciences (2400 Ridge Road, Berkeley, CA 94709; $35/yr.). For *Pascal Centre Notebook,* contact the Pascal Centre (at Redeemer College, 777 Highway 53 East, Ancaster, Ontario, L9K 1J4, Canada); a four-volume set of conference proceedings from the Centre has also appeared (Van der Meer, 1995a-d). *Science and Religion News* is published by IRAS but has a separate address (65 Hoit Rd., Concord, NH 03301).

Green Cross comes with membership in the Christian Society of the Green Cross (10 East Lancaster Ave., Wynnewood, PA 19096; $25/yr.). Addresses of over forty Christian denominational and interdenominational groups concerned with environmental and ecological issues are listed in an appendix of Van Dyke, et al. (1996).

Discovering our Closest Colleagues: On the American Scientific Affiliation, see Close-Up 3. The Director of Graduate Student Ministries for IVCF is Cam Anderson (P.O. Box 7895, Madison, WI 53707). Examples of local ministry: the McLaurin Institute at Minnesota and Veritas Forum at Harvard (Monroe, 1996). Veritas lecture tapes from various universities are available from AudioMission (tel.: 800-874-8730).

IVCF Faculty Ministries, headed by Terry Morrison (P.O. Box 7895, Madison, WI 53707), publishes a quarterly *Faculty Newsletter* and other resources, including a *Faculty Handbook* ($5), *Models of Ministry* ($2) and a list of nearly forty Christian professional organizations (free on request).

Christian Leadership Ministries (CLM, 3440 Sojourn Drive, Suite 200, Carrollton, TX 75006), directed by Stan Oakes, publishes a quarterly newsletter, *The Real Issue.* "Leadership University" is CLM's "virtual campus" on the Internet. Through its site on the World Wide Web, CLM hopes to provide access to 100,000 articles by scholars and 10,000 annotated bibliographies.

To find a Christian group in your field, try the *Encyclopedia of Associations* (Jaszczak, 1996) or contact the headquarters of ASA, IVCF Faculty Ministries or CLM (addresses above).

Formation of a Council of Christian Scholarly Societies actually seems to be underway, stimulated by the Institute for Advanced Christian Studies (IFACS, P.O. Box 241, Wheaton, IL 60189). IFACS, a granting institution known for its support of evangelical scholars and their work, is not the same as the Institute for Christian Studies (ICS, 229 College St., Toronto, Ontario M5T 1R4, Canada), a graduate school granting a Master of Worldview Studies degree. ICS publishes a newsletter, *Perspective,* available on request, and scholarly works from a Reformed perspective.

The Coalition for Christian Colleges and Universities (CCCU, 329 Eighth St. NE, Washington, DC 20002) was founded in 1976 as the Christian College Coalition. Harvey Fellowships are funded by the Mustard Seed Foundation; application forms are available annually (after April 15) from CCCU. The Coalition is also a sponsor of the Au Sable Institute of Environmental Studies in Mancelona, Michigan, an important center for Christian studies of environmental concerns.

Some think tank addresses: CTNS, 2400 Ridge Rd., Berkeley, CA 94709 (see Peters, 1989), Institute for Theological Encounter with Science and Technology (ITEST), 221 North Grand, St. Louis, MO 63103 (Faith/Science Press catalog on request). Ecumenical Roundtable (917 Forest Ave., Pittsburgh, PA 15202) has begun to sponsor a booth at the AAAS Annual Meeting and Science Innovation Exhibition (AMSIE). The Presbyterian Church (USA), United Church of Christ and Evangelical Lutheran Church in America science groups have held conferences and produced publications.

Sample missionary service groups: Agape Movement or Food for the Hungry (agricultural assistance and community development), MAP International (medical assistance), Technoserve or Missionary Electronics (general technical assistance), Missions Advanced Research and Communications Center (studies of the mission enterprise), Moody Institute of Science (production and distribution of science-based films), Jungle Aviation and Radio Service Division of Wycliffe Bible Translators.

Sample referral groups: Intercristo, 19303 Fremont Ave., N., Seattle, WA 98133; Global Opportunities, 1600 Elizabeth St., Pasadena, CA 91104; Educational Resources and Referrals—China, 2606 Dwight Way, Berkeley, CA 94704.

A Life of Adventure: Toward the beginning of my career, some of the most helpful books I discovered were by British authors, including chemist R. E. D. Clark (1950, 1958, 1960, 1961, 1967) and the distinguished mathematician C. A. Coulson (1956, 1960). A huge void was filled by *Modern Science and Christian Faith* (ASA, 1948), followed by Ramm (1954) and Barbour (1960, 1968a). Articles in ASA's journal also helped fill that void, many exploring ideas later incorporated into books.

For an argument for "care" as the ultimate clue to the universe, see Turner (1978). On the meaning of excellence in academic life, see Bube (1987) and Bradley (1996).

Close-Up 1: The Core of Christian Faith

For a comparison of foundationalistic and holistic (web) models of knowledge, see N. Murphy (1990), drawing on the philosophical work of Imre Lakatos. Murphy's definition of theology is taken from page 196.

The responses of C. S. Lewis (1956) to critics are taken from the Preface of his *Mere Christianity.* Other useful distillations of Christian doctrine are found in Stott (1975) and Packer (1973; new ed., 1993).

To compare theological variations within even closely related Christian traditions, see Dayton and Johnston (1992). To compare the whole spectrum of Christianity with other religious traditions, see the chapter on "Christianity" in H. Smith (1958, 1991).

Close-Up 2: The Bible & Science

The general question of biblical interpretation is treated in hundreds of commentaries and reference works. From an evangelical point of view, see, for example, Atkinson (1990) or Wenham, et al. (1994). Ramm (1954) is a classic work still in print and still a good starting point for evangelicals. See also Stek (1990) and Hummel (1986). For an example of literalist interpretation of Genesis 1, see Morris (1976, 1993); for a concordist interpretation, see Wiester (1983); for a broader view, see Hyers (1984).   ʹ

On "not taking anybody's word," scientists show respect for the *authority* of prior authorship, but reject *authoritarian* encroachment on their thinking. Founders of the Royal Society were so committed to experimentation that they chose as their motto, "Nothing in words." The spelling of the Latin form varies, but evidently Robert Hooke used *Nullius in verba* in a paper read to the Society on July 25, 1694; a paragraph with the Latin motto is quoted in Greene (1959, p. 48) from *The Posthumous Works of Robert Hooke,* edited by Richard Waller in 1705.

Close-Up 3: The American Scientific Affiliation

The quote about Irwin Moon's concern is from Numbers (1992, p. 159). Numbers's chapter on "Evangelicals and Evolution in North America" (pp. 158-183) deals with ASA's earliest years and its internal debates over fiat creation, progressive creation and theistic evolution. Documentary sources and commentary on ASA history are found in Kalthoff (1995), part of a ten-volume documentary set (Numbers, 1995).

For information on ASA Annual Meetings, affiliated groups (Affiliation of Christian Biologists, Affiliation of Christian Geologists), local sections, commissions (e.g., bioethics, science education, history of science, social sciences), and publications, request a current brochure from the Ipswich address. ASA publications have included symposia such as *Modern Science and Christian Faith* (ASA, 1948) and Mixter (1959). Publications currently available from ASA are an annotated bibliography (ASA, 1992) and a guidebook for high school teachers (ASA-CISE, 1986; 4th ed., 1993).

For a modern translation of the Apostles' Creed cited in ASA's Statement of Faith, see Bray (1984, pp. 204-205). According to Bray, the Apostles' Creed closely resembles a very early pattern of baptismal confession. On the value of venerable Christian creeds to a modern physicist, see Polkinghorne (1994).

Close-Up 4: On to the Internet

On the founding of the Internet's precursor and on ArpaNet's potential as perceived in the early 1980s, see Newell and Sproull (1982).

On freedom and control, the Internet has played a role in political liberation movements, as in the People's Republic of China. It is also used by militia movements in the U.S.; directions have been posted for making the kind of bomb that blew up a federal building in Oklahoma in 1995. Longtime Internet users regard much of what is available now as junk cluttering up the system. The "Infobahn" has been compared to a Los Angeles freeway during rush hour (Germain, 1996). If that is already happening, what of the future? For an optimistic view, see Gates (1995); for skeptical views, see Brook and Boal (1995). For concerns about effects on personal and social life, see Turkle (1995) and Stoll (1995).

On Internet costs: institutional costs for access can run to tens of thousands of dollars a year. For individuals, commercial on-line services (America Online, CompuServe, Prodigy, Microsoft Network, Netcom, The Well, etc.) are like little internets that can also provide access to the big Internet. They have different rate structures (usually $10 to $20/month) and keep adding new features.

For an overview of scientific communication, including the problem of costs, see Taubes (1996). Facing tens of thousands of research journals, librarians must see in electronic publishing a realistic solution to budget and shelf-space limitations.

The American Chemical Society (1155 Sixteenth St., NW, Washington, DC 20036) has a home page at http://www.acs.org and also a Publications Division with its own home page at http://www.pubs.acs.org. That division has published *The Internet: A Guide for Chemists* (Bachrach, 1995) but also a booklet titled *Will Science Publishing Perish?* On the ferment in Web technology and the explosion of new chemical information, see Krieger (1996). A recent special issue of *Science* on computers (August 2, 1996) was devoted to their use in biology; see Germain (1996). On ongoing developments in science communication, see Bloom (1996a, 1996b) and Lepkowski (1996).

The information on Christian colleges is from Crider (1995). The IVP Web page is at http://www.ivpress.com.

The ASA began with an Internet address and now has its own Web page. To interact with others on the ASA list, send an e-mail to majordomo@calvin.edu with "subscribe asa" in the body of your message. To get off the list, send an e-mail to the same address with "unsubscribe asa" in the message. For a HELP document for Majordomo software, send an e-mail to the same address with the word "help" in the message. To ASA's Web address at http://www.calvin.edu/chemistry/ASA/ add papers.html to get an index of selected papers from the journal, which can be read by adding PSCF.html to the basic ASA Web site string. Adding resources/index.html brings up a general listing of all you can reach through that site.

For assessments of the Internet in *The Real Issue,* see Vitz (1995), Gill (1995), Baker (1995) and Forsberg (1995). Baker pointed to the operation of ICLnet, established by the Institute for Christian Leadership, publisher of *Faculty Dialogue* (12753 SW 68th Ave., Suite 299, Tigard, OR 97223). ICLnet (http://www.iclnet.org/lu) is being used by Christian Leadership Ministries (CLM, 3440 Sojourn Drive, Suite 200, Carrollton, TX 75006) as a link between CLM staff and some eleven thousand faculty members who receive *The Real Issue*. The electronic address of *The Real Issue* archive is http://www.iclnet.org/clm/menus/ri.html.

The Real Issue for April/May 1996 included an interview with an engineering professor who makes use of the Internet to communicate with students in his courses, a page of recommended Web sites, an explanation of how Leadership University functions as a virtual campus, and a stirring challenge to academics to "adapt to the Internet or die" (Holtzman, 1996).

Close-Up 5: Good Company

McIntyre: For a profile of Jack McIntyre, see W. R. Hearn (1991a). See also McIntyre (1992). Charles Townes won the 1964 Nobel Prize in physics for inventing the maser (microwave amplification by stimulated emission of radiation) and laser (light amplification by stimulated emission of radiation). As an advisor to the secretary of defense in the 1980s, he served on a committee dealing with the MX missile. The quote is from Townes (1992, p. 5).

Schaefer: Soon after moving to Georgia, Fritz Schaefer made headlines by giving three extracurricular lectures showing that many scientists have believed in God and the Bible. When a professor charged that he had used a classroom illegally, the *Atlanta Constitution* aired the controversy. One story quoted Schaefer as saying that his most important discovery had come outside the laboratory when he became a Christian in 1973. Having taught at Berkeley, he was astonished that anyone in Georgia would think it illegal to express one's views on anything. Fritz concluded that his critics had labeled him a "creationist" simply because it was a pejorative term. For a sample of his views, see Schaefer (1994, 1995).

Burgus: Roger Burgus's chemical detective work in the heated race to identify hypothalamic peptides acting on the pituitary has been recounted by Nicholas Wade (1981). Nobelist Guillemin called Burgus "one of those people who are the salt of the earth; Burgus and honesty are the same word" (Wade, 1981, p. 112). Yet before Burgus left that group, he was treated not as a collaborator but as a competitor—because other endocrinologists began seeing him as "a mainstay of the Guillemin team" (Wade, p. 248).

Collins: At Michigan, Francis Collins was one of some sixty faculty and staff members signing their names to an Easter advertisement in the campus newspaper, attesting to faith in the historical resurrection of Jesus Christ. A profile in the University of Michigan alumni magazine quoted Collins as saying, "For me, science is the chance to discover something that no man has known before, but God has known all along. In some ways you can almost think of it as a form of worship" (Rogers, 1993).

Lincoln: Ken Lincoln worked with the Jet Propulsion Laboratory (JPL) group responsible for the instrument package on Galileo's Jupiter probe and in late 1995 helped celebrate Galileo's arrival "on target." Ken has long been active in IVCF and ASA activities in the San Francisco Bay Area.

Swearengen: On his return from Washington, D.C., Jack Swearengen worked on problems of safely dismantling atomic warheads. He has brought both a Christian perspective and technical expertise to his writings about nuclear weapons and arms control (Swearengen, 1992). He has engaged in friendly debate with those who think that Christians should have no part in weapons development, including his own son (Swearengen and Swearengen, 1990).

Kaita: Robert Kaita has written of opportunities his work has given him for Christian witness in the former Soviet Union and the People's Republic of China (Kaita, 1993). An *ASA Brief*, "The Search for a New Source of Energy from Nuclear Fusion" (September/October 1995 ASA newsletter), quoted Bob as saying that the idea that the universe has a designer "makes scientific research—the search for the rules established by that designer—a rational activity."

Everitt: Francis Everitt wrote a biography of James Clerk Maxwell, a "great Christian as well as a great nineteenth-century physicist" (Everitt, 1975). In an essay comparing science and religion (Everitt, 1991), Francis gave a positive and personal answer to Sir Nevill Mott's question, *Can a Scientist Believe?* (Mott, 1991).

Prance: On his forays into tropical forests Ghillean Prance encountered some missionaries oblivious to the ecological problems of the people they served, but praised those who sought to produce believers "able to thrive in their own native surroundings" (Prance, 1982). He is now on the editorial board of the Christian environmental magazine *Green Cross*. For his full story see Langmead (1995).

Walker: Laurence Walker has written that God understands the ecological succession that follows harvesting of forest products "better than His creatures seem to," adding: "Beauty will return. The cross was made of wood; so too was the manger" (Walker, 1990). See also Walker (1991) and the story of his life as a forester (Walker, 1995), dedicated to "The Faithful Friend who guided me all along The Way, though seldom was I aware of His presence." Larry has pastored two small country churches since stepping down from his deanship of the College of Forestry.

Page: For the story of Robert Page's technical contributions to radar, see Page (1962). A more recent article, "The Road to Radar," credited him with installing the Navy's first working radar gear, noting that as the seventh of nine children in a Minnesota family, Page "had first trained for the ministry but, on the urging of his college physics professor, transferred into science" (Chiles, 1987).

Everest: F. Alton Everest was awarded an honorary Doctor of Science degree in 1959 by Wheaton College in Illinois. Some of the films he produced for Moody Institute of Science (MIS) are still being shown around the world; much of their scientific footage is incorporated in a set of three one-hour video cassettes, *The Wonders of God's Creation* (available from MIS, 820 N. LaSalle St., Chicago, IL 60610). Everest, a founder and first president of ASA, edited *Modern Science and Christian Faith* (ASA, 1948), though his name did not appear on the cover. His *Master Handbook of Acoustics* (Everest, 1994) is in its third edition. For a profile, see W. R. Hearn (1988c).

Olsen: Kenneth Olsen has moved on to another company now, but during his leadership of DEC, *Fortune* magazine called him "America's most successful entrepreneur." His photo was on the cover (October 27, 1986) and the nine-page profile covered not only DEC's fortunes and Olsen's management style, but also his life as a Christian. Brought up in a conservative Christian home, Ken was president of his IVCF group as an electrical engineering student at the Massachusetts Institute of Technology. Ken said that as a young engineer his first "management experience" came from being given the task of supervising the Sunday school program of Park Street Church in Boston.

Hickernell: In 1987, on a tour of the People's Republic of China by ASA scientists, Fred Hickernell gave a seminar at the Optics Institute of the Academia Sinica, similar to our National Academy but maintaining research institutes all over China. In 1994 he was president of ASA.

Pike: Kenneth Pike has received honorary doctorates from many academic institutions, including the University of Chicago and René Descartes University at the Sorbonne. An account of his life up to 1981 (E. V. Pike, 1981) contained a seventeen-page bibliography of his writings. For an introduction to his theory of language, see K. L. Pike (1981, 1982). Ken's "home base" is the Summer Institute of Linguistics (SIL, 7500 W. Camp Wisdom Rd., Dallas, TX 75236). By 1995, SIL had over five thousand people working in Bible translation, literacy or linguistics in 1,355 languages in fifty countries.

Halver: In his preface to ASA's *Teaching Science in a Climate of Controversy,* John Halver said that if, instead of "just happening," the universe was created, "We can view ourselves as purposeful creatures bearing the stamp of God's intentions. Human life takes on a sacred dimension. We become obligated to treat each other with dignity and respect." Some other NAS members, upset that he had expressed his belief in the Creator in that public way, threatened to make an issue of it. Other NAS members came to his defense, especially those in the applied biology section who knew him well, so the issue never came up officially.

Griffiths: Robert Griffiths participated in a 1987 Consultation on "The Church and Contemporary Cosmology" that brought scientists and theologians together under auspices of the Presbyterian Church (USA). After some of the theologians expressed excitement over a paper on the status of quantum and statistical physics, Bob chided them for taking the metaphysical implications of quantum paradoxes more seriously than physicists do. For papers given at that consultation, see Miller and McCall (1990).

van der Ziel: Aldert van der Ziel once remarked that those who see the gradation from pure to applied science to engineering to technology as a kind of hierarchy generally put themselves at the top. Aldert accepted the idea of science as "the pursuit of truth" but considered that definition loaded because it suggested that only science is true. In his theological works (van der Ziel, 1960, 1965), following Karl Barth, he took a dim view of "natural theology." He looked instead to the Bible for God's revelation. For a profile, see W. R. Hearn (1991c).

Gingerich: For Owen Gingerich's Dwight Lecture in Christian Thought at the University of Pennsylvania, see Gingerich (1983); for his Gross Memorial Lecture at Valparaiso University, see Gingerich (1993). Having translated Johannes Kepler's *Astronomia nova* and other works, Owen sees Kepler's life as evidence that "an individual can be both a creative scientist and a believer in divine design in the universe," with motivation for research stemming "from a desire to trace God's handiwork" (Gingerich, 1994, p. 29).

Cole: At Berkeley, David Cole investigated the histone proteins associated with DNA in cell nuclei and served as a consultant in a study of ethical issues of the human genome project at the Center for Theology and the Natural Sciences (CTNS). He was also an active member of the board of New College Berkeley, an evangelical center for Christian studies.

Hoshiko: Tomuo Hoshiko has given papers at ASA annual meetings on a wide range of ethical issues, including the use of animals in biomedical research. His 1989 paper on "Forbidden Knowledge" asked whether any areas are, or should be, closed to scientific investigation.

Anderson: Elving Anderson teamed with a philosopher to produce a Christian ethic for biology (Reichenbach and Anderson, 1995), a book sponsored by the Institute for Advanced Christian Studies (IFACS) in a series called "Studies in a Christian World View." Elving has served on the IFACS board for many years. For a profile, see W. R. Hearn (1989b).

MacKay: Donald MacCrimmon MacKay, an editor of *Experimental Brain Research* and *International Handbook of Sensory Physiology,* was widely known for his arguments for "logical indeterminacy" as a basis for understanding human freedom. A seminal essay by MacKay (1965a) was included in his edited volume, *Christianity in a Mechanistic Universe* (1965b). Besides many significant books (MacKay, 1974, 1978, 1979, 1980), he contributed chapters to nearly fifty others. His thinking about science and Christian faith remained crisp—he wrote four articles in 1986 for the *Journal of the American Scientific Affiliation*—despite a brain tumor that killed him at age sixty-four in February 1987. A book based on his 1986 Gifford Lectures at the University of Edinburgh was edited posthumously by his wife Valerie (MacKay, 1991). For a critique, see Thorson (1992); for an appreciation of MacKay and a selected bibliography, see Haas (1992).

Bube: Richard Bube's editorships have included that of ASA's journal, where he served from 1968 to 1983. For some important works, see Bube (1968, 1971, 1985, 1995). At Stanford he mentored over fifty Ph.D. students and for twenty-five years also taught an undergraduate seminar on "Interactions Between Modern Science and Christianity" (Bube, 1989b). For a four-page version of his life, see W. R. Hearn (1990b); for a 530-page version, see Bube (1994).

Bradley: Engineer and materials scientist Walter Bradley might seem out of his field doing calculations on energy requirements for the origin of life, but he reasons that "if life began on its own from nonliving stuff, those materials had to obey the same laws as the materials I study" (quoted in W. R. Hearn, 1988b). So far, he says, there is simply no way to solve the "configurational entropy problem" to produce a realistic scenario for the origin of life. See Thaxton et al. (1984) and Bradley (1988). For his views on academic careers, see Bradley (1996).

Offner: David Offner's bionics textbook uses specific examples of "design in nature" to show students how to create systems fulfilling prescribed functions. Along with technical diagrams and equations are touches of whimsy, as in certain acronyms: GOD stands for "Grand Omni Designer"; NATURE for "Numerous Activities That Underline Ruler's Existence"; and ATHEIST for "Anyone That Himself Enthrones, Idolizing Self-generated Theories" (Offner, 1995).

Weiss: Kurt Weiss served on the councils of the Society for Experimental Biology and Medicine and the Gerontological Society, as president of the Southwestern Section of the American Physiological Society, and on the Governor of Oklahoma's Advisory Committee on Aging. At Oklahoma's medical school he was awarded the David Ross Boyd Professorship for "outstanding teaching and guidance of students." The A. Kurt Weiss Memorial Lectureship is now an annual event at the University of Oklahoma Health Sciences Center in Oklahoma City. Sponsored by the Christian Medical Coalition, the lectures challenge students and faculty with "the true basis for moral and ethical reasoning in medicine."

Dormer: Since his initial visit to Kenya, Kenneth Dormer has returned several times as an ASA representative on the board of the African Institute for Science, Research, Education, and Development (AISRED), organized by African Christians to work on some of the technical problems of their countries. Ken has encouraged his AISRED colleagues to make use of the Internet for information exchange, despite their extremely low-tech research environment. Ken was president of ASA in 1992.

Jones: Gareth Jones's book on coping with controversy (Jones, 1994) grew out of an unpleasant experience when an earlier book (Jones, 1984) was maligned as "pro-abortion." The book, mostly about other issues, stated the author's opposition to all abortions except in a very few cases under extreme conditions. Threats from an antiabortion activist group led to the book's withdrawal from the American market, though it was later picked up by another Christian publisher (Eerdmans). For details of the story, see Jones (1985). On other biomedical ethics issues, see Jones (1981, 1987).

Price: Martin Price keeps friends and supporters informed in *ECHO Update,* available on request (ECHO, 17430 Durrance Road, N. Ft. Myers, FL, 33917). *ECHO Development Notes* supplies information to agricultural workers in Third World countries; the fiftieth issue appeared in 1995.

Mills: Gordon Mills has written extensively about the complexity of biochemical systems. Molecular geneticists can trace variations in cytochrome-C structure from a "primitive" cytochrome, but the system producing that molecule in yeast cells seems no less intricate than the analogous system in humans. To Mills, although "nearly everything else can be explained in terms of natural causes," an "intelligent cause" must have come into play in cosmological and biological origins. See Mills (1992, 1994, 1995) and Mills and Kenyon (1996). For a profile, see W. R. Hearn (1991b).

Bohon: Part of Robert Bohon's job at 3M was to work with European counterparts on technical solutions to environmental problems. He was a charter member of a subcommittee on dangerous chemicals, part of the U.S. Business and Industry Advisory Council of the Organization for Economic Cooperation and Development (OECD). Musically gifted, Bob has been a violinist in the 3M company orchestra in addition to serving as choir director for his church. For a profile, see W. R. Hearn (1988e).

Lee: Chi-Hang Lee's book on *The Challenge of Science to Christianity* (in Chinese) includes over twenty of his essays (Lee, 1992). It was published in Taiwan but copies can be ordered from the author at 120 Brandywine Way, Walnut Creek, CA 94598. Chi-Hang Lee was president of ASA in 1982.

Hunt: Ann Hunt turned to full-time research after teaching at the college level and spending her summers in a National Science Foundation-sponsored program of research for college teachers. Before moving to Eli Lilly in 1978, she earned a Master of Theological Studies degree at Gordon-Conwell Theological Seminary in Massachusetts and was a research fellow at Harvard Medical School. For a profile, see W. R. Hearn (1989a).

Berg: Many of Marie Berg's early adventures were dreadful. Born in 1909, she lived through

World War I, terrible inflation and the rise of the Nazis. As a non-Aryan student, she had to be careful; people disappeared but no one dared talk about it lest they, too, be taken away. Marie got her Ph.D. just two weeks before it was too late; by then she had become a Christian, but to the Nazis she was a Jew. She worked in a shoe polish factory, improvising substitutes for ingredients no longer available. With escape routes blocked, she and her husband spent time in a "voluntary" work camp before relatives could get them out via Italy. Marie Berg's story makes the troubles of most young scientists in America today seem trivial.

Van Leeuwen: Mary Stewart Van Leeuwen has argued that Christian social scientists should consider a more "hermeneutic" or value-critical approach in their work (Van Leeuwen, 1988). Her books include works on the meaning of persons (Van Leeuwen, 1985) and the significance of gender (Van Leeuwen, 1990). For a biographical sketch and appreciation, see Bishop (1988).

Adeney: Miriam Adeney's Bookwriting Project has produced books by natives of the Philippines, Brazil, Nepal and India. She consults on communications strategies all over the world, including Africa and Eastern Europe, and has written several books applying Christian faith to practical problems (M. Adeney, 1984, 1987).

Myers: For some of David Myers's popular works, see Myers (1978, 1980, 1992). The 1978 book, subtitled *Psychological Research and Christian Belief,* was the first volume in a series sponsored by the Christian Association for Psychological Studies (CAPS). Myers and Jeeves (1987) is in the Through the Eyes of Faith series sponsored by what is now the Coalition for Christian Colleges and Universities (CCCU).

Jeeves: Malcolm Jeeves wrote a significant book based on papers given at the 1965 Oxford conference (Jeeves, 1969). For more recent works, see Jeeves (1976, 1994).

Lindquist: Stanley Lindquist is now director emeritus of Link Care Center, which continues to offer psychological services to missionary-sending groups and to help "recycle" troubled missionaries. A newsletter, *Heartbeat,* is free on request (Link Care Center, 1734 W. Shaw Ave., Fresno, CA 93711). For a profile, see W. R. Hearn (1988d).

Moberg: David Moberg has focused on the spiritual quality of human nature, trying to quantify certain aspects of it (1967a-b). Many of his three hundred or so publications deal with the relationship between spiritual maturity and aging (e.g., Moberg, 1995). Moberg has authored several books (Moberg, 1965, 1979, 1985).

Behe: Biochemist Michael Behe says that believers in the theory of materialistic evolution have gone beyond what the data warrant to build "a great edifice of pseudo-knowledge which, like cotton candy, is spun from a little bit of sugar and a lot of air" (Buell and Hearn, 1994, p. 149). For more, see Behe (1994) and especially Behe (1996).

Epstein: Chemist Michael Epstein has been active in a Washington, D.C., group affiliated with the Committee for the Scientific Investigation of Claims of the Paranormal (CSICOP, publishers of *Skeptical Inquirer*). Seeing my published note (which identified me as an ASA member) in *SI* about a weird claim I had encountered, Mike wrote to me, introducing himself as a fellow Christian interested in exposing pseudoscience.

Cantore: Enrico Cantore founded the Institute for Scientific Humanism in 1974 at Fordham University, adding the term "World" in 1980. WISH has challenged scientists to offer the world more than technical competence, namely the humane values of true science. "Sapiential attitude" is Cantore's equivalent of biblical wisdom, characterized by realistic experiential openness, attentive reflection, and respectful response, with Jesus Christ as our exemplar of true wisdom (Cantore, 1985). See also Enrico's magnum opus (Cantore, 1977).

Young: Davis Young was a founder and first president of the Affiliation of Christian Geologists. Besides his own books (Young, 1977, 1982, 1995), he has contributed to other works critical of "scientific creationism" (Van Till, et al., 1988, 1990). He argues that an old-earth interpretation of Genesis 1—3 should not be seen as an accommodation to modern science, since in the fifth century Augustine was already open to that interpretation (Young, 1988). For a profile, see W. R. Hearn (1989c).

Wonderly: Daniel Wonderly's books focus exclusively on sedimentary evidence for an ancient earth because young-earth creationists, to whom they are addressed, do not trust radiometric dating methods (Wonderly, 1977, 1987).

Mixter: Russell L. Mixter edited ASA's "Darwin Centennial" volume (Mixter, 1959). For an account of his long career, see the paper profiling him presented at ASA's 50th anniversary meeting at Wheaton College (Chappell, 1992).

Brand: Raymond Brand served on the faculty committee guiding the Human Needs and Global Resources (HNGR) program at Wheaton. At ASA's 1985 Oxford conference, Ray urged all scientists to serve the needs of people in less developed countries (Brand, 1987). Sheaffer and Brand (1980) was an early effort to raise the environmental consciousness of Christians, which Ray has continued to stir as one of the *al.* in Van Dyke et al. (1996). For a profile, see W. R. Hearn (1990a).

Wilcox: David Wilcox once paraphrased Theodosius Dobzhansky's famous dictum ("Nothing in biology makes sense apart from evolution") by arguing that nothing in evolutionary biology makes sense apart from the will of God. "Science has proved neither that the material universe is undirected, nor that our material explanations are adequate" (Wilcox, 1994, p. 205). Dave has emphasized that the information coded on DNA, not DNA itself, is the essence of life (Wilcox, 1989). His range of interests includes paleoanthropology (Wilcox, 1996).

Van Till: Howard Van Till has coauthored several collaborative works (Van Till et al., 1988, 1990) besides writing a book of his own (Van Till, 1986). He has argued for the "functional integrity of the universe" in a number of articles, including "When Faith and Reason Meet" (Van Till, 1993), originally published as "Is Special Creationism a Heresy?" in *Christian Scholar's Review.*

Maatman: Russell Maatman has seen one of his books, *The Bible, Natural Science, and Evolution* (Maatman, 1980), translated into Korean, Russian and Ukrainian. See also Maatman (1978, 1985).

Hartzler: Harold Hartzler is regarded as a patriarch of ASA for his faithful attendance, loyal service and general enthusiasm for Christian fellowship in the sciences. He was ASA's first executive secretary. Three of his papers dealt with ASA history (Hartzler, 1955, 1983, 1985).

Flora: Marilyne Flora has raised two daughters with her physicist husband Bob; Bob's brother Stephen does software design for the family enterprise (W. R. Hearn, 1990c). The Physiogrip for measuring muscle functions and Cardiocomp for electrocardiograms are two products available from Intellitool (P. O. Box 459, Batavia, IL 60510).

Martin: Helen Martin has served on the Board of Directors of the National Board for Professional Teaching Standards and was saluted as an outstanding teacher in ASA's *Teaching Science in a Climate of Controversy.*

Zipf: Elizabeth Zipf has been president of the Council of Biology Editors and secretary-general of the International Federation of Scientific Editors' Associations. She has also been active in various organizations of women in science.

Lepkowski: Wil Lepkowski went to Bhopal, India, in 1985 to report the aftermath of a chemical plant explosion that killed at least 1,800 people and affected probably a third of the city's one million inhabitants. He followed up with a 1988 story on litigation winding its way through the courts. Wil has reported many of the trends affecting science in the 1990s (Lepkowski, 1991, 1996).

Ehlers: Vernon Ehlers participated in the initial year (1977-1978) of the Calvin Center for Christian Scholarship, which produced *Earthkeeping* (Wilkinson, 1980). Revised and retitled (Wilkinson, 1995), it is a biblically based call for responsible environmental stewardship. As ASA keynoter in 1987, Michigan state senator Vernon Ehlers spoke on "applied earthkeeping." He had learned that writing reasonable environmental laws and getting them passed was much harder than merely standing up for the right principles.

Frost: At Baylor, Robert Frost (not the poet) and I often brown-bagged our lunches in his lab or mine, praying together and speaking of our faith, sometimes with medical or graduate students. After "hanging up his lab coat," one of Bob's books on the Spirit-filled life was titled *The Biology of the Holy Spirit* (Frost, 1975).

Thaxton: Charles Thaxton reports that students in countries formerly behind the iron curtain tend to know only what communist propaganda taught them, including the idea that science is the enemy of Christian belief. They are surprised to learn from such sources as Pearcey and Thaxton (1994) of Christianity's role in inspiring the development of science. That book and Thaxton, et al. (1984) have been translated into several eastern European languages.

Allen: Gary Allen's scientific credentials have gained him respect among UN diplomats from many countries, including countries closed to Christian missionaries. They see that if Gary gave up work in which he was making a name for himself, what he gave it up for must be important.

Ross: Hugh Ross did postdoctoral research on quasars and galaxies at the California Institute of Technology before beginning his evangelistic ministry, Reasons to Believe, in the mid-1980s at Sierra Madre Congregational Church. His positive spin on scientific discoveries strengthens biblical faith and points unbelievers to God's power and majesty (Ross, 1989, 1996). Hugh has proposed holding a council like those of the early church to face the issue of the age of the earth (Ross, 1994). A catalog of publications and the quarterly *Facts & Faith* are available on request (RTB, P.O. Box 5978, Pasadena, CA 91117).

Russell: Robert Russell is an ordained minister in the United Church of Christ (Congregational) who has written extensively on the impact of quantum physics and cosmology on theology (R. J. Russell, 1988, 1989). For the story of Bob's personal integrative pilgrimage, reprinted from the Autumn 1988 *CTNS Bulletin,* see R. J. Russell (1990).

Newman: Robert Newman has an M.Div. and S.T.M. in Old Testament. In an interview (Barrett and Fisher, 1984, pp. 119-30), Newman spoke of his debt to pastor Herman J. Eckelmann Jr., with whom he published an interpretation of Genesis in 1977 (Newman and Eckelmann, 1989). Eckelmann, an electrical engineer who worked at Cornell University's Center for Radiophysics and Space Research while pastoring Faith Bible Church of Ithaca, led to Christ many students of science and engineering and influenced many to turn to specifically Christian work. IBRI, which Newman directs, sponsors symposia and publishes monographs on science/faith issues; catalog available on request (IBRI, P.O. Box 423, Hatfield, PA 19440). See Newman (1988, 1995).

Dembski: William Dembski frequently brings philosophical arguments to bear against scientisms (Dembski, 1990, 1994, 1996). Dembski is an associate editor of the new journal *Origins & Design.*

Neidhardt: Jim Neidhardt, on his "theological sabbatical," traced similarities in the work of physicist Niels Bohr (1885-1962) and theologian Karl Barth (1886-1968), who, though unaware of each other, both seemed to be influenced by Søren Kierkegaard (Neidhardt, 1986). For his appreciation of theologian Thomas Torrance, see Neidhardt (1989). See also Loder and Neidhardt (1992).

Pursey: Barbara Pursey serves on the board of the Presbyterian Association on Science, Technology, and the Christian Faith. She and her husband Derek, who remains active in collaborative physics research after retiring from Iowa State University, have both participated in ecumenical round tables on science and faith.

Murphy: George Murphy has been a prolific writer on science and Christian faith at both scholarly and popular levels. For his adult religious education materials on taking science seriously, see G. L. Murphy (1986). See also G. L. Murphy (1991, 1996).

Herrmann: Robert Herrmann spent three years in postdoctoral research at the Massachusetts Institute of Technology before replacing Isaac Asimov at Boston University's School of Medicine (when Asimov left biochemistry to become a full-time writer). In 1976 Herrmann moved to Oklahoma to help Oral Roberts University establish its schools of medicine and dentistry. In an interview, Bob told of his Christian motivation for studying the effects of aging on DNA (Barrett and Fisher, 1984, pp. 164-171). See Templeton and Herrmann (1989, 1994).

Munro: Don Munro was chair of the Houghton College biology department when he resigned in 1994 to become ASA's executive director. Like his predecessor Bob Herrmann, he is interested in biomedical ethics and is also an adjunct professor of biology at Gordon College and advisor to premedical students.

Barclay: For many years Oliver Barclay was general secretary of InterVarsity Fellowship in England. His empirical approach was evident in a book of apologetics he wrote for university students (Barclay, 1974).

Hummel: Charles Hummel took a novel approach in his book on the history of science (the story of Galileo), using that history to lay a groundwork for resolving present conflicts between science and the Bible (Hummel, 1986). The book includes a tribute to French mathematician and physicist Blaise Pascal (1623-1662) as an exemplar of personal integration of faith and scientific work.

Morrison: Terry Morrison took over IVCF's faculty ministries in 1990. He travels extensively, encouraging faculty at universities all over the United States to serve Christ wholeheartedly in professional work and in witness to colleagues and students. Terry welcomes examples of creativity in those areas for updating IVCF's "Models of Ministry."

Templeton: Born in Tennessee, John Templeton now lives in Nassau and holds British citizenship. A business college he endowed at Oxford is named for him and he has been knighted by the Queen of England. For a biography and account of the first Templeton prizes, see Proctor (1983). On "Humility Theology" see an appendix in Templeton (1995). The Templeton Foundation continues to invest in creative projects to stimulate the interaction of science and religion. For a description of programs, see Templeton (1995, pp. 129-39). For current information on lectureships, awards for papers, courses in science and religion, etc., request the bimonthly *Progress in Theology* (P.O. Box 797, Ipswich, MA 01938). Wiener (1995) took a jaundiced view of the Science and Religion Course Program.

Suppe: John Suppe is one of several Christian professors at Princeton interviewed by Thomas Woodward, a Princeton alumnus, in a video called *The Princeton Chronicles* distributed by the Foundation for Thought and Ethics (FTE, P.O. Box 830721, Richardson, TX 75083). In that video John and his colleagues explain how they came to believe in Jesus Christ and how they bring their faith and academic work together. For John Suppe's views on theism and naturalism, see Suppe (1996).

References Cited

Some Abbreviations

AAAS	American Association for the Advancement of Science
ASA	American Scientific Affiliation
ASA-CISE	ASA Committee for Integrity in Science Education
CCCU	Coalition for Christian Colleges and Universities
JASA	Journal of the American Scientific Affiliation
NAS	National Academy of Sciences
NAS-COSAC	NAS Committee on Science and Creationism
NAS-COSEPUP	NAS Committee on Science, Engineering and Public Policy
PSCF	*Perspectives on Science and Christian Faith*

Adeney, B. 1995. *Strange Virtues: Ethics in a Multicultural World.* Downers Grove, Ill.: InterVarsity Press.

Adeney, M. 1984. *God's Foreign Policy: Practical Ways to Help the World's Poor.* Grand Rapids, Mich.: Eerdmans.

————. 1987. *A Time for Risking: Priorities for Women.* Portland, Ore.: Multnomah Press.

American Men and Women of Science. 1995-1996. 17th ed. New York: Bowker.

Arveson, P., and W. Hearn. 1979. "God and the Scientists: Reflections on the Big Bang." *Radix* 11 (July/August): 9-14.

ASA. 1948. *Modern Science and Christian Faith: The Christian Student's Science Symposium.* Wheaton, Ill.: Van Kampen. 2nd ed. 1950. Wheaton, Ill.: Scripture Press.

————. 1992. *Contemporary Issues on Science and Christian Faith: An Annotated Bibliography.* Ipswich, Mass.: ASA.

ASA-CISE. 1986. *Teaching Science in a Climate of Controversy: A View from the American Scientific Affiliation.* Ipswich, Mass.: ASA. 4th ed. 1993.

Asimov, I. 1976. *Isaac Asimov's Biographical Encyclopedia of Science and Technology.* New York: Avon.

Atkinson, D. 1990. *The Message of Genesis 1—11.* Downers Grove, Ill.: InterVarsity Press.

Bachrach, S. M., ed. 1995. *The Internet: A Guide for Chemists.* Washington, D.C.: American Chemical Society.

Baker, J. W. 1995. "Crossroads on the Electronic Highway." *The Real Issue* 14 (November/December): 8-11.

Banks, R. 1984. *The Tyranny of Time.* Downers Grove, Ill.: InterVarsity Press.

Barbour, I. G. 1960. *Christianity and the Scientist.* New York: Association Press.

————. 1968a. *Issues in Science and Religion.* Englewood Cliffs, N.J.: Prentice-Hall.

————, ed. 1968b. *Science and Religion: New Perspectives on the Dialogue.* New York: Harper.

————. 1974. *Myths, Models and Paradigms.* New York: Harper & Row.

————. 1980. *Technology, Environment and Human Values.* New York: Praeger.

————. 1990. *Religion in an Age of Science.* San Francisco: Harper & Row.

————. 1991. *Ethics in an Age of Technology.* San Francisco: Harper & Row.

Barclay, O. R. 1974. *Reasons for Faith.* Downers Grove, Ill.: InterVarsity Press.

Barr, S. M. 1995. "The Atheism of the Gaps." *First Things* 57 (November): 50-53.

Barrett, E. C., and D. Fisher, eds. 1984. *Scientists Who Believe.* Chicago: Moody Press.

Bauman, M., ed. 1993. *Man and Creation: Perspectives on Science and Theology.* Hillsdale, Mich.: Hillsdale College Press.

Behe, M. J. 1994. "Experimental Support for Regarding Functional Classes of Proteins To Be Highly Isolated from Each Other." In *Darwinism: Science or Philosophy?* ed. J. Buell and V. Hearn, pp. 60-71. Richardson, Tex.: Foundation for Thought and Ethics.

———. 1996. *Darwin's Black Box: The Biochemical Challenge to Evolution.* New York: Free Press.

Bergman, J. 1993. "Censorship in Secular Science: The Mims Case." *PSCF* 45 (March): 37-43.

Berland, T. 1962. *The Scientific Life.* New York: Coward-McCann.

Bernbaum, J. A., and S. M. Steer. 1986. *Why Work? Careers and Employment in Biblical Perspective.* Grand Rapids, Mich.: Baker.

Berry, R. J., ed. 1991. *Real Science, Real Faith.* Eastbourne, England: Monarch.

Beveridge, W. I. B. 1957. *The Art of Scientific Investigation.* New York: Random House.

Bishop, D. R. 1988. "Integrating Psychology and Christianity: A Biographical Sketch of Mary Stewart Van Leeuwen." *PSCF* 40 (December): 229-31.

Blaiklock, E. M., ed. 1971. *Why I Am Still a Christian.* Grand Rapids, Mich.: Zondervan.

Bloom, F. E. 1996a. "Refining the On-line Scholar's Tools." *Science* 271 (January 26): 429.

———. 1996b. "An Enhanced Perspective." *Science* 271 (February 9): 741.

Boulding, K. E. 1980. "Our Common Heritage." *Science* 207 (February 22): 831-36.

Braben, D. 1994. *To Be a Scientist.* New York: Oxford University Press.

Bradley, W. L. 1988. "Thermodynamics and the Origin of Life." *PSCF* 40 (June): 72-83.

———. 1996. "The Calling of a Christian Professor." *The Real Issue* 15 (September/October): 2-5.

Brand, R. H. 1987. "At the Point of Need." *PSCF* 39 (March): 2-8.

Bray, G. 1984. *Creeds, Councils and Christ.* Leicester, England: Inter-Varsity Press.

Brennan, M. B. 1996. "Women Chemists Reconsidering Careers at Research Universities." *Chemical & Engineering News* 74 (June 10): 8-15.

Broad, W., and N. Wade. 1982. *Betrayers of the Truth: Fraud and Deceit in the Halls of Science.* New York: Simon & Schuster.

Brockman, J. 1995. *The Third Culture.* New York: Simon & Schuster.

Brook, J., and I. A. Boal, eds. 1995. *Resisting the Virtual Life: The Culture and Politics of Information.* San Francisco: City Lights Books.

Brush, S. G. 1991. "Women in Science and Engineering." *American Scientist* 79 (September/October): 404-19.

Bube, R. H., ed. 1968. *The Encounter Between Christianity and Science.* Grand Rapids, Mich.: Eerdmans.

———. 1971. *The Human Quest: A New Look at Science and Christian Faith.* Waco, Tex.: Word.

———. 1985. *Science and the Whole Person.* Ipswich, Mass.: ASA.

———. 1987. "On the Pursuit of Excellence: Pitfalls in the Effort To Become No. 1." *PSCF* 39 (June): 67-76.

———. 1989a. "So You Want to Be a Science Professor? The Education Business: Things My Mother Never Taught Me." *PSCF* 41 (September): 143-51.

———. 1989b. "Obtaining Approval for a Seminar on Science and Christianity in a Secular University: A Case Study." *PSCF* 41 (December): 206-12.

———. 1991. "How Can a Scientist Be a Christian in Today's World?" In *Can Scientists Believe?* ed. N. Mott, pp. 109-20. London: James & James.

———. 1994. *One Whole Life: The Personal Memoirs of Richard H. Bube.* Privately printed by author (753 Mayfield Ave., Stanford, CA 94305).

———. 1995. *Putting It All Together: Seven Patterns for Relating Science and the Christian Faith.* Lanham, Md.: University Press of America.

Buber, M. 1970. *I and Thou.* Trans. W. Kaufman. New York: Scribner.

Buell, J., and V. Hearn, eds. 1994. *Darwinism: Science or Philosophy?* Richardson, Tex.: Foundation for Thought and Ethics.

Bullock, W. L. 1988. "Scientists Decry a Slick New Packaging of Creationism: A Reply to William Bennetta." *PSCF* 40 (September): 165-7.

Bush, V. 1945. *Science, the Endless Frontier.* Reprint New York: Arno, 1980.

Calvin, J. 1948. *Calvin's Commentaries on the Book of Genesis.* Grand Rapids, Mich.: Eerdmans.

Cantore, E. 1977. *Scientific Man: The Humanistic Significance of Science.* New York: ISH Publications.

———. 1985. "The Christic Origination of Science." *PSCF* 37 (December): 211-22.

Capon, R. F. 1967. "The Secular and the Sacred." *America* (March 4): 307-12. Reprinted in *The Sacred and the Secular,* ed. M. J. Taylor. Englewood Cliffs, N.J.: Prentice-Hall, 1968.

Carr, J. 1992. *The Art of Science: A Practical Guide to Experiments, Observations and Handling Data.* San Diego, Calif.: Hightext.

Chalk, R., ed. 1988. *Science, Technology and Society: Emerging Relationships.* Washington, D.C.: AAAS.

Chappell, D. F. 1992. "Christian, Teacher, Scientist, Mentor: Dr. Russell L. Mixter, Visionary for the Role of Science in Christian Higher Education." *PSCF* 44 (March): 10-16.

Chiles, J. R. 1987. "The Road to Radar." *American Heritage of Invention & Technology* (Spring): 24-30.

Clareson, T. D. 1961. *Science and Society: Midcentury Readings.* New York: Harper.

Clark, R. E. D. 1950. *Darwin: Before and After—The Story of Evolution.* London: Paternoster. First pub. 1948.

———. 1958. *Creation.* London: Tyndale Press. First pub. 1946.

———. 1960. *Christian Belief and Science: A Reconciliation and a Partnership.* London: English Universities Press.

———. 1961. *The Universe: Plan or Accident? The Religious Implications of Modern Science.* London: Paternoster. First pub. 1949.

———. 1967. *The Christian Stake in Science.* London: Paternoster.

Clarke, W. N. 1988. "Is a Natural Theology Still Possible Today?" In *Physics, Philosophy and Theology: A Common Quest for Understanding,* ed. R. J. Russell, W. R. Stoeger and G. V. Coyne, pp. 103-23. Notre Dame, Ind.: University of Notre Dame Press.

Cobern, W. W. 1988. "A Values Framework for Teaching Global Science." *PSCF* 40 (December): 204-9.

Coulson, C. A. 1956. *Science and Christian Belief.* New York: Oxford University Press. First pub. 1955.

———. 1960. *Science, Technology and the Christian.* New York: Abingdon.

Cox, H. 1965. *The Secular City.* New York: Macmillan.

———. 1968. "The Christian in a World of Technology." In *Science and Religion: New Perspectives on the Dialogue,* ed. I. G. Barbour, pp. 261-80. New York: Harper.

Cramer, J. A. 1985. "Science, Scientism and Christianity: The Ideas of D. M. MacKay." *JASA* 37 (September): 142-8.

Cramer, J. A., and D. M. MacKay. 1976. "Dialogue: *The Clockwork Image* Controversy." *JASA* 28 (September): 123-5.

Crider, S. 1995. "Cruising the Infobahn—Christian Colleges Get 'Wired.' " *The News* (a publication of CCCU), April, p. 1.

Darwin, C. 1859. *On the Origin of Species by Means of Natural Selection, or the Preservation of Favoured Races in the Struggle for Life.* Facsimile ed., Cambridge, Mass.: Harvard

University Press, 1975.

———. 1892. *The Autobiography of Charles Darwin and Selected Letters,* ed. F. Barlow. Reprint. New York: Dover, 1958.

Davies, P. C. 1992. *The Mind of God: The Scientific Basis for a Rational World.* New York: Simon & Schuster.

Dawkins, R. 1976. *The Selfish Gene.* New York: Oxford University Press.

———. 1986. *The Blind Watchmaker.* New York: W. W. Norton.

———. 1996. *Climbing Mount Improbable.* New York: W. W. Norton.

Dayton, D. W., and R. K. Johnston. 1992. *The Variety of American Evangelicalism.* Downers Grove, Ill.: InterVarsity Press.

Dembski, W. A. 1990. "Converting Matter into Mind: Alchemy and the Philosopher's Stone in Cognitive Science." *PSCF* 42 (December): 202-26.

———. 1994. "The Incompleteness of Scientific Naturalism." In *Darwinism: Science or Philosophy?* ed. J. Buell and V. Hearn, pp. 79-94. Richardson, Tex.: Foundation for Thought and Ethics.

———. 1996. "Teaching Intelligent Design as Religion or Science?" *The Princeton Theological Review* 3 (May): 14-18.

Dennett, D. C. 1995. *Darwin's Dangerous Idea: Evolution and the Meanings of Life.* New York: Simon & Schuster.

Denton, M. 1985. *Evolution: A Theory in Crisis.* London: Burnett.

Dickerson, R. E. 1992. "The Game of Science: Reflections After Arguing with Some Rather Overwrought People." *PSCF* 44 (June): 137-38.

Dowley, T., ed. 1977. *Eerdmans Handbook to the History of Christianity.* Grand Rapids, Mich.: Eerdmans.

Drake, S. 1978. *Galileo at Work: His Scientific Biography.* Chicago: University of Chicago Press.

Draper, J. W. 1875. *History of the Conflict between Religion and Science.* New York: Appleton.

Ellul, J. 1964. *The Technological Society.* Trans. J. Wilkinson. New York: Knopf.

———. 1980. *The Technological System.* Trans. J. Neugroschel. New York: Continuum.

———. 1990. *The Technological Bluff.* Trans. G. W. Bromiley. Grand Rapids, Mich.: Eerdmans.

Elmer, D. 1994. *Cross-Cultural Conflict: Building Relationships for Effective Ministries.* Downers Grove, Ill.: InterVarsity Press.

Everest, F. A. 1994. *Master Handbook of Acoustics.* 3rd ed. Blue Ridge Summit, Penn.: TAB Books.

Everitt, C. W. F. 1975. *James Clerk Maxwell: Physicist and Natural Philosopher.* New York: Scribner.

———. 1991. "Faith and Mystery in Science, Reason and Scepticism in Religion." In *Can Scientists Believe?* ed. N. Mott, pp. 163-78. London: James & James.

Ferngren, G. B., and R. L. Numbers. 1996. "C. S. Lewis on Creation and Evolution: The Acworth Letters, 1944-1960." *PSCF* 48 (March): 28-33.

Feshbach, M., and A. Friendly Jr. 1992. *Ecocide in the USSR: Health and Nature under Siege.* New York: Basic Books.

Forsberg, G. E. 1995. "Working with Students in a Technological Age." *The Real Issue* 14 (November/December): 12-14.

Frey, R. 1986. "Semantic Problems in the Creation-Evolution Debate." *JASA* 38 (September): 206-7.

Frost, R. C. 1975. *The Biology of the Holy Spirit.* Tappan, N.J.: Fleming H. Revell.

Frye, R. M., ed. 1983. *Is God a Creationist? The Religious Case Against Creation Science.* New York: Scribner.

Gates, B., with N. Myhrvold and P. Rinearson. 1995. *The Road Ahead.* New York: Viking.

Geisler, N. L., and J. K. Anderson. 1987. *Origin Science: A Proposal for the Creation-Evolution*

Controversy. Grand Rapids, Mich.: Baker.

Germain, E. 1996. "Fast Lanes on the Internet." *Science* 273 (August 2): 585-88.

Ghiselin, B., ed. 1955. *The Creative Process*. New York: Mentor.

————. 1963a. "Ultimate Criteria for Two Levels of Creativity." In *Scientific Creativity: Its Recognition and Development*, ed. C. W. Taylor and F. Barron, pp. 30-43. New York: Wiley.

————. 1963b. "The Creative Process and Its Relation to the Identification of Creative Talent." In *Scientific Creativity: Its Recognition and Development*, ed. C. W. Taylor and F. Barron, pp. 355-64. New York: Wiley.

Gilkey, L. 1985. *Creationism on Trial: Evolution and God at Little Rock*. Minneapolis: Winston.

Gill, D. W. 1989. *The Opening of the Christian Mind: Taking Every Thought Captive to Christ*. Downers Grove, Ill.: InterVarsity Press.

————. 1995. "The Moral Character of Means and Ends." *The Real Issue* 14 (November/December): 4-7.

Gingerich, O. 1983. "Let There Be Light: Modern Cosmogony and Biblical Creation." In *Is God a Creationist? The Religious Case Against Creation Science*, ed. R. M. Frye, pp. 119-37. New York: Scribner.

————. 1993. "Where in the World Is God?" In *Man and Creation: Perspectives on Science and Theology*, ed. M. Bauman, pp. 209-29. Hillsdale, Mich.: Hillsdale College Press.

————. 1994. "Dare a Scientist Believe in Design?" In *Evidence of Purpose: Scientists Discover the Creator*, ed. J. M. Templeton, pp. 21-32. New York: Continuum.

Gorman, C. 1991. "The Double Take on Dioxin." *Time*, August 26, p. 52.

Gould, S. J. 1992. "Impeaching a Self-Appointed Judge." *Scientific American* 267 (July): 118-20.

Gratzer, W. 1989. *A Literary Companion to Science*. New York: Norton.

Greene, J. C. 1959. *The Death of Adam: Evolution and Its Impact on Western Thought*. Ames: Iowa State University Press.

————. 1961. *Darwin and the Modern World View*. Baton Rouge: Louisiana State University Press.

Gross, P. R., and N. Levitt. 1994. *Higher Superstition: The Academic Left and Its Quarrels with Science*. Baltimore: Johns Hopkins University Press.

Haas, J. W., Jr. 1983a. "Complementarity and Christian Thought—an Assessment: The Classical Complementarity of Niels Bohr." *JASA* 35 (September): 145-51.

————. 1983b. "Complementarity and Christian Thought—an Assessment: Logical Complementarity." *JASA* 35 (December): 203-9.

————. 1986. "Integrity in Science: A Christian Response." *JASA* 38 (September): 204-6.

————. 1992. "Donald MacCrimmon MacKay (1922-1987): A View from the Other Side of the Atlantic." *PSCF* 44 (March): 55-60.

Haddam, J. 1996. "Art, Reason and Reality." *Skeptical Inquirer* 20 (September/October): 57-59.

Hamman, P. E., ed. 1985. *The Sacred in a Secular Age*. Berkeley: University of California Press.

Hanson, R. W., ed. 1986. *Science and Creation: Geological, Theological and Educational Perspectives*. Issues in Science and Technology (AAAS series). New York: Macmillan.

Harris, S. 1989. *Einstein Simplified: Cartoons on Science and Scientists*. New Brunswick, N.J.: Rutgers University Press.

————. 1990. *You Want Proof, I'll Give You Proof: Sidney Harris Laughs at Science*. San Francisco: W. H. Freeman.

————. 1992. *Chalk Up Another One: The Best of Sidney Harris*. Washington, D.C.: AAAS.

Hartzler, H. H. 1955. "The American Scientific Affiliation: History and Purposes." *JASA* 7 (September): 3-5.

————. 1983. "The Relationship Between the American Scientific Affiliation and the Creation Research Society." *JASA* 35 (June): 107-9.

————. 1985. "Forty Years with ASA." *JASA* 37 (June): 2-6.

Hatfield, C., ed. 1973. *The Scientist and Ethical Decision*. Downers Grove, Ill.: InterVarsity Press.

Hawking, S. W. 1988. *A Brief History of Time*. New York: Bantam.

Hayes, B. 1996. "The End of Science Writing?" *American Scientist* 84 (September/October): 495-96.

Haynes, R. D. 1994. *From Faust to Strangelove: Representations of the Scientist in Western Literature*. Baltimore: Johns Hopkins University Press.

Hearn, V. 1974. *What They Did Right: Reflections on Parents by Their Children*. Wheaton, Ill.: Tyndale House.

―――. 1989. "God Language: Some Personal Reflections." *Catalyst: A Forum for Scriptural Christianity Within the United Methodist Church*, March, p. 2.

Hearn, W. R. 1968. "Biological Science." In *The Encounter between Christianity and Science*, ed. R. H. Bube, pp. 199-223. Grand Rapids, Mich.: Eerdmans.

―――. 1971. "A Biochemist Shares His Faith." In *Why I Am Still a Christian*, ed. E. M. Blaiklock, pp. 64-80. Grand Rapids, Mich.: Zondervan.

―――. 1972. "Chemistry." In *Christ and the Modern Mind*, ed. R. W. Smith, pp. 273-84. Downers Grove, Ill.: InterVarsity Press.

―――. 1973. "Whole People and Half Truths." In *The Scientist and Ethical Decision*, ed. C. Hatfield, pp. 83-96. Downers Grove, Ill.: InterVarsity Press.

―――. 1988a. "Where Can Truth Be Found?" *Radix* 18, no. 3: 8-11, 27-30.

―――. 1988b. "Texas Professor Probes Life's Mystery: Walter L. Bradley." *Search* 1 in *PSCF* 40 (March): 32, insert.

―――. 1988c. "For Half a Century, He's Figured Out How: F. Alton Everest." *Search* 2 in *PSCF* 40 (June): 96, insert.

―――. 1988d. "He Put Psychology to Work for Missions: Stanley E. Lindquist." *Search* 3 in *PSCF* 40 (September): 160, insert.

―――. 1988e. "He Works (and Plays) in Industry: Robert L. Bohon." *Search* 4 in *PSCF* 40 (December): 224, insert.

―――. 1989a. "She Solves Chemical Puzzles: Ann H. Hunt." *Search* 5 in *PSCF* 41 (March): 32, insert.

―――. 1989b. "He Tracks Inherited Diseases: V. Elving Anderson." *Search* 6 in *PSCF* 41 (September): 160, insert.

―――. 1989c. "He's Still a 'Rock-Hound': Davis A. Young." *Search* 7 in *PSCF* 41 (December): 224, insert.

―――. 1990a. "He Cares About God's Creatures: Raymond H. Brand." *Search* 8 in *PSCF* 42 (March): 36, insert.

―――. 1990b. "He's Fond of Photons: Richard H. Bube." *Search* 10 in *PSCF* 42 (September): 168, insert.

―――. 1990c. "A Born Biology Teacher: Marilyne Sally Flora." *Search* 11 in *PSCF* 42 (December): 232, insert.

―――. 1991a. "From Atom Smashing to Nuclear Medicine: John A. McIntyre." *Search* 12 in *PSCF* 43 (March): 32, insert.

―――. 1991b. "Biochemist Known for 'Humanity, Scholarship, Research': Gordon C. Mills." *Search* 13 in *PSCF* 43 (June): 128, insert.

―――. 1991c. "Physicist, Engineer, Biblical Scholar: Aldert van der Ziel." *Search* 14 in *PSCF* 43 (September): 158, insert.

―――. 1991d. "Science, Selves and Stories." *CTNS Bulletin* 11 (Spring): 26-31.

―――. 1992a. "Scientific Gamesmanship." *PSCF* 44 (June): 138-39.

―――. 1992b. "Review of *Darwin on Trial*." *CTNS Bulletin* 12 (Winter): 33-36.

―――. 1993. "Reprise" (poem). *Radix* 22, no. 1: 31.

―――. 1994. "Evidence of Purpose in the Universe." In *Evidence of Purpose: Scientists*

Discover the Creator, ed. J. M. Templeton, pp. 57-69. New York: Continuum.

Hearn, W. R., and R. A. Hendry. 1959. "The Origin of Life." In *Evolution and Christian Thought Today,* ed. R. L. Mixter, pp. 53-70. Grand Rapids, Mich.: Eerdmans.

Hefley, J. C. 1967. *Adventurers with God: Fifteen Scientists Share Their Christian Faith.* Grand Rapids, Mich.: Zondervan.

Holden, C. 1991. "Career Trends for the '90s." "Science Careers," pull-out section in *Science* 252 (May 24): 1110-17.

Holmes, A. F. 1983. *Contours of a World View.* Grand Rapids, Mich.: Eerdmans.

————, ed. 1985. *The Making of a Christian Mind: A Christian World View and the Academic Enterprise.* Downers Grove, Ill.: InterVarsity Press.

Holtzman, F. 1996. "Trends of the Revolution: Education and the Worldwide Web." *The Real Issue* 14 (April/May): 10-13.

Hooykaas, R. 1972. *Religion and the Rise of Modern Science.* Grand Rapids, Mich.: Eerdmans.

Hopler, T., and M. Hopler. 1993. *Reaching the World Next Door: How to Spread the Gospel in the Midst of Many Cultures.* Downers Grove, Ill.: InterVarsity Press.

Horgan, J. 1996. *The End of Science: Facing the Limits of Knowledge in the Twilight of the Scientific Age.* New York: Addison-Wesley.

Hull, D. L. 1988. *Science as a Process: An Evolutionary Account of the Social and Conceptual Development of Science.* Chicago: University of Chicago Press.

————. 1992. "Review of *Darwin on Trial.*" *CTNS Bulletin* 12 (Winter): 31-33. Reprinted from *Nature* 352 (1991): 485-6.

Hummel, C. E. 1986. *The Galileo Connection: Resolving Conflicts Between Science and the Bible.* Downers Grove, Ill.: InterVarsity Press.

Hunt, K., and G. Hunt. 1991. *For Christ and the University: The Story of InterVarsity Christian Fellowship of the U.S.A./1940-1990.* Downers Grove, Ill.: InterVarsity Press.

Hyers, C. 1984. *The Meaning of Creation: Genesis and Modern Science.* Atlanta: John Knox.

Jackson, C. I. 1992. *Honor in Science.* Research Triangle Park, N.C.: Sigma Xi, the Scientific Research Society.

Jaki, S. L. 1978. *The Road of Science and the Ways to God.* Chicago: University of Chicago Press.

————. 1992. *Universe and Creed.* Milwaukee, Wis.: Marquette University Press.

Jaroff, L. 1991. "Crisis in the Labs." *Time,* August 26, pp. 45-51.

Jaszczak, S., ed. 1996. *Encyclopedia of Associations.* Detroit: Gale Research.

Jeeves, M. A. 1969. *The Scientific Enterprise and Christian Faith.* Downers Grove, Ill.: InterVarsity Press.

————. 1976. *Psychology and Christianity: The View Both Ways.* Downers Grove, Ill.: Inter-Varsity Press.

————. 1994. *Mind Fields: Reflections on the Science of the Mind and Brain.* Grand Rapids, Mich.: Baker.

Johnson, P. E. 1991. *Darwin on Trial.* Downers Grove, Ill.: InterVarsity Press. 2nd ed. 1993.

————. 1993a. "Creator or Blind Watchmaker?" *First Things* 34 (January): 8-14. Responses in April issue, p. 2.

————. 1993b. "The Religion of the Blind Watchmaker." *PSCF* 45 (March): 46-48.

————. 1995. *Reason in the Balance: The Case Against Naturalism in Science, Law and Education.* Downers Grove, Ill.: InterVarsity Press.

Jones, D. G. 1981. *Our Fragile Brains: A Christian Perspective on Brain Research.* Downers Grove, Ill.: InterVarsity Press.

————. 1984. *Brave New People: Ethical Issues at the Commencement of Life.* Grand Rapids, Mich.: Eerdmans.

————. 1985. "The View from a Censored Corner." *PSCF* 37 (September): 169-77.

————. 1987. *Manufacturing Humans: The Challenge of the New Reproductive Technologies.*

Leicester, England: Inter-Varsity Press.

———. 1994. *Coping with Controversy: Conflict, Censorship and Freedom Within Christian Circles.* Dunedin, New Zealand: Vision.

Judson, H. F. 1979. *The Eighth Day of Creation.* New York: Simon & Schuster.

Kaita, R. 1993. "Obstacles and Opportunities in Science for Christian Witness." *PSCF* 45 (June): 112-5.

Kalthoff, M. A. 1993. "God and Creation: An Historical Look at Encounters Between Christianity and Science." In *Man and Creation,* ed. M. Bauman. Hillsdale, Mich.: Hillsdale College Press.

———. 1995. *Creation and Evolution in the Early American Scientific Affiliation,* Creationism in Twentieth-Century America 10. Ed. R. L. Numbers. Hamden, Conn.: Garland.

Kaplan, R. D. 1996. *The Ends of the Earth: A Journey at the Dawn of the Twenty-first Century.* New York: Random House.

Kass-Simon, G., and P. Farnes. 1990. *Women of Science: Righting the Record.* Bloomington: Indiana University Press.

Keller, E. F. 1983. *A Feeling for the Organism: The Life and Work of Barbara McClintock.* New York: W. H. Freeman.

———. 1985. *Reflections on Gender and Science.* New Haven: Yale University Press.

Kennedy, R. 1995. *Faith at State: A Handbook for Christians at Secular Universities.* Downers Grove, Ill.: InterVarsity Press.

Klaw, S. 1968. *The New Brahmins: Scientific Life in America.* New York: Morrow.

Krieger, J. H. 1996. "Genomic Information, Web Technology Drive Chemical Software Development." *Chemical & Engineering News* 74 (April 22): 10-17.

Kurtz, P. 1986. *The Transcendental Temptation: A Critique of Religion and the Paranormal.* Amherst, N.Y.: Prometheus.

Lakoff, S. A., ed. 1966. *Knowledge and Power: Essays on Science and Government.* New York: Free Press.

Langmead, C. 1995. *A Passion for Plants: From the Rainforests of Brazil to Kew Gardens.* Oxford: Lion.

Lapp, R. E. 1965. *The New Priesthood: The Scientific Elite and the Uses of Power.* New York: Harper & Row.

Larson, E. J. 1985. *Trial and Error: The American Controversy over Creation and Evolution.* New York: Oxford University Press.

Lasby, C. G. 1966. "Science and the Military." In *Science and Society in the United States,* ed. D. D. Van Tassel and M. G. Hall, pp. 251-82. Homewood, Ill.: Dorsey.

Laudan, L. 1984. *Science and Values: The Aims of Science and Their Role in Scientific Debate.* Berkeley: University of California Press.

———. 1988. "The Demise of the Demarcation Problem." In *But Is It Science? The Philosophical Question in the Creation/Evolution Controversy,* ed. M. J. Ruse, pp. 337-350. Amherst, N.Y.: Prometheus.

Lederman, L. 1991. *Science: The End of the Frontier?* Washington, D.C.: AAAS. Supplement to *Science,* January.

Lee, C.-H., ed. 1992. (in Chinese) *The Challenge of Science to Christianity.* Taipei, Taiwan: Christian Arts Press.

Lepkowski, W. 1991. "Debate over Federal Funding of Academic Research Intensifies." *Chemical & Engineering News* 69 (January 14): 20-21.

———. 1996. "On-line Service to Supply Science News." *Chemical & Engineering News* 74 (April 22): 8.

Lewis, C. S. 1956. *Mere Christianity.* New York: Macmillan.

Lindberg, D. C. 1992. *The Beginnings of Western Science: The European Scientific Tradition in Philosophical, Religious and Institutional Context.* Chicago: University of Chicago Press.

——, and R. L. Numbers, eds. 1986. *God and Nature: Essays on the Encounter Between Christianity and Science.* Berkeley: University of California Press.

Lindskoog, K. 1994. *Light in the Shadowlands.* Sisters, Ore.: Questar. Now pub. Pasadena, Calif.: Hope Publishing House.

Lingenfelter, S. 1996. *Agents of Transformation: A Guide for Effective Cross-Cultural Ministry.* Grand Rapids, Mich.: Baker.

Loder, J. E., and W. J. Neidhardt. 1992. *The Knight's Move: The Relational Logic of the Spirit in Theology and Science.* Colorado Springs: Helmers & Howard.

Ludwig, M. A. 1993. *Computer Viruses, Artificial Life and Evolution.* Tucson, Ariz.: American Eagle.

Maatman, R. W. 1978. *The Unity of Creation.* Sioux Center, Iowa: Dordt College Press.

——. 1980. *The Bible, Natural Science and Evolution.* Sioux Center, Iowa: Dordt College Press.

——. 1985. *Chemistry: A Gift of God.* Sioux Center, Iowa: Dordt College Press.

MacKay, D. M. 1965a. "Man as a Mechanism." In *Christianity in a Mechanistic Universe,* ed. D. M. MacKay, pp. 49-69. London: Inter-Varsity Fellowship.

——, ed. 1965b. *Christianity in a Mechanistic Universe.* London: Inter-Varsity Fellowship.

——. 1974. *The Clockwork Image.* Downers Grove, Ill.: InterVarsity Press.

——. 1978. *Science, Chance and Providence.* 1977 Riddell Memorial Lectures. New York: Oxford University Press.

——. 1979. *Human Science and Human Dignity.* Downers Grove, Ill.: InterVarsity Press.

——. 1980. *Brains, Machines and Persons.* London: Collins.

——. 1986a. "MacKay vs. Cramer: A Rebuttal." *JASA* 38 (March): 62-63.

——. 1986b. "Christian Priorities in Science." *JASA* 38 (June): 78-87.

——. 1986c. "Summing Up of ASA/RSCF Conference (Oxford University, July 1985)." *JASA* 38 (September): 195-203.

——. 1986d. "The Health of the Evangelical Body: What Can We Learn from Recent History?" *JASA* 38 (December): 258-65.

——. 1991. *Behind the Eye.* Cambridge, Mass.: Basil Blackwell.

Marsden, G. M. 1991. *Understanding Fundamentalism and Evangelicalism.* Grand Rapids, Mich.: Eerdmans.

——. 1994. *The Soul of the American University.* New York: Oxford University Press.

Matsumura, M., ed. 1995. *Voices for Evolution.* 2nd ed. Berkeley: National Center for Science Education.

McCarthy, M. 1951. *The Groves of Academe.* New York: Harcourt Brace.

McGrath, A. 1996. *A Passion for Truth: The Intellectual Coherence of Evangelicalism.* Downers Grove, Ill.: InterVarsity Press.

McIntyre, J. A. 1992. "It's Time to Rejoin the Scientific Establishment." *PSCF* 44 (June): 124-7.

McMullin, E. 1988. "Natural Science and Belief in a Creator." In *Physics, Philosophy and Theology: A Common Quest for Understanding,* ed. R. J. Russell, W. R. Steiger and G. V. Coyne, pp. 49-79. Notre Dame, Ind.: University of Notre Dame Press.

——. 1993. "Evolution and Special Creation." *Zygon* 28 (September): 299-335.

Medawar, P. B. 1979. *Advice to a Young Scientist.* New York: Harper & Row.

Medvedev, Z. A. 1969. *The Rise and Fall of T. D. Lysenko.* Trans. I. M. Lerner. New York: Columbia University Press.

Menninga, C. 1988. "Coping with Controversy." *PSCF* 40 (September): 191.

Merton, R. K. 1973. *The Sociology of Science.* Chicago: University of Chicago Press.

Miller, J. B., and K. E. McCall, eds. 1990. *The Church and Contemporary Cosmology.* Pittsburgh: Carnegie-Mellon University Press.

Mills, G. C. 1992. "Structure of Cytochrome C and C-like Genes: Significance for the Modification and Origin of Species." *PSCF* 44 (December): 236-45.

————. 1994. "The Molecular Evolutionary Clock: A Critique." *PSCF* 46 (September): 159-68.

————. 1995. "A Theory of Theistic Evolution as an Alternative to the Naturalistic Theory." *PSCF* 47 (June): 112-22.

Mills, G. C., and D. Kenyon. 1996. "The RNA World: A Critique." *Origins & Design* 17 (Winter): 9-16.

Mixter, R. L., ed. 1959. *Evolution and Christian Thought Today.* Grand Rapids, Mich.: Eerdmans.

Moberg, D. O. 1965. *Inasmuch: Christian Social Responsibility in Twentieth Century America.* Grand Rapids, Mich.: Eerdmans.

————. 1967a. "The Encounter of Scientific and Religious Values Pertinent to Man's Spiritual Nature." *Sociological Analysis* 28 (Spring): 22-23.

————. 1967b. "Science and the Spiritual Nature of Man." *JASA* 19 (March): 12-17.

————. 1979. *Spiritual Well-Being: Sociological Perspectives.* New York: University Press of America.

————. 1985. *Wholistic Christianity: An Appeal for a Dynamic, Balanced Faith.* Elgin, Ill.: Brethren Press.

————. 1995. "Spiritual Maturity and Aging." *Theology, News and Notes* (a publication of Fuller Theological Seminary) 42 (December): 3-5, 21.

Monroe, K. 1996. *Finding God at Harvard: Spiritual Journeys of Thinking Christians.* Grand Rapids, Mich.: Zondervan.

Monsma, S. V., ed. 1986. *Responsible Technology: A Christian Assessment.* Grand Rapids, Mich.: Eerdmans.

Moreland, J. P. 1989. *Christianity and the Nature of Science.* Grand Rapids, Mich.: Baker.

————, ed. 1994. *The Creation Hypothesis: Scientific Evidence for an Intelligent Designer.* Downers Grove, Ill.: InterVarsity Press.

Morris, H. M. 1976. *The Genesis Record.* El Cajon, Calif.: Master Books.

————. 1993. *Biblical Creationism: What Each Book of the Bible Teaches About Creation and the Flood.* Grand Rapids, Mich.: Baker.

Mott, N. 1991. *Can Scientists Believe? Some Examples of the Attitude of Scientists to Religion.* London: James & James.

Mouw, R. J. 1992. *Uncommon Decency: Christian Civility in an Uncivil World.* Downers Grove, Ill.: InterVarsity Press.

Murphy, G. L. 1986. *The Trademark of God.* Wilton, Conn.: Morehouse-Barlow.

————. 1991. "Time, Thermodynamics and Theology." *Zygon* 26 (September): 359-72.

————. 1996. "Possible Influences of Biblical Beliefs upon Physics." *PSCF* 48 (June): 82-87.

Murphy, N. 1990. *Theology in the Age of Scientific Reasoning.* Ithaca, N.Y.: Cornell University Press.

————. 1993. "Phillip Johnson on Trial: A Critique of His Critique of Darwin." *PSCF* 45 (March): 26-36.

Myers, D. G. 1978. *The Human Puzzle: Psychological Research and Christian Belief.* New York: Harper & Row.

————. 1980. *The Inflated Self: Human Illusions and the Biblical Call to Hope.* New York: Seabury.

————. 1992. *The Pursuit of Happiness.* New York: Morrow.

Myers, D. G., and M. A. Jeeves. 1987. *Psychology Through the Eyes of Faith.* New York: Harper & Row.

NAS-COSAC. 1984. *Science and Creationism: A View from the National Academy of Sciences.* Washington, D.C.: National Academy Press. 2nd ed. 1995.

NAS-COSEPUP. 1965. *Basic Research and National Goals.* Washington, D.C.: National Academy Press.

————. 1989. *On Being a Scientist: Responsible Conduct in Research.* Washington, D.C.:

National Academy Press. 2nd ed. 1995.

———. 1992. *Responsible Science: Ensuring the Integrity of the Research Process.* Washington, D.C.: National Academy Press.

Neidhardt, W. J. 1986. "The Creative Dialogue Between Human Intelligibility and Reality: Relational Aspects of Natural Science and Theology." *The Asbury Theological Journal* 41, no. 2: 59-83.

———. 1989. "Thomas F. Torrance's Integration of Judeo-Christian Theology and Natural Science: Some Key Themes." *PSCF* 41 (June): 87-98.

Nelkin, D. 1988. *Selling Science: How the Press Covers Science and Technology.* New York: W. H. Freeman.

Newell, A., and R. F. Sproull. 1982. "Computer Networks: Prospects for Scientists." *Science* 215 (February 12): 843-52.

Newman, R. C. 1988. "Self-Reproducing Automata and the Origin of Life." *PSCF* 40 (March): 24-31.

———. 1995. "Scientific and Religious Aspects of the Origins Debate." *PSCF* 47 (September): 164-75.

———, and H. J. Eckelmann Jr. 1989. *Genesis One and the Origin of the Earth.* Hatfield, Penn.: Interdisciplinary Biblical Research Institute. First pub. 1977. Downers Grove, Ill.: InterVarsity Press.

Nicholas, R. 1985. *Good Things Come in Small Groups.* Downers Grove, Ill.: InterVarsity Press.

Nisbet, R. 1980. *History of the Idea of Progress.* New York: Basic Books.

Noll, M. 1994. *The Scandal of the Evangelical Mind.* Grand Rapids, Mich.: Eerdmans.

Numbers, R. L. 1992. *The Creationists: The Evolution of Scientific Creationism.* New York: Knopf.

———, ed. 1995. *Creationism in Twentieth-Century America.* 10 vols. Hambden, Conn.: Garland.

Offner, D. H. 1995. *Design Homology: An Introduction to Bionics.* Privately printed by author (1502 S. Maple St., Urbana, IL 61801).

Olby, R. C. 1974. *The Path to the Double Helix.* New York: Macmillan.

Oliver, J. E. 1991. *The Incomplete Guide to the Art of Discovery.* New York: Columbia University Press.

Olson, E. A. 1996. "A Response to Richard Wright's 'Tearing Down the Green.' " *PSCF* 48 (June): 74-81.

Packer, J. I. 1973. *Knowing God.* Downers Grove, Ill.: InterVarsity Press. 20th anniversary ed. 1993.

Page, R. M. 1962. *The Origin of Radar.* New York: Doubleday/Anchor.

Pannenberg, W. 1988. "The Doctrine of Creation and Modern Science." *Zygon* 23 (March): 3-21.

———. 1996. "How to Think About Secularism." *First Things* 64 (June/July): 27-32.

Peacocke, A. 1993. *Theology for a Scientific Age: Being and Becoming—Natural, Divine and Human.* 2nd ed. Minneapolis: Fortress.

Pearcey, N., and C. B. Thaxton. 1994. *The Soul of Science: Christian Faith and Natural Philosophy.* Wheaton, Ill.: Crossway.

Penrose, R. 1994. *Shadows of the Mind: A Search for the Missing Science of Consciousness.* New York: Oxford University Press.

Perkowitz, S. 1996. "Moving the Goalposts." *Scientific American* 84 (September/October): 426-7.

Perutz, M. F. 1989. *Is Science Necessary? Essays on Science and Scientists.* New York: E. P. Dutton.

Peters, T., ed. 1989. *Cosmos as Creation: Theology and Science in Consonance.* Nashville: Abingdon.

Peterson, D. J. 1993. *Troubled Lands: The Legacy of Soviet Environmental Destruction.* Boulder,

Colo.: Westview.

Pike, E. V. 1981. *Ken Pike: Scholar and Christian*. Dallas: Summer Institute of Linguistics.

Pike, K. L. 1981. *Tagmemics, Discourse and Verbal Art*. Michigan Studies in the Humanities. Ann Arbor: University of Michigan Press.

———. 1982. *Linguistic Concepts: An Introduction to Tagmemics*. Lincoln: University of Nebraska Press.

Plantinga, A. 1991. "When Faith and Reason Clash: Evolution and the Bible." *Christian Scholar's Review* 21 (September): 8-32.

Polanyi, M. 1958. *Personal Knowledge*. Chicago: University of Chicago Press.

———. 1964. *Science, Faith and Society*. Chicago: University of Chicago Press.

———. 1969. *Knowing and Being: Essays by Michael Polanyi*. Ed. M. Greene. Chicago: University of Chicago Press.

Polkinghorne, J. 1984. *The Quantum World*. Princeton, N.J.: Princeton University Press.

———. 1986. *One World: The Interaction of Science and Theology*. Princeton, N.J.: Princeton University Press.

———. 1988. *Science and Creation: The Search for Understanding*. Boston: New Science Library.

———. 1989. *Science and Providence: God's Interaction with the World*. Boston: New Science Library.

———. 1991. *Reason and Reality: The Relationship Between Science and Theology*. Philadelphia: Trinity Press International.

———. 1992. *The Way the World Is*. London: Triangle. First pub. 1983. Grand Rapids, Mich.: Eerdmans.

———. 1994. *The Faith of a Physicist: Reflections of a Bottom-Up Thinker*. Princeton, N.J.: Princeton University Press.

Pollard, W. G. 1961. *Physicist and Christian*. Greenwich, Conn.: Seabury.

Poole, M. 1990. *Guide to Science and Belief*. Batavia, Ill.: Lion.

Prance, G. T. 1982. "Missionaries as Earthkeepers." *Radix* 14 (November/December): 22-25.

Price, D., J. L. Wiester and W. R. Hearn. 1990. "Science and Something Else: Religious Aspects of the NAS Booklet 'Science and Creationism.' " *PSCF* 42 (June): 115-18.

Price, D. K. 1954. *Government and Science: Their Dynamic Relation in American Democracy*. New York: New York University Press. Paper ed. 1962. New York: Oxford University Press.

———. 1965. *The Scientific Estate*. Cambridge, Mass.: Harvard University Press.

Proctor, W. 1983. *The Templeton Touch*. New York: Doubleday.

Provine, W. 1988. "Scientists, Face It: Science and Religion Are Incompatible." *The Scientist* 2 (September 5): 5.

Quebedeaux, R. 1979. *I Found It! The Story of Bill Bright and Campus Crusade*. San Francisco: Harper & Row.

Ramm, B. 1954. *The Christian View of Science and Scripture*. Grand Rapids, Mich.: Eerdmans

Ratzsch, D. 1986. *The Philosophy of Science*. Downers Grove, Ill.: InterVarsity Press.

———. 1996. *The Battle of Beginnings: Why Neither Side Is Winning the Creation-Evolution Debate*. Downers Grove, Ill.: InterVarsity Press.

Reichenbach, B. R., and V. E. Anderson. 1995. *On Behalf of God: A Christian Ethic for Biology*. Grand Rapids, Mich.: Eerdmans.

Rescher, N. 1984. *The Limits of Science*. Berkeley: University of California Press.

Roe, A. 1953. *The Making of a Scientist*. New York: Dodd, Mead.

Rogers, T. 1993. "On the Track of the Stuff of Life (Profile of Francis S. Collins)." *Michigan Alumnus*, January/February, pp. 19-23.

Rolston, H., III. 1988. *Environmental Ethics: Values in and Duties to the Natural World*. Philadelphia: Temple University Press.

———. 1989. *Philosophy Gone Wild*. Amherst, N.Y.: Prometheus.

————. 1991. "Respect for Life: Christians, Creation and Environmental Ethics" and "Genes, Genesis and God in Natural History." *CTNS Bulletin* 11 (Spring): 1-8, 9-23.

Rosenberg, T. 1995. *The Haunted Land: Facing Europe's Ghosts After Communism.* New York: Random House.

Ross, H. 1989. *The Fingerprint of God: Recent Scientific Discoveries Reveal the Unmistakable Identity of the Creator.* Orange, Calif.: Promise.

————. 1994. *Creation and Time: A Biblical and Scientific Perspective on the Creation-Date Controversy.* Colorado Springs: NavPress.

————. 1996. *Beyond the Cosmos: The Extra-dimensionality of God.* Colorado Springs: NavPress.

Ruse, M. J., ed. 1988. *But Is It Science? The Philosophical Question in the Creation/Evolution Controversy.* Amherst, N.Y.: Prometheus.

Russell, C. 1985. *Cross-Currents: Interactions Between Science and Faith.* Grand Rapids, Mich.: Eerdmans.

Russell, R. J. 1988. "Quantum Physics in Philosophical and Theological Perspective." In *Physics, Philosophy and Theology: A Common Quest for Understanding,* ed. R. J. Russell, W. R. Stoeger and G. V. Coyne, pp. 343-368. Notre Dame, Ind.: University of Notre Dame Press.

————. 1989. "Cosmology, Creation and Contingency." In *Cosmos as Creation: Theology and Science in Consonance,* ed. T. Peters, pp. 177-209. Nashville: Abingdon.

————. 1990. "Christian Discipleship and the Challenge of Physics: Formation, Flux and Focus." *PSCF* 42 (September): 139-54.

Russell, R. J., W. R. Steiger and G. V. Coyne, eds. 1988. *Physics, Philosophy and Theology: A Common Quest for Understanding.* Notre Dame, Ind.: University of Notre Dame Press.

Sagan, C. 1980. *Cosmos.* New York: Random House.

Salomon, J. J. 1973. *Science and Politics.* Cambridge, Mass.: MIT Press.

Sayre, A. 1975. *Rosalind Franklin and DNA.* New York: W. W. Norton.

Schaefer, H. F., III. 1994. "Stephen Hawking, the Big Bang and God: Part I." *The Real Issue* 13 (November/December): 8-10. "Part II." *The Real Issue* 14 (March/April 1995): 4-8.

Schideler, E. W. 1966. *Believing and Knowing: The Meaning of Truth in Biblical Religion and in Science.* Ames: Iowa State University Press.

Shamos, M. H. 1995. *The Myth of Scientific Literacy.* New Brunswick, N.J.: Rutgers University Press.

Sheaffer, J. R., and R. H. Brand. 1980. *Whatever Happened to Eden? Earth's Energy-Environment Crisis Opens Doors to New Prosperity.* Wheaton, Ill.: Tyndale House.

Sider, R. J. 1980. *Living More Simply: Biblical Principles and Practical Models.* Downers Grove, Ill.: InterVarsity Press.

Sigma Xi. 1993. *Ethics, Values and the Promise of Science.* Research Triangle Park, N.C.: Sigma Xi, The Scientific Research Society.

Sime, R. L. 1996. *Lise Meitner: A Life in Physics.* Berkeley: University of California Press.

Sire, J. W. 1988. *The Universe Next Door: A Basic World View Catalog.* 2nd ed. Downers Grove, Ill.: InterVarsity Press. 1st ed. 1976. 3rd ed. 1997.

————. 1990. *Discipleship of the Mind.* Downers Grove, Ill.: InterVarsity Press.

————. 1994. *Why Should Anyone Believe Anything at All?* Downers Grove, Ill.: InterVarsity Press.

Skinner, B. F. 1971. *Beyond Freedom and Dignity.* New York: Knopf.

Smith, H. 1958. *The Religions of Man.* New York: Harper & Row.

————. 1976. *Forgotten Truth: The Primordial Tradition.* New York: Harper & Row.

————. 1982. *Beyond the Post-modern Mind.* Wheaton, Ill.: Quest. 2nd ed. 1989.

————. 1991. *The World's Religions.* Revision of *The Religions of Man.* San Francisco: HarperCollins

———. 1994. "Bubble Blown and Lived In: A Theological Autobiography." *CTNS Bulletin* 14 (Summer): 10-15.

Smith, P. 1990. *Killing the Spirit.* New York: Viking.

Smith, R. W., ed. 1972. *Christ and the Modern Mind.* Downers Grove, Ill.: InterVarsity Press.

Snow, C. P. 1958. *The Search.* New York: Scribner. First pub. 1934.

———. 1961. *The Two Cultures and the Scientific Revolution.* New York: Cambridge University Press.

Sonnert, G., and G. Holton. 1996. "Career Patterns of Men and Women in the Sciences." *American Scientist* 84, no. 1 (January/February): 63-71.

Stafford, T. 1987. "Cease-Fire in the Laboratory: Working Scientists Find That Science and Faith Are Less and Less in Conflict." *Christianity Today,* April 3, pp. 17-21.

Stek, J. 1990. "What Says the Scripture?" In *Portraits of Creation: Biblical and Scientific Perspectives on the World's Formation,* ed. H. Van Till et al., pp. 203-65. Grand Rapids, Mich.: Eerdmans.

Stoll, C. 1995. *Silicon Snake Oil: Second Thoughts on the Information Superhighway.* New York: Doubleday.

Stott, J. R. 1975. *Basic Christianity.* Downers Grove, Ill.: InterVarsity Press.

Suppe, J. 1996. "In Response to the Question of J. W. Haas Jr., 'Are Evangelical Scientists Practical Atheists?' " *PSCF* 48 (September): 184-85.

Swearengen, J. C. 1992. "Arms Control and God's Purpose in History." *PSCF* 44 (March): 25-35.

Swearengen, J. C., and A. P. Swearengen. 1990. "Comparative Analysis of the Nuclear Weapons Debate: Campus and Developer Perspectives." *PSCF* 42 (June): 75-85.

Taubes, G. 1996. "Science Journals Go Wired." *Science* 271 (February 9): 764-66.

Taylor, C. W., and F. Barron, eds. 1963. *Scientific Creativity: Its Recognition and Development.* New York: Wiley.

Taylor, M. J. 1968. *The Sacred and the Secular.* Englewood Cliffs, N.J.: Prentice-Hall.

Teich, A. H., and M. S. Frankel. 1991. *Good Science and Responsible Scientists: Meeting the Challenge of Fraud and Misconduct in Science.* Washington, D.C.: AAAS.

Teilhard de Chardin, P. 1959. *The Phenomenon of Man.* Trans. B. Wall. New York: Harper.

Templeton, J. M., ed. 1994. *Evidence of Purpose: Scientists Discover the Creator.* New York: Continuum.

———. 1995. *The Humble Approach: Scientists Discover God.* Rev. ed. New York: Continuum. Original ed. 1981.

Templeton, J. M., and R. L. Herrmann. 1989. *The God Who Would Be Known: Revelations of the Divine in Contemporary Science.* New York: Continuum.

———. 1994. *Is God the Only Reality?* New York: Continuum.

John Templeton Foundation, ed. 1996. *Who's Who in Theology and Science.* Framingham, Mass.: Winthrop. 1st ed. 1992.

Thaxton, C. B., W. L. Bradley and R. L. Olsen. 1984. *The Mystery of Life's Origin: Reassessing Current Theories.* New York: Philosophical Library.

Thorson, W. R. 1992. "An I *Behind the Eye:* Donald MacKay's Gifford Lectures." *PSCF* 44 (March): 49-54.

Tipler, F. 1994. *The Physics of Immortality.* New York: Doubleday.

Tobias, S., D. E. Chubin and K. Aylesworth. 1995. *Rethinking Science as a Career: Perceptions and Realities in the Physical Sciences.* Tucson, Ariz.: Research Corporation.

Torrance, T. F. 1989. *The Christian Frame of Mind: Reason, Order and Openness in Theology and Natural Science.* Colorado Springs: Helmers & Howard.

Townes, C. H. 1992. "Reflections on My Life as a Physicist." *CTNS Bulletin* 12 (Summer): 1-7.

Turkle, S. 1995. *Life on the Screen: Identity in the Age of the Internet.* New York: Simon & Schuster.

Turner, D. 1978. *Commitment to Care: An Integrated Philosophy of Science, Education and*

Religion. Old Greenwich, Conn.: Devin-Adair.

Van der Meer, J. M., ed. 1995a. *Facets of Faith and Science.* Vol. 1, *Historiography and Modes of Interaction.* Lanham, Md.: University Press of America.

———. 1995b. *Facets of Faith and Science.* Vol. 2, *The Role of Beliefs in Mathematics and the Natural Sciences.* Lanham, Md.: University Press of America.

———. 1995c. *Facets of Faith and Science.* Vol. 3, *The Role of Beliefs in the Natural Sciences.* Lanham, Md.: University Press of America.

———. 1995d. *Facets of Faith and Science.* Vol. 4, *Interpreting God's Action in the World.* Lanham, Md.: University Press of America.

van der Ziel, A. 1960. *The Natural Sciences and the Christian Message.* Minneapolis: Denison.

———. 1965. *Genesis and Scientific Inquiry.* Minneapolis: Denison.

Van Dyke, F., et al. 1996. *Redeeming Creation: The Biblical Basis for Environmental Stewardship.* Downers Grove, Ill.: InterVarsity Press.

Van Leeuwen, M. S. 1985. *The Person in Psychology: A Contemporary Christian Appraisal.* Grand Rapids, Mich.: Eerdmans.

———. 1988. "North American Evangelicalism and the Social Sciences: A Historical and Critical Appraisal." *PSCF* 40 (December): 194-203.

———. 1990. *Gender and Grace: Love, Work and Parenting in a Changing World.* Downers Grove, Ill.: InterVarsity Press.

Van Tassel, D. D., and M. G. Hall, eds. 1966. *Science and Society in the United States.* Homewood, Ill.: Dorsey.

van 't Hoff, J. H. 1967. *Imagination in Science.* Trans. G. F. Springer. Berlin: Springer-Verlag. First pub. 1901.

Van Till, H. J. 1986. *The Fourth Day: What the Bible and the Heavens Are Telling Us About the Creation.* Grand Rapids, Mich.: Eerdmans.

———. 1993. "When Faith and Reason Meet." In *Man and Creation: Perspectives on Science and Theology,* ed. M. Bauman, pp. 141-64. Hillsdale, Mich.: Hillsdale College Press.

———. D. A. Young and C. Menninga. 1988. *Science Held Hostage: What's Wrong with Creation Science and Evolutionism.* Downers Grove, Ill.: InterVarsity Press.

———. et al. 1990. *Portraits of Creation: Biblical and Scientific Perspectives on the World's Formation.* Grand Rapids, Mich.: Eerdmans.

Vitz, P. C. 1995. "New Technology and the Old University." *The Real Issue* 14 (November/December): 1-3.

Wade, N. 1981. *The Nobel Duel.* New York: Doubleday/Anchor.

Walker, L. C. 1990. *Forests: A Naturalist's Guide to Trees and Forest Ecology.* New York: Wiley.

———. 1991. *The Southern Forest: A Chronicle.* Austin: University of Texas Press.

———. 1995. *Excelsior: Memoir of a Forester.* Nacogdoches, Tex.: College of Forestry, Stephen F. Austin State University.

Walsh, B. J., and J. R. Middleton. 1984. *The Transforming Vision: Shaping a Christian World View.* Downers Grove, Ill.: InterVarsity Press.

Watson, J. D. 1968. *The Double Helix.* New York: Atheneum.

Weaver, W. 1959. "A Scientist Ponders Faith." *Saturday Review* (January 3): 8-10, 33. Reprinted in *Science and Society: Midcentury Readings,* ed. T. D. Clareson, pp. 293-301. New York: Harper, 1961.

———. 1970. *Scene of Change: A Lifetime in American Science.* New York: Scribner.

Wenham, G. J., et al., eds. 1994. *New Bible Commentary.* 4th ed. Downers Grove, Ill.: InterVarsity Press.

White, A. D. 1896. *A History of the Warfare of Science with Theology in Christendom.* 2 vols. New York: Appleton.

White, M., and J. Gribbin. 1992. *Stephen Hawking: A Life in Science.* New York: Plume/Penguin.

Wiener, J. 1995. "Cash for Courses." *Lingua Franca* 6 (November/December): 68-73.

Wiester, J. L. 1983. *The Genesis Connection.* Hatfield, Penn.: Interdisciplinary Biblical Research Institute.

———. 1988. "Response to Reviews of *Teaching Science in a Climate of Controversy:* 'Did the Universe Have a Beginning?' and 'Where Did the First Animals Come From?' " *PSCF* 40 (September): 162-65.

Wilcox, D. L. 1986. "A Taxonomy of Creation." *JASA* 36 (December): 244-50.

———. 1989. "Of Messages and Molecules: What Is the Essence of Life?" *PSCF* 41 (December): 227-31.

———. 1994. "A Blindfolded Watchmaker: The Arrival of the Fittest." In *Darwinism: Science or Philosophy?* ed. J. Buell and V. Hearn, pp. 195-209. Richardson, Tex.: Foundation for Thought and Ethics.

———. 1996. "Adam, Where Are You? Changing Paradigms in Paleoanthropology." *PSCF* 48 (June): 88-96.

Wilkinson, L., ed. 1980. *Earthkeeping: Christian Stewardship of Natural Resources.* Grand Rapids, Mich.: Eerdmans.

———, ed. 1995. *Earthkeeping in the Nineties: Stewardship of Creation.* Grand Rapids, Mich.: Eerdmans.

Wilson, E. B. 1952. *An Introduction to Scientific Research.* New York: McGraw-Hill.

Wilson, E. O. 1971. *Sociobiology: The New Synthesis.* Cambridge, Mass.: Harvard University Press.

Wonderly, D. E. 1977. *God's Time-Records in Ancient Sediments.* Flint, Mich.: Crystal.

———. 1987. *Neglect of Geologic Data: Sedimentary Strata Compared with Young-Earth Creationist Writings.* Hatfield, Penn.: Interdisciplinary Biblical Research Institute.

Woodward, J., and D. Goodstein. 1996. "Conduct, Misconduct and the Structure of Science." *American Scientist* 84 (September/October): 479-90.

Wright, R. T. 1989. *Biology Through the Eyes of Faith.* New York: Harper & Row.

———. 1995. "Tearing Down the Green: Environmental Backlash in the Evangelical Sub-Culture." *PSCF* 47 (June): 80-91.

Wuthnow, R. 1985. "Science and the Sacred." In *The Sacred in a Secular Age,* ed. P. E. Hominid, pp. 187-203. Berkeley: University of California Press.

Young, D. A. 1977. *Creation and the Flood: An Alternative to Flood Geology and Theistic Evolution.* Grand Rapids, Mich.: Baker.

———. 1982. *Christianity and the Age of the Earth.* Grand Rapids, Mich.: Zondervan.

———. 1988. "The Contemporary Relevance of Augustine's View of Creation." *PSCF* 40 (March): 42-45.

———. 1995. *The Biblical Flood: A Case Study of the Church's Response to Extra-biblical Knowledge.* Grand Rapids, Mich.: Eerdmans.

Ziman, J. 1994. *Prometheus Bound: Science in a Dynamic Steady State.* New York: Cambridge University Press.